INFORMATION LANDSCAPES FOR A LEARNING SOCIETY

Networking and the Future of Libraries 3

An International Conference held at the University of Bath, 29 June–1 July 1998

Edited by

Sally Criddle, Lorcan Dempsey and **Richard Heseltine**

Published in association with the UK Office for Library and Information Networking, University of Bath

Library Association Publishing
London

Published by
Library Association Publishing
7 Ridgmount Street
London WC1E 7AE

Library Association Publishing is wholly owned by The Library Association.

Published 1999

British Library Cataloguing in Publication Data
A catalogue record for this book is available from the British Library

ISBN 1-85604-310-X

UKOLN is jointly funded by the British Library Research and Development Department and the Joint Information Systems Committee of the Higher Education Funding Councils. More information about UKOLN and its activities can be found at:
<URL: http://www.ukoln.bath.ac.uk>.

Typeset in 11/13pt Elegant Garamond and CastleT from authors' disk by Library Association Publishing.
Printed and made in Great Britain by Bookcraft (Bath) Ltd, Midsomer Norton, Somerset.

Contents

Contributors

David Baker Director of Information Strategy and Services and University Librarian, University of East Anglia, Norwich NR4 7TJ, UK.
<d.baker@uea.ac.uk>

David Bearman Partner, Archives and Museum Informatics, 2008 Murray Avenue, Suite D, Pittsburgh, PA 15217, USA.
<dbear@archimuse.com>

Lars Bjornshauge Director, Technical Knowledge Centre of Denmark, PO Box 777, DK 2800 LYNGBY, Denmark.
<lbj@dtv.dk>

Andrew Blau formerly Director, Communications Policy, Benton Foundation, currently Program Director, The Markle Foundation, 75 Rockefeller Plaza, Suite 1800 New York, NY 10019, USA.
<Andrew_Blau@markle.org>

Lorcan Dempsey Director, UKOLN, University of Bath BA2 7AY, UK.
<l.dempsey@ukoln.ac.uk>

John Dolan Head of Birmingham Central Library, Chamberlain Square, Birmingham B3 3HQ, UK.
<johndolan@dial.pipex.com>

Biddy Fisher Head of Academic Services and Development, Sheffield Hallam University, Pond Street, Sheffield S1 1WB, UK.
<b.m.fisher@shu.ac.uk>

Daniel Greenstein Director, Arts and Humanities Data Service, King's College Library, London WC2R 2LS, UK.
<daniel.greenstein@ahds.ac.uk>

Hilary Hammond formerly Director of Arts and Libraries, Norfolk County Council, currently working as an independent consultant.
<h2c2@clara.net>

Richard Heseltine   Director of Academic Services and Librarian, University of Hull, Hull HU6 7RX, UK.
<r.g.heseltine@lib.hull.ac.uk>

David Kay   Strategic Development Director, Fretwell-Downing Informatics, 861 Ecclesall Road, Sheffield S11 7AE, UK.
<dkay@fdgroup.co.uk>

Grace Kempster   County Librarian, Essex County Council, Goldlay Gardens, Chelmsford CM2 0EW, UK.
<grace.kempster@essexcc.gov.uk>

Ray Lester   Head of Library and Information Services, The Natural History Museum, Cromwell Road London SW7 5BD, UK.
<r.lester@nhm.ac.uk>

Peter Lyman   University Librarian, University of California, Berkeley, 245 Doe Library, Berkeley CA 94720-6000, USA.
<plyman@sims.berkeley.edu>

Clifford Lynch   Executive Director, Coalition for Networked Information, 21 Dupont Circle, Suite #800, Washington DC 20036-1109, USA.
<clifford@cni.org>

Andrew McDonald   Director of Information Services, University of Sunderland, Chester Road Library, Sunderland SR1 3ED, UK.
<andrew.mcdonald@sunderland.ac.uk>

Mike Stapleton   Technical Director, System Simulation Limited, 250M Bedford Chambers, Covent Garden, London WC2E 8HA, UK.
<mike@ssl.co.uk>

Jennifer Trant   Partner, Archives and Museum Informatics, 2008 Murray Avenue, Suite D, Pittsburgh, PA 15217, USA.
<jtrant@archimuse.com>

Sarah Tyacke   Keeper of Public Records, The Public Record Office, Kew TW9 4DU, UK.
<styacke.pro.kew@gtnet.gov.uk>

Frank Webster   Professor of Sociology, Oxford Brookes University, Gipsy Lane Campus, Headington, Oxford OX3 0BP, UK.
<f.webster@brookes.ac.uk>

Cris Woolston   Director, Teaching and Learning Support, University of Hull, Hull HU6 7RX, UK
<c.j.woolston@acs.hull.ac.uk>

Introduction

Lorcan Dempsey

A glass web spans the globe which is transforming commercial, social and cultural life in ways we do not fully understand. The emergence of new digital information spaces alongside the existing physical places of public life is posing challenges for policy and service developers. We are seeing the creation and recreation of markets and economic activity; of political and public discourse; of cultural, research and learning work.

These challenges are being addressed in a range of national and other policy initiatives addressing 'information and learning society' issues, in research and technical development programmes, and in organizational strategic plans. At the same time, practitioners are seeking points of contact and comparison as they work to reduce uncertainty in the planning of future services.

The UK national policy context is provided by significant reports into Higher and Further Education, such as those by Dearing[1] and Kennedy,[2] by proposals for a National Grid for Learning,[3] a University for Industry,[4] and imminent proposals about lifelong learning. A range of ambitious millennium projects join other regional and local initiatives in the creation of digital services. The library world has seen *New library: the people's network*,[5] the Digital Libraries Programme of the British Library,[6] and the maturation and extension of the Electronic Libraries Programme[7] of the Joint Information Systems Committee of the Higher Education Funding Councils (JISC),[8] and proposals for a National Electronic Library for Health.[9]

Libraries and related organizations face particular challenges. How will they construct digital information spaces which enrich the lives of their users? How will they construct services that continue to provide business and research intelligence, nourish the imagination, and preserve the memory and knowledge of new and existing communities? How will they reach into the lives of a fragmented, mobile, and diverse constituency of users? How will they support new patterns of learning and information use? How will they unify access to an intellectual record scattered across physical and digital places? How will they build bridges with other service providers as their roles change in the network society?

These issues were discussed at this, the third in the *Networking and the future of libraries* conference series. It takes as its starting point the construction of 'information and learning landscapes'. If emerging network places are to support rich learning experiences they must be designed, organized and supported in ways that make people want to be there. Libraries and other organizations already provide a range of network services. They must now take those and weave them into a fabric that supports discovery, navigation, and use of diverse information and learning resources; that supports new forms of reading, writing and communication; that turns a series of unconnected opportunities into a library service.

It is this fabric that we have tried to suggest with the phrase 'information landscape', and several contributions in this volume unpick or extend the metaphor. However, it is posed as a question not as an answer. We have little real sense yet of what hybrid or digital libraries will be like. The other phrase in the title, 'the learning society', is also, in a sense, a question. We recognize 'information society' or 'learning society' as shorthand labels for a set of changes, or as a part of political vocabulary, but not as a worked out shared understanding.

For this reason, much of the discussion is exploratory or tentative, suggesting the possibly provisional nature of our current positions, or acknowledging that we are taking first steps in uncertain directions. The opening and closing key-notes, by Richard Heseltine and Clifford Lynch respectively, emphasize such questions and also the connections between technical decisions, service direction, and behavioural change. The conference interests have four broad foci:

Systems and architectural issues. The Internet provides a pervasive, predictable transport. The web provides a pervasive predictable presentation and user access medium. However, poor support for organization and management of network resources creates difficulties for information providers and frustration for information users. It is the need for such support that is driving digital library and information architecture initiatives. We focused on an important emerging aspect of this wider spectrum: the design and construction of 'broker' services which aim to unify access to multiplying resources in rich network spaces.

Information landscapes. Current information and learning systems exist as functional islands, a series of individual, unconnected opportunities. The information landscapes of the future will weave together electronic services and existing services in ways that join users to the materials and tools that they need, when they need them. How will these landscapes support users and how will they relate to existing places and services? How will library services combine physical places and digital information spaces, the print and the electronic, learning and information?

The public sphere. Libraries have existed in the public sphere: they are instruments of learning, of an informed citizenry, of civilization. How will this mission be maintained in a network society which is increasingly globalized, where the unconnected are increasingly disadvantaged, where new costs are changing patterns of accessibility? How inclusive will the landscapes be? How can libraries ensure that their role is recognized in the emerging policy framework that is driving national and international information society initiatives?

Change. How will libraries and other knowledge exchanges change themselves to change the lives of their users? How will they create active community and learning?

Discussion at the conference highlighted the inevitably cross-sectoral and international nature of these questions. It demonstrated points of contact and comparison between those responsible for cultural heritage, learning and information services, as well as the changing world of publishing. It underlined the need for dialogue and shared approaches which allow the flow of information and learning opportunities, and which encourage collaboration as we design our collective future. It emphasized the connection between professional and sectoral concerns and the wider political issues of a 'learning age', and the crucial need to lobby, inform, and demonstrate value in actual services.

This conference was special in that it marked 21 years during which a 'centre' has been funded at the University of Bath. UKOLN is now supported by the Joint Information Systems Committee of the Higher Education Funding Councils, by the British Library Research and Innovation Centre, and by the University of Bath, where it is based. During this period conferences have been important features of our work, and we look forward to working with our funders and our many collaborators in organizing many more in the coming 21 years!

References

1   Dearing, R., *Higher education in the learning society: report of the National Committee of Inquiry into Higher Education*, London, HMSO, 1997. Available at <URL: http://www.leeds.ac.uk/niche/index.html>.

2   Kennedy, H., *Learning works. Main report of the Widening Participation Committee*, Coventry, The Further Education Funding Council, 1997.

3   Department for Education and Employment, *Connecting the learning society: national grid for learning; the government's consultation paper*, London, Department for Education and Employment, 1997. Also available at <URL: http://open.gov.uk/dfee/grid/index.htm>.

4   The University for Industry is set out in the Green Paper, *The Learning age: a renaissance for a new Britain* (Cm 3790, 1998). See also <URL: http://open.gov.uk/dfee/grid/index.htm>.

5   Library and Information Commission, *New library: the people's network*, London, Library and Information Commission, 1997. Also available at <URL: http://www.ukoln.ac.uk/services/lic/newlibrary/>.

6   See <URL: http://www.ukoln.ac.uk/services/bl/>.
7   See <URL: http://www.ukoln.ac.uk/services/elib/>.
8   See <URL: http://www.jisc.ac.uk/>.
9   National Electronic Library for Health. *See Information for health: an information strategy for the modern NHS.* Available at <URL: http://omni.ac.uk/mirrored/nhs/info-strategy/>.

Opening keynote address

Opening keynote address

ALICE THROUGH THE LOOKING GLASS: INFORMATION SPACES FOR A NEW
LEARNING GENERATION

Richard Heseltine

Following Alice

This conference promises to be a landmark conference – a conference which
takes our shared understanding of the issues involved in networked information
onto a new and higher level. Indeed, when we first began planning the conference it was very much in our minds to push back the boundaries of the debate
about networked information. Of course, you will still find papers concerned
with technical issues, with metadata, with architectural matters, and rightly so.
But we wanted to go beyond technical issues regarding the organization of access
to information, and start to address sociological issues, to consider the cultural
and political landscape of the information society. For the sociological and the
technological are not mutually exclusive. As the great cultural historian and commentator Raymond Williams once observed,[1] a technology is more than a technique. A particular technical invention can be seen, and temporarily interpreted,
as if it were autonomous, but a technology embraces a whole range of knowledge,
skills, devices and applications. It is a sphere of social activity, necessarily in complex and variable connection with other social relations and institutions. If there
is a unifying theme to this conference, it is about placing information in its social
context, while at the same time exploring the technical underpinnings needed to
make the information society, the learning society, work. You cannot construct the
information society, or the learning society, on rhetoric alone. But by the same
token you cannot construct technical solutions in a social vacuum.

I want to cover four main areas in this paper. First, I want to elaborate on my
view that the commonplace notion of the virtual library, or digital library, has a
tendency to decontextualize information. This is a retrograde step that ignores
the potential of communications and information technology (C&IT) to integrate multiplicities of information and communication services in real, contextu-

alized working environments. I plan to offer the concept of a *landscape* as a better way of conceptualizing the organization of these services.

Second, I want to highlight some features of the underlying technical architecture which will be required to underpin the new learning and working environments which I envisage. In this respect, I want to signpost the more detailed consideration which will be given later in this conference to the MODELS Information Architecture.

Third, I want to introduce a very different dimension, which is reflected in the reference in my title to a new learning generation. I want to give some preliminary consideration to the fact that a generation is 'growing up digital' to steal the title of Don Tapscott's latest book,[2] and that this generation exhibits quite different learning styles from previous generations which did not grow up with computers as an everyday part of life. This impacts on the kinds of learning landscapes which we, or rather they, will want to develop.

Finally, I want to look at the landscape metaphor in more detail, and give some practical examples of what I understand by the concept.

I had better say something about Alice. You may recall the opening of *Alice's adventures in Wonderland*: ' . . . "and what is the use of a book", thought Alice, "without pictures or conversations?".'[3] As a child with a progressive learning style, she goes on to explore wonderland, and although she is often confused by it, she does not try to reorganize it in her own conventional terms. We meet Alice again at the beginning of *Through the looking glass*.[4] She enters here into another dimension, into a new landscape, and again she explores, without too much prejudice, this new landscape, until at the end she becomes a queen. Now, for many of us, the world of electronic information has over the last few years been a kind of wonderland. But unlike Alice, because we have different learning styles, we have tried to reorganize it in our own traditional terms. What I want to suggest throughout this paper, and when, by way of conclusion, I come back to Alice, is that we perhaps need to climb through the looking glass, to see the world in different terms, and to embrace it as might a child – not a Victorian child, but as a child who has 'grown up digital'.

Let us consider the scene in *Jurassic Park* where the small girl discovers a Unix system ('I know this', she says) and succeeds in restoring the island's power supply. We have the girl – clearly a member of the generation which has grown up digital. She has a problem to solve, and it is a fairly pressing problem with dinosaurs at the door, but she does not need a manual to tackle it. She gets in there, she explores, she finds out. And how is the information she needs represented? Not as a dataset, or as a series of command options, but as a three-dimensional landscape which she can readily appreciate and navigate. So there we have a new learner navigating an information landscape – and doing something useful at the same time.

Vices of the virtual library

I will now turn to the concept of the virtual library. In a recent paper on the MODELS project the authors quote Alberto Manguel, the author of *A history of reading*. Manguel describes traditional libraries as 'ordainers of the universe' – an epithet apparently used by the Sumerians. Manguel dwells on the efforts of Callimachus to ordain the order of books at the library of Alexandria, and he quotes in turn the opinion of the French critic Christian Jacob that Callimachus' library was the first example of 'a utopian place of criticism, in which the texts can be compared, opened side by side.'[5]

This narrative provides some interesting insights into the nature of libraries. First, they are physically separate, as by definition they must be by virtue of their role as storehouses of books. A good example of this is the recently opened new British Library, which stands in St Pancras as a magnificent celebration of the physicality of the library and of its transcendence of the concerns of the day. It represents the literal incorporation of knowledge, standing above the temporal conflicts and strivings which led to the production of that knowledge. In the second place, we have the notion of the librarian as 'ordainer' of the universe, and a classification scheme is just that: it is a predetermined, decontextualized, abstract representation of knowledge. It must be abstract in order to last, otherwise we would need continuously to reorder our collections of books to fit passing practical concerns. Thirdly, we find in that narrative a context of sorts for the information contained in the library, and that context is provided by the classic purpose of research, the pursuit of knowledge for its own sake. The library is a utopian place of criticism.

These three essential characteristics of the library of Callimachus remain highly relevant to the physical libraries of today, and the concept of the virtual library represents an effort, unconscious perhaps, to reproduce the essentials of the library of Alexandria in an electronic environment.

The virtual library is certainly separate. It exists in a universe of its own, bound by its own rules of organization. It is preordained. Often it is discussed as if it is an artefact in its own right – something that can almost be seen and touched. It certainly encourages the aggrandizing instincts of librarians. Just when they had become used to the idea that, no, they could not all build the library of Alexandria, here comes the Internet with the promise that, yes, after all, they can provide something bigger and richer than anyone else. And it probably won't burn down. And the virtual library supports a classical research agenda. It aims to lay out a utopian place of criticism – a decontextualized resource to be drawn on for the finer purposes of scholarship.

This separation of information from education and work is unhealthy, because people can best use information resources when they are placed in context. It can be argued that the role of the educator is precisely to place information in context. It is not just a resource to be drawn on but something to be embedded in learning. It needs to be intimately connected with problem-solving and the acquisition of skills, so that the raw material which it represents can be more readily transformed into useful and lasting knowledge. With books that is hard to do. With C&IT, however, it does become possible to build these integrated, contextualized environments.

At a more practical level, this contextualizing also means bringing access to information resources into association with other activities. We might think about integrating information access with systems for the production, storage and management of documents, with systems for the sharing of documents within workgroups, with communication systems, which might include e-mail, telephony or synchronous conferencing systems, and with commercial trading places. By clinging to the concept of the virtual library, thereby rebuilding the walls of the traditional library, we risk separating information spaces from work spaces. C&IT has the capacity to unite information and work spaces to create rich working and learning environments which are given substance by being embedded in practical, non-abstract contexts.

And that is where the concept of a landscape comes in. I shall return to this concept later, but for the moment I shall define a landscape provisionally as a means of representing a personal working environment so that it embraces both work spaces and information spaces. A landscape provides a personal, adaptable view of the world. As a metaphor, it appears to provide a powerful way of enabling people to make sense of virtual territory. Whereas the concept of the virtual library detaches information resources from real activities, the concept of a landscape can reintegrate them.

Virtues of the MODELS Information Architecture (MIA)

So far I have been talking about contextualizing information, and about integrating different kinds of services within that context. I shall now consider the underlying architecture of the environments created on that basis. Three years ago at the last UKOLN conference I made the following statement:

> End users are being confronted now by a multiplicity of systems and services: for obtaining information; for communicating; for taking delivery of documents; and for producing documents. We need to have much better models of how all these services should fit together from the point of view of the end user. What are the key standards? What are the most effective means of presenting services? This is not just a matter of user interfaces but of bringing everything together in a real working environment.[6]

The MODELS Information Architecture (MIA), which has been developed through the MODELS project, now gives us that framework, at least as far as information services are concerned. The MIA will be considered in detail later in this conference, and should be regarded as a very powerful tool both for understanding and for developmental work. For the moment let me highlight two features.

First, the concept of a landscape is firmly embedded in the architecture. So although the MIA is still mainly concerned with information services, it has the potential to underpin the wider context – the broader learning or working environment which I envisage. The landscape metaphor will serve that purpose. We could easily imagine the architecture being extended to link with something like Lotus Learning Space, which provides its own set of integrated tools for undertaking learning tasks, for communications and so forth.

Second, this architecture is capable of adapting dynamically to change. Many current attempts to bring together diverse resources rely on customizing the solution to a predefined set of resources. But we need to be able to bring in new resources, and perhaps to take old ones out. So the solution needs to be generic, it needs to be open, and it needs to be standards-based. The MODELS Information Architecture appear to meet these criteria, and therefore stands a good chance of providing the underpinning architecture we require. The MIA appears to be sustainable, extensible and scaleable.

Growing up digital

Let us now consider the theme of 'growing up digital'. I personally went to a very traditional English grammar school. The very first lesson I was ever given there was on the parsing of an English sentence. I was trained to think in a particular way. I was trained to think in terms of clear categories and hierarchies. I was trained to absorb information that was handed down to me, to analyse it, to synthesize it and to reproduce it. I was not trained to explore, to experiment, to solve problems, to work in groups, to think laterally or to interact creatively with my knowledge environment.

All those of my generation, and of earlier generations, experienced much the same kind of education. That is why we are comfortable with the notion of a separate information space which is organized according to predetermined rules. That is why we still expect every new piece of software to come with a set of instructions.

That kind of school experience is no longer current. Methods of teaching have changed to encourage the experimental, the exploratory, and we are grappling with some of the consequences of that. As any parent knows, the current generation can scarcely spell, has no idea of grammar, and has difficulty saying the times tables. But they can do wonderful things which we could not, especially if you put them in front of a computer.

Anyone, from David Blunkett down, who thinks we can revert to a world of broadcast education, where students are the passive recipients of preordained categories of information, is living in a timewarp. As Don Tapscott has argued in his book *Growing up digital*,[7] the children of today's Net Generation (as he calls them), are learning, playing, communicating, working and creating communities very differently from their parents. Digital media enhance these new approaches, these new learning styles. Perhaps they drive them. Or perhaps what we are seeing is a releasing of the natural learning styles of children – styles which were previously beaten out of them, or trained out of them.

Games playing provides us with many examples of the way in which children learn differently in a digital environment. They do not read instructions: they explore; they experiment; they find out for themselves. They do not want, nor do they need, preconstructed, preordained information spaces. They just do it. Some of you may know the computer game called Myst. It is one of many problem-solving software environments of a kind that children love. Its successor is called Riven which outdistances Myst in both its scale and complexity (it comes on five CD-ROMs) and in the brilliance of its graphics.

Here is what is said about Riven in the magazine *Wired*:

> *Riven* is gamemaking at its most audacious. Visual and audio effects aside, the effort put into making the experience intellectually immersive is staggering. The programmers have created a civilisation, and then dropped you, the unwitting player, into it. You can never be sure whether a building is a temple, a control room, or a simple shelter, because everything has larger cultural significance. In one room, bronze beetles on the wall snap open to reveal Byzantine-style religious scenes: a book falling from the sky; a messiah figure casting his followers into an abyss. Acclimatising to *Riven* is like learning to read – you must learn to synthesise the scattered symbolism of the game into a useful visual alphabet.[8]

There are no explanatory notes to Riven. There is no obvious objective. There are no clear signposts. Yet children will deal with this quite happily. All *my* training prevents me from doing so. Children who grow up digital are comfortable with this kind of intellectually immersive environment. They show us the *real* potential of the technology. Never before have we had the ability to create learning environments like this.

When *we* construct tools to access networked information, we inevitably do so in terms of our own training and aptitudes. Our children, however, will do things differently, and will not invent digital libraries. As Tapscott argues,[9] the people, companies and nations which succeed in the new economy will be those who listen to their children. We should listen to their views on the world. We should learn from their effortless mastery and application of new tools. The challenge is not to create digital libraries, but to envision integrated learning environments which are designed for the learning styles of a digital generation. The makers of products such as Myst and Riven are rising to this challenge. In education, particularly in higher education, we just do not get it. So our best response to the emergence of the Internet is to try to catalogue it.

Landscapes for a learning generation

I shall now bring all these themes together by returning to the concept of landscapes. They are an immensely important idea, and one that is gaining currency. A landscape is the user's personal view of the information universe. It is much more than an interface. It is a kind of map but more dynamic than a map. It not only shows the user where appropriate and relevant information resources can be found, it also amends the map as new resources are discovered, and dynamically alerts the user to the availability of new things. And it is about more than information resources as we understand them. It is intended to represent a complete working environment.

The software to develop this kind of landscape – this kind of working environment – is starting to become available in the context of the Internet. There is already a parallel in the use of the landscape metaphor by companies such as GeoCities, which provide Internet users with facilities to construct their own personal websites, or 'homesteads', on the Internet 'frontier'. You can even choose to build your web 'home' in a specific 'neighbourhood' of like-minded people. The concept of a landscape is evidently a powerful way of enabling people to make sense of virtual territory.

The landscape metaphor can also be individualized to suit people's real working needs. Information resources, which are a part but only a part of the landscape, are firmly integrated into people's working and learning environments. They are not separated out as standalone items Whereas the concept of the virtual library detaches information resources from real activities, the concept of an information landscape reintegrates them.

A simple one-dimensional example of a landscape is found within an online learning environment called Merlin, which has been developed at the University of Hull. A pathway represents a set of learning tasks, with assessment exercises at the end of each stage. It has embedded e-mail-based conferencing software, and is capable of incorporating synchronous audio and video. It includes Internet resources, and means of producing and distributing documents, and of storing them within personal or shared portfolios. It was originally designed for students taking distance-taught English language courses, and thus provides students following such a course with a landscape which gives a personal view of their learning world.

There is a garden design software package that allows users to draw up a one-dimensional plan of a garden, and to populate it with their own chosen plants and objects. You might just want a shrub or tree from a particular genus, but you could also select from a large database to pick a particular species which meets own requirements. By analogy, you could construct an information garden, and choose a generic BIDS service, or you might want a customized version of that service. You can then take the plan, and see it in three dimensions, you can alter your perspective and even walk around within it. Thus we are starting to produce the kind of immersive environment that was spoken about earlier. And finally, you can show the garden changing through the seasons, and over time. So the garden model is dynamic, just as learning landscapes need to be dynamic and adaptable. So in this concept of a landscape, we have moved far away from an interface, and are approaching the immersive environment which is so well adapted to the learning styles of a digital generation.

Lewis Carroll, the sad librarian

I shall conclude by returning to Lewis Carroll's Alice. Alice featured in the Follett Report.[10] She was the student in one of the Report's little vignettes – little scenarios of the future – and she did some interesting things. From the computer in her bedroom, she could check her diary, exchange e-mail with her tutor, consult the library catalogue, order documents, and download videos of lectures. But you get the impression this was really a series of single, unintegrated actions. To approach a more integrated, more highly contextualized, more intellectually immersive environment, we need to liberate Alice by taking her through the looking glass into a new world, into a new landscape.

That leaves us with Lewis Carroll, the sad librarian. For as sub-librarian of Christ Church, Oxford, Carroll used a small room overlooking the deanery garden where the Liddell children played croquet. 'How often he must have watched them', one commentator has suggested, 'longing to escape from the dark halls of Oxford into the bright flowers and cool fountains of childhood's Eden.'[11] And that is a lesson for librarians.

Consider a scene from a film called 'Dead poets society' in which Robin Williams, playing the new teacher at an exclusive and traditional boys' school, instructs his pupils to rip up the stultifying introduction written by J. Evans Pritchard PhD to a book of poetry. Librarians too, in their own ways, should make history of J. Evans Pritchard PhD – no longer slaves to Dewey, or Library of Congress subject headings; no longer imagining that subject gateways are the only way into the world; ready to learn as Alice in the garden of talking flowers;

thinking less about information and more about learning – in short seeing through the looking glass.

References

1   Williams, R., 'Communication technologies and social institutions', in *Contact: human communications and its history*, London, Thames and Hudson, 1981, 226–38.

2   Tapscott, D., *Growing up digital: the rise of the net generation*, New York, McGraw-Hill, 1998.

3   Carroll, L. (alias Dodgson, C. L.), *Alice's adventures in wonderland*, 1865 (several editions).

4   Carroll, L. (alias Dodgson, C. L.), *Through the looking glass: and what Alice found there*, 1872 (several editions).

5   Manguel, A., *A history of reading*, London, HarperCollins, 1996, quoted in Dempsey, L., Russell, R. and Murray, R., 'A Utopian place of criticism?: brokering access to network information', *Journal of documentation*, **55** (1), 1999.

6   Heseltine, R., 'Resource discovery and systemic change: a UK perspective', in Dempsey, L., Law, D. and Mowat, I., (eds.) *Networking and the future of libraries 2: managing the intellectual record*, London, Library Association Publishing, 1995.

7   Tapscott, D. *op. cit.*

8   Ward, J., 'Worlds away', *Wired*, **6** (3), 1998. Also available at <URL: http://www.wired/archive/6.03/streetcred.html?pg=6>.

9   Tapscott, D. *op. cit.*

10 Report of the Joint Funding Council's Libraries Review Group, chairman Sir Brian Follett. (The Follett Report). The 'Alice' vignette appears in Chapter 7 – Information Technology. Available at <URL: http://back.niss.as.uk/education/hefc/follett/>.

11 Gardner, M., *The annotated Alice: Alice's adventures in wonderland, and Through the looking glass*, London, Blond, 1960.

Part 1

Information architectures:
constructing the digital library

1

The library, the catalogue, the broker

Lorcan Dempsey

Introduction

In his chapter on libraries and librarians in *A history of reading*,[1] Alberto Manguel calls librarians 'ordainers of the universe', an epithet used, he tells us, by the Sumerians. He discusses the efforts of Callimachus to ordain the order of books at The Library of Alexandria and notes that 'With Callimachus, the library became an organized reading-space'.

These phrases are useful handles on which to hang a view of what it is libraries do. Libraries may no longer aim to collect and classify all documented knowledge, but their selection and acquisition policies have 'ordained' the view of knowledge and learning their readers have had, as well as which materials have become a part of the intellectual record libraries jointly create with archives, museums and others. The library has further organized these materials in ways that are useful to their users; it is not merely an unordered aggregation. In this paper I want to explore some aspects of this organization in a new environment. What 'organized reading-spaces' will libraries create in a network society?

Organization, libraries and catalogues

Organization is central to what libraries do, and is a large part of the value they add. As such it is not surprising that the 'organizaton of knowledge' has been central to the disciplinary claims of librarianship and an elaborate apparatus of cataloguing, classification and bibliography has developed. Indeed, Callimachus stands near the head of this tradition. He was responsible for the production of a work in 240 BC which Norris describes in her *History of cataloguing* as 'a classified catalogue, a bibliography and a biographical dictionary all in one'.[2] The subsequent history of the catalogue provides interesting examples of discussion and argument about the value, and the cost, of such organizational skills and labour. Norris traces the development from systematic-classed lists of the ancient world ('ordainers' of the universe as they sought to capture all knowledge in their classifications), through the inventories of the medieval period, to the realization that the catalogue had to be more than a mere listing, it 'was a key to the library'. The construction of such a key required a specialist art and governing rules. Of central interest here is the debate surrounding the catalogue of the British Museum, and the opposition between Anthony Pannizzi who developed his seminal 91 rules for the construction of the British Museum Catalogue and various lay proponents of a simpler – cheaper and quicker – list-based approach.

Why is a simple list not enough? Because neither the effective disclosure of library materials nor the user's best interests are well served by such a list. Much discussion of the nature and function of the catalogue go back to the celebrated 'objects' described by Cutter.[3] Simply stated, these are that the catalogue supports the finding function (by known author, title or subject), and the gathering function (by author, or subject or kind of literature), and the selecting function (as to edition or as to character). An inventory or list will not support these functions very well. Authors may have different names. Works appear in many manifestations (*Hamlet* is a work; there are many manifestations of this work in different editions, compilations, formats, and so on). Works may not have titles or authors, or their titles or authors may not be clear. In a world where the description and collocation of works, manifestations, authors and subjects may be quite complicated, the organizational investment represented in the catalogue, and the skills and rules which enable it, are required to support the realization of Cutter's objects. Going beyond Cutter, some argue that the role of the catalogue is to bring to the surface through such organizational devices the knowledge that is represented in the collection, by allowing the user to navigate using subjects, works and authors.

Libraries have also organized the materials themselves, and in open access libraries this typically follows a classified approach. The reader can browse in 'ordained' ways. The format of the materials – books and journals – is well known and has co-evolved with the development of libraries and the reading patterns of their users. These materials present further organizational devices – contents pages, indexes, bibliographies – which provide other avenues into the literature.[4] However, alongside the book collections are others – reports, slides, journals, special collections, archives – which are typically not well integrated into the catalogue itself or, physically, into the classified sequence on the shelves. They may be internally organized islands, where such organization is not consistent across collections. Each island may involve a different pattern of organization and use. They may have separate catalogues or other finding tools, and may be arranged in various ways, slides one way, for example, EU documentation another.

Until recently, these collections have been physically co-located in library buildings. In the largely print-based world, readers are accustomed to the labour of interacting with the apparatus of different collection types. The special collections, or the archives, or the slide collection, or the standards collection, might be in different places, with different levels of catalogue. Readers recognize that the catalogue deals with books, and that to discover whether a particular journal article is available may involve several steps in different tools. They move between the collections themselves, finding tools, conversation with colleagues, and advice from the librarian – that 'living catalogue only waiting to be consulted'.[5] A large part of the sustained experience of any library comes from the relationship between the various finding tools, the collections, and the places they collectively occupy.[6] These exist in complex relation, and complex practices and behaviours have developed around them, often specific to particular libraries. As in any complicated system, much use is directed by tacit understanding developed through custom and experiment. In fact, we know surprisingly little about such behaviour in the round: research tends to focus on the use of the catalogue, or on browsing behaviour, or on some other individual component; similarly, the progress of automation has been piecemeal, task by task. This is one reason why, despite several years of attention, we do not have very well developed views of what digital or hybrid libraries will be like. It is also a reason for occasional misunderstanding between reader and library over a particular change: where the latter might see a specific improvement or saving, the former might see disruption in a pattern of behaviour or expectation.

As digital resources multiply, organizational and behavioural practices are being modified, typically, at present, in ad hoc ways. Such resources introduce new 'islands': they are usually not part of the traditional organizational apparatus, whether realized in the catalogue or through physical arrangement. There may be an electronic reserve collection; a collection of CD-ROMs; document discovery and delivery services (FirstSearch, BIDS, etc.); access to collections of specialist data sets (through the Arts and Humanities Data Service, or MIDAS (Manchester Information Datasets and Associated Services), or the Data Archive, for example). The multiplication of such islands has several drawbacks. For users, it means that the use of resources becomes complicated. There may be diversity of organization of resources (different collection types, different catalogues); diversity of user interface and interaction pattern; there may be diversity of logins and conditions of use. Such diversity is a barrier to use: it erects fences, wastes time and dampens demand. For libraries, it means that there are additional demands in terms of training, support and collection management: as diversity increases, scale economies diminish.

How do these new developments relate to the traditional organizational techniques, the catalogue and the physical arrangement of materials?

The catalogue has only ever provided access to a part of the collection. Typically, the non-book 'islands' have not been represented in it. Of particular significance here is the absence of journal literature. It may contain title information, but typically not article details. As the volume and variety of non-book material increases, the catalogue increasingly becomes one resource among many. It is less and less the complete 'key to the library'. Terry Hanson has discussed the motivation for developing an 'access catalogue' which describes a range of resources to users,[7] and the LASER (Library Access to Selected Electronic Resources) system at Leeds is an interesting example of this.[8] However, the user now also has access to other resource description databases: for journals, for Internet resources, for electronic texts, and so on.

Clearly, these new resources are not physically integrated as part of a physical classified sequence. The experience may be partly replicated by providing web pages which present resources organized in simple ways. Increasingly, as suggested above, there may be databases of resource descriptions which may be used to present views of what is available. In this way, the intellectual and the physical arrangements come together. But there are some interesting ways in which the arrangement of digital resources differs from the physical. I have suggested that electronic resources do not currently have the uniformity of treatment which has developed with print resources. Each may have to be 'learned' or handled in special ways. Furthermore, materials in the print world arrive in discrete packages, which are managed and used individually. Because of their 'physicality', the user or the library has to makes the connections or links. In the new network space, resources may communicate, connections may be made, resources may change shape or be reconfigured. So, for example, documents, bibliographic references, or scientific data may be imported into a user workspace. An intermediate system may interact with several resources on behalf of a user, as happens with the 'clump' projects, where several catalogues are queried in parallel.[9] Data may be automatically collected and indexed, as happens with the web robots. Processes may be automated through communication between applications, as where data is passed between a search service, a document delivery service, and an accounting system, without the need for manual intervention.

We are only in early stages of such developments, but this variety of resource, and of organizational approach, is characteristic of what is coming to be known as the 'hybrid library'. The hybrid library can be understood as an organized attempt to come to terms with the multiple islands that library services are increasingly becoming and to reduce the difference in patterns of access and management between those islands.

To finish this part of the discussion, I want to pick up two points. The first is to do with the implications of some of this change for the 'organization of knowledge' tradition of libraries. The second takes forward the remark made earlier about value and cost.

I began by talking about the goals of the catalogue, as elaborated by Cutter. An apparatus of codes and practices has developed to realize these goals: so that the assignment of headings, and perhaps, further authorities work, bring together names, works and subjects; descriptions allow retrieval of manifestations; and so on. Of course, these goals may be imperfectly and variably realized in today's catalogues. Furthermore, cataloguing theory has been developed in an environment where the catalogue typically exposed the content of a particular collection under a single organization's control, where that collection typically contained books, and where the catalogue was realized by manual means. The structure of the catalogue may not be apparent in some automated catalogues, and is not very effective across collections. In fact, the information retrieval approach, and its extension in network protocols such as Z39.50, involves a 'flattening' of structure: the model is one of individual, unrelated records which describe information objects. So, the catalogue may not be well equipped to satisfy these theoretical cataloguing objectives. Increasingly, readers may be allowed to search across several catalogues, individually or as a federated resource, meaning that differences in practice between libraries and catalogues may be apparent. In a new development, the catalogue may be looked at alongside resources created within different curatorial traditions (archival finding aids) or from different sectors (abstracting and indexing services, online book sellers), where the same structuring apparatus may not be used. These issues raise serious questions for libraries and their practices – both in terms of their theoretical basis and their practical application – but further exploration is beyond my scope here.

Whatever the current state of the catalogue, a more general form of the argument advanced above in its defence remains relevant. The hybrid library cannot be a mere collocation of services, a listing on a web page. Where is the added value the library provides? The value of the library is that it saves users' time, that it releases the value of the resources it manages, that it effectively brings together users and resources over time. Organization continues to be central, but the techniques used need to develop with the needs of the user and the characteristics of the materials. In particular it is becoming clear that it is not enough for the library to provide access to a part of its collection through a catalogue; another through a set of annotated web links or resource database; another indirectly through abstracting and indexing services; and so on; with no relation between them. It is likely that the collections and services will be brought together at some higher level. Furthermore, It will be increasingly difficult to consider these services separately from the wider fabric of resources that is available. And, it is becoming more important to support other services than just searching or discovery: network resources can communicate with each other, and this involves further thinking about how to present and support user services. I consider some of these issues further in later sections. The purpose of the comparison with the catalogue is to highlight that the 'added value' may not be obvious, nor may it emerge directly from user requirements. Indeed, its value may need to be promoted and defended.

Organization, libraries and networked information

I want to consider some of the characteristics of network resources, and of the environment in which they are used. Let us take first, as an example, the resources that might be available to the reader who is interested in books and journals: catalogues; abstracting and indexing services; document delivery services; and so on. Some of the characteristics of available resources are:

- They are heterogeneous, and are growing in volume and variety. Services have different access characteristics, may require individual login, use diverse data schema and exchange formats, and so on. The experience of using a subject gateway like EEVL (Edinburgh Engineering Virtual Library) for example, is different from using an abstracting service on CD-ROM, which is different from using a network abstracting service through Edina. Services require the user to have significant advance knowledge of what is available, and some persistence if they wish to use several. Services have different terms and conditions attached to their use.
- They are autonomously managed; they have developed independently, responsive to different service and business goals. This means that within any information process, it may be necessary to interact with several services which do not coordinate their activities. Until recently, these services have been conceived and designed as standalone systems, rather than as parts of a fabric of information resources on a network. So, for example there are network services which accept document requests (such as that provided by the British Library), there are packages which can format requests for dispatch to such services, there are services which allow people discover the documents of use to them. These may not be linked up in such a way that an end-to-end process can be automated. Data may not cross boundaries, or may have to be re-keyed or transcribed by user or by staff.
- They are individually controlled. Information providers wish to protect the value of resources they make available. There may be a need to confirm the identity of users or the integrity of resources. A framework for commerce needs to be in place. At present these needs are provided on a service-by-service basis. When these issues of security, control and commerce achieve

widely deployed common solutions we can expect another surge in the availability of networked information.

- They represent different aggregations of function. For example, a union catalogue allows people to discover (and locate) journal articles. An integrated service from the British Library or BIDS (Bath Information Data Service) allows a user to discover, locate, and request documents and have them delivered. An abstracting and indexing service allows users to discover the existence of documents. Some services may be offered as 'one stop shops'. 'One shop stop' might be a more accurate characterization. Although some organizations now offer services which include discover, locate, request and deliver facilities, they are still just components within this potentially distributed document supply service since no server will meet all coverage or quality of service criteria. This is not to say that 'one stop shops' are not locally useful, but they provide inevitably partial solutions.

This lack of organized access has some implications:

- Network resources do not release their full value. There is some evidence, summarized by Bell for example,[10] that variety inhibits effective use for casual users who do not have the time or inclination to become familiar with more than a few different approaches, and who do not stray from familiar paths. This variety also presents a management issue for libraries: different technical characteristics may require different approaches, training needs are duplicated, the technology is very much on the surface rather than disappearing into a coherent environment of use. Similar issues can be raised in relation to other information providers, where variety of technical or service approach may reduce demand or raise the cost of supply.
- Users are not well served. Relevant resources may not be visible, or will be ignored. The learning or social opportunity is diminished.
- The opportunity of networking is missed. The opportunity now posed by the developing technologies is not just to automate particular tasks but to automate end-to-end processes in ways that support effective use, and deliver integrated services into working environments.

This is the situation within the area traditionally looked after by libraries. However, library users might expect organized access to a wider range of materials. Libraries now operate in a shared network space which brings together users, service providers and resources in new combinations and balances. So, there are new divisions of labour in the learning and information domains. Take the example of document supply, where publishers, libraries and aggregators are realigning the pattern of delivery; or the creation of new learning environments, which may bring together learning technologists, library and information people, and so on, in the creation of a new type of service. There are new forms of user behaviour and expectation, as, for example, where communication technologies are reaching into writing and learning environments. There are also cross-domain convergences, where previously distinct activities may be brought into new relation. For example, we are likely to see much greater collaboration in relation to cultural heritage and local history, where libraries, archives and museums recognize shared access and preservation concerns. Or, again, greater link-up between the library and booksellers, publishers, or other suppliers of materials, as they recognize a shared interest in providing services which meet the various needs of users. Some libraries have bookshops on their premises; why not link their online services also?

These influences again point to an environment in which heterogeneous, autonomously managed information resources continue to increase in volume and variety. We can suggest some characteristics of this wider environment and its relationship to library services:

- The user workspace. I used the expression 'network space' earlier, and metaphors of landscape and ecology have threaded discussion at this conference. What these phrases suggest is an emerging awareness that it is reasonable to see such spaces as living and working places. We can see a progressive shift in perception from a computer, to a workspace, to an environment. This will continue as the environment becomes richer in services we wish to see, as computational devices and the means of connecting them become more pervasive, and as technologies for security and commerce mature. Increasingly, the user of services will expect them to be available within their own communications space, to be able to reuse, combine, and link, without barriers, fences or arbitrary difference. In an interesting discussion of the future of computing, Terry Winograd talks of the historical shift from 'computing machinery to interaction design' as the focus of computing. He suggests that this requires a shift from seeing the machinery to 'seeing the lives of the people using it'.[11] Viable digital information spaces will depend on the ability to allow the user richer interactional abilities. This in turn depends on presenting opportunity effectively and creating the ability for components of the network space to communicate. It also suggests the need for greater personalization services.
- The role of the library. Libraries need to consider their response to these changes within the network space. Unlike some other players, libraries have a dual role. They manage their own collections and make them available, but they also have a role in guiding their users to resources and services out of their direct control. In many cases this distinction becomes less clear as a

model based on the purchase of rights in the use of materials, with particular terms and conditions, replaces a model based the direct purchase and circulation of materials themselves. Nor should it be forgotten that libraries are part of larger institutions, whose mission they support. Libraries co-evolve with these wider institutions which in turn are being transformed. There are important and far-reaching discussions about the management of learning and research, the provision of digital information services for the citizen, the place of cultural heritage services, and the 'informationalization' of business and industrial processes. Again, this suggests greater variety of practice and partnership.

- Technical change. A difficulty for those currently developing network information services is accelerated technical change, and the risk associated with investment in a volatile environment. The current web environment is document-centric, with limited support for interaction and structured applications which exploit the richness of the resources that are made available. Alongside this, structured approaches exist which have developed within particular domains (Z39.50, SGML, EDI, and so on). There is limited support for some of the technologies required to build new long-term institutions within the network space (distributed authentication, security, commerce). However, we are seeing the rapid development of a more 'structured web' within which it is likely that existing structured approaches to work will be re-engineered or integrated. The 'web' will support richer applications, distributed objects, security and commerce services. The goal should be for an applications framework to be able to support rich enough services that the technology disappears into the environment. We are still some way from that.

I suggested above that the goal of the hybrid library was somehow to overcome the fragmentation of the library service into multiple islands. We can now recognize that there are also multiple other islands in the network space the user occupies, and that the library needs to work to provide effective access to some of these also. This is in the midst of rapid organizational, service and technical change which makes taking decisions difficult. As other communities are facing some of these issues, and as libraries may have to try to provide access to resources outside of their control, common approaches at various levels would be useful. However, at the moment, as discussed by Ray Lester elsewhere in this volume, there is limited opportunity to seek consensus across these communities.

How might we move forward? What does integration mean? Some examples of what it might cover are:

- Information landscape. For the moment, I introduce this term to suggest the shift in emphasis which sees information resources organized around user interests rather than around particular technical or media characteristics. What this might mean in practice is discussed further below.

- Collection description. Libraries do not typically describe resources at the collection level. I have loosely spoken about collections already. I mean such things as physical collections of documents, slides, tapes, and so on. However, they might also include such things as databases (the catalogue for example), electronic journals, websites. The notion is vague until decisions are made in some service context. Describing which collections are available and under what conditions would provide some higher level integration which is currently lacking.

- Authentication. The library as a place has certain controls built in: membership cards, single points of entry and exit, supervision. Open distributed control in the digital information space is still a research and development challenge. Authentication and authorization information needs to be exchanged at various stages. Support for commercial activity will have to be provided. The integrity and privacy of exchanged information may have to be assured. The usefulness of an information landscape will be severely mitigated without distributed authentication services which mean that the client need only 'prove' themselves once. Multiple challenges (passwords) erect fences in the landscape which inhibit use. They are potentially relevant at various points in information exchanges. This issue is not discussed further.

- System interworking. We might identify two related aspects. The first could be called intra-function integration, where there is working across different systems which provide the same function. So for example, one might be able to cross-search heterogeneous resources, or have a message dispatched to heterogeneous request services. The oft-mentioned desire to be able to look at several services through a similar interface is an example of this. The second could be called inter-function integration, where there is working between systems which provide different functions. Typically, this might involve handing data between functions, as where, for example, an identifier or citation is passed from a search function to a locate function. (A locate function might resolve the identifier to discover locations, or match a citation against a holdings file, or use some other technique.) Inter-function communication is required if end-to-end processes are to be automated, reducing expensive manual effort.

- Semantic interworking. Different islands may employ different subject vocabularies and schema, different data schema, different conventions with regard to identification, and so on. A variety of mappings may be required, and it is likely that some issues here will remain intractable.

In recent years, 'broker' services have emerged which aim to provide some or all of these integration services. In the next section I explore broker systems, with particular reference to the library issues. Typically a broker will provide support for projecting a unified service across some part of the independently produced, distributed resources we have been discussing.

Organization, libraries and brokers

Building blocks

In his discussion of networked heritage information in Chapter 3, Mike Stapleton provides a useful list of building blocks. I repeat this here with my own gloss. Mike's text is in quotation marks.

- Databases. 'For creating and managing online catalogues and content repositories.' We could add other services here, a document requesting service for example.
- Gateways. 'Provide interfaces to the repositories and deliver content in different forms.' The use of 'gateway' here shows how unsettled our vocabulary is. In this use, it refers to how the resource is made network accessible. In this discussion I have used 'interface' or 'service' rather than 'gateway' for sense proposed here. So, a document requesting service may have an interface that implements the Inter Library Loan protocol. A catalogue may be made available through Z39.50, telnet and web interfaces, and so on. Historically, library resources have been made network aware in one of the following ways:
  - Terminal access to remote services. Users login to a monolithic application with its own user interface and request commands. Data may be downloaded using special, separate procedures or by some form of screen capture.
  - World Wide Web access. The service provider presents its own user interface and request commands, this time through a web form. The gain is that there is some consistency of presentation in a consistently navigable environment. Although the web is becoming a richer environment, dominant current use is for transfer of static information in the form of web pages, or for the unstructured output from databases. As with terminal access, the client just responds to user interface directives such as 'display this text in bold italics' etc. These services are largely oriented around providing services to human users, who then have to process the results.
  - Client/Server access. This architecture is significantly different in that the client has some understanding of the data it is handling. Proprietary

approaches may be in use within certain systems. The use of open standards such as Z39.50 is growing but not widespread. When the client understands the data it is handling, it can be reused in various ways, the results can be processed. The client is responsible for the re-presentation of that data to the user, and is capable of shielding the user from differences between servers. It can be reformatted for display alongside records from other resources, can be passed to other applications, and so on.

- For completeness, I note here significant developments in the web community which will provide support for the exchange of structured data, for distributed objects, and for a range of other services which will significantly enhance the development of web-based information processing applications. Resources may be dynamic and distributed.
- Brokers. 'Provide a common point of access to a range of repositories and data sources.' These will be discussed in greater detail below.
- Delivery platforms. 'Provide users with an interface appropriate for the task at hand.' The current dominant delivery platform is the web browser.
- Protocols. 'Connect it all together on the networks.'

Brokers

Some examples of brokers from the library and related domains are listed in this section. In each case, an application, or 'external mediator', facilitates access to diverse resources and supports data flow. The broker will be designed to support a particular business need, which determines what types of integration it supports. The term 'broker' may be familiar from a distributed object environment, but I intend no specialized meaning here. A broker may be a set of annotated web links; it may deploy a more sophisticated apparatus which supports a richer business model or quality of service. The examples given here do rather more than provide a set of web links or resource database, even if they are still rather early examples.

- LIDDAS (Local Interlending and Document Delivery Administration System) is an Australian project looking at managing interlending and document delivery operations. It will broker access to databases for search and location of desired items, services for request and delivery of items, directory services for environment and business information, and authentication services, passing data between applications as appropriate. The model is very much one of 'single service – multiple systems'.[12]
- The eLib 'hybrid library' and 'clump' projects are looking at broker-type services in their particular application areas. Clumps provide virtual union catalogue services across different underlying OPACs.[13] The hybrid library

projects are variously conceived, looking at providing integration services across particular sets of resources.

- Aquarelle is an EU project which provides a 'mediator' or broker service for museum repositories. It searches across heterogeneous cultural resources providing some central services to support that operation. Mike Stapleton describes Aquarelle in Chapter 3.
- The Arts and Humanities Data Service (AHDS) Gateway projects a unified picture of the AHDS based on a federation of five underlying, autonomously managed service providers. The Gateway provides a service which hides the different access mechanisms of the heterogeneous systems in use at service provider sites, and provides authenticated document requesting services. Daniel Greenstein describes the AHDS gateway in Chapter 2.
- The ROADS cross-searching service. ROADS (Resource Organization And Discovery in Subject-based services) is an eLib funded project which is providing a set of tools for the UK subject gateways, databases of descriptions of Internet resources. The cross-searching service provides a query routing and referral service between the autonomously managed subject gateways.[14] In a related initiative, the CHIC (Cooperative Heirarchical Indexing Coordination) project has developed a service which searches across Z39.50, WHOIS++, and Harvest resources.[15]

The focus of some of these developments is discovery: to varying degrees, they hide differences and collate the results from several different underlying discovery systems. Some go beyond this to address several functional areas and allow data to flow between them. For example, the hybrid library project Agora aims to pass data about selected articles from a discovery to a 'locate' function where it may be matched against some holdings data; data may then be passed to a request function, where it forms the basis of a request message. It hides the difference between different discovery systems and different request systems.

These examples prompt some comments, before discussing brokers in more general terms:

- Human and machine access. Services will be provided which may be accessible to human users through the web, or to intermediate or broker systems through some machine protocol. In the latter case, machine-readable structured data will be returned for reuse in some context; in the former human-readable results will be returned for reading. For example, an OPAC may have a web interface for human access, and a Z39.50 interface for 'clump' access or hybrid library access. Human access is the dominant model.
- Lack of standard interfaces. What characterizes these initiatives is that they support standard machine interfaces which allows them to interact with arbi-

trary services which support the same interfaces. Of course not all services or databases of interest will be available through such standard interfaces. In some cases it may be necessary to write applications which will talk to particular service interfaces, and there is a trend for services to make APIs (application programming interfaces) public to facilitate this. In many cases only human interfaces may be available, so the broker will not be able to retrieve structured data, or may have to try and capture and analyse screen-based data.

- While these examples are largely 'bespoke' applications with standard interfaces to the outside world, we may gradually see more fully distributed applications emerge based on distributed components specialized by function which communicate within one of the distributed object approaches.

MODELS and brokers

This discussion draws on work still developing with our MODELS (MOving to Distributed Environments for Library Services) project which is describing the MODELS Information Architecture (MIA).[16] MODELS started from the view that the development of a high-level architecture was a useful support to discussions of interworking in the library area. It has moved forward through a series of invitational workshops, desk research, and it has influenced the development of several systems and services in the UK and beyond. The MIA provides a common frame of reference and vocabulary which has achieved some currency. The current state of the MIA is described in Chapter 4 and I do not propose to discuss it in detail here.[17] The initial work described a high level broad framework (see Figure 1.1), this now being refined with a view to implementation, and it will be further reported elsewhere.

The broker provides infrastructure for managed access to physically distributed resources. MODELS has generalized the services provided by such 'brokers' in the following way:

- User access – managing interaction with the user. 'Information landscape' is a term that was introduced within the MODELS context to describe the presentation of information environments to users. It might be seen as a potential beneficiary of 'interaction design'. The landscape will project the underlying business processes in a user-oriented way. The 'information landscape' will describe the resources available, provide navigation and selection support, and may be configured to reflect particular styles, policies and collections. A minimal landscape may have links to resources; richer landscapes will gradually emerge which are constructed on the basis of forward knowledge of available services, user profiles, and other data. For example, there has been some discussion of matching user profiles (which record preferences

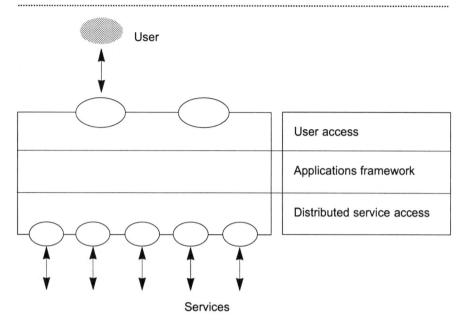

Fig. 1.1 *High level view of MIA*

and privileges) against collection descriptions to personalize the landscape. In a hybrid environment, it will also be important to provide routes in to the print and the digital environments here. The landscape also merges what was previously intellectual and physical access to collections. The California Digital Library provides an interesting example of a landscape (though it does not use the term).[18] Collections (databases, electronic journals, finding aids) and services are described, can be examined in search and classified browse mode. Individuals and institutions can customize their views. Raising 'landscape' in these terms focuses some questions on how it might be provided: it is an area of active research and development, rather than an answer. The landscape is dependent on the other services the broker can support. We have discussed landscape presentation, user profiling, client access (in theory, a broker might be accessible to client as well as to a human user) as part of a user access layer.

- Applications framework – programs and data to support business logic. There needs to be a framework which orchestrates the service components that the broker provides in support of business functions. Operations we might envisage here are: bringing together the user requests with appropriate services; merging and manipulating data for presentation to a user or to pass between functions; and implementing the particular business processes needed (e.g. distributed document delivery, clump, cross-domain resource discovery, etc.).

To do this it requires knowledge about data schemas and formats, and services and collections to which it brokers access. This might be locally configured or provided to it through directory or registry services. The richness of the services here will influence the quality of service provided by the broker.

- Distributed service interfaces – managing interaction with services and resources. Various resources and services require different modes of interaction. Ideally, the broker will abstract the mechanics of these interactions. A reader may request an item to be delivered; the system will decide whether this needs an HTTP 'get', an ILL request, or a note saying to go to the reference collection. A reader may wish to locate some items; the system will present some options for searching, will open up a Z39.50 session, or a web browser, or whatever is required. The system will deal appropriately with delivered items. The variety of services and resources mean that a variety of modes of interaction will be possible. The broker will support interfaces appropriate to its application area. As noted above, in a real-world environment, the absence of widespread deployment of standard machine interfaces means that a broker may have customized or specialized interfaces to particular services. There are clearly advantages in minimizing the number of interfaces which have to be supported.
- Control of access – authentication, commerce. These are included here for completeness. Distributed, open solutions are needed, which the broker can call on as services.

These are logical functional groups which have worked well when measured against a range of emerging developments. The advantage of such an approach is that it separates different aspects. So if a service is offered through a different protocol, or if a new service is added, it should not be necessary to change the user access level. The appropriate transformations will be effected in the middle layer. Similarly, users may see available resources through different landscapes without having to alter the way in which those resources are organized. We begin to see how new resources might be routinely 'shelved' by being added to the lower layer. We can also see how the flexibility introduced in the user access layer makes it plausible to consider a variety of customized approaches into the available resources.

We can also see the advantages of increasing modularization. The broker may be able to call service components from various places to provide its service. For example, terminology services (thesauri) might be used in query expansion.

This is a somewhat idealized presentation, and current brokers in the areas under discussion are rather less well developed than this sketch suggests. The purpose of MIA has been to provide some common ground for discussion of these issues. It is also clear that in implementation many difficulties will be experi-

enced. These brokers are typically working with large, diverse collections of legacy data.

A note on metadata

In the library domain, discussion has tended to focus on so-called 'item' level metadata (descriptions of individual books, articles, and so on). The new environment has new requirements. The broker needs to have access to various types of metadata to support its operation. This is data about its environment and the resources in it. It should be clear that metadata is of central importance. Agility in a distributed environment depends on the ability to identify and use components, and this increasingly relies on metadata. Metadata will be pervasive of distributed information environments.[19] Metadata will be associated with information objects, with applications, with people, with organizations. It will support operations by people and by programs, providing them with advance knowledge of the characteristics of objects of interest and supporting sensible behaviour. In relation to brokers we can note:

- Collection descriptions. Typically information objects exist in collections, where a collection comprises similar information objects. These collections might be databases, websites, document supply centres or libraries. They may be particular collections within a library, or the catalogue for such collections. Such collections are also, of course, information objects, and collections may contain other collections. Collections will also have different terms and conditions associated with their use. They are embedded in particular organizational and business practices, which may impose additional technical requirements on any networked solution, for charging for example. Typically collections will be managed by organizations. Information objects may be 'data' or 'metadata'. How to characterize collections is a poorly defined area at the moment, where a variety of approaches exist and for which consensual approaches are urgently required. This is especially so in the service environment we have sketched above where a range of broker services are emerging. Each of these will have to provide ways of describing the collections and services which are available to users of their systems. 'Collection descriptions' provide forward knowledge about the resources that are available to a user, allowing sensible discrimination between them and their effective use. These may be intellectually created. There is also some interest in automatically generated representations. For example, centroids are inverted index style representations of database content used to support query routing. They are defined by the Common Indexing Protocol,[20] and are used to support cross searching of the UK subject gateways.

- Application (or service, or interface) description. Collections will be made available through some machine interface which needs to be described. Such descriptions will permit brokers and clients to connect to arbitrary resources. Several approaches exist, which cover such attributes as host name, port number, etc. Other services may also need to be described in this way.
- Schema descriptions. If a system is to broker access to heterogeneous metadata collections, to render heterogeneous content in some way, or to map between interchange formats, it needs to have access to schema data which supports this activity.
- User profiles. We have discussed these above.

In the current environment it is likely that brokers may be configured with this type of data. In due course it will be stored in directory and registry services which the broker queries.

There are various ways to create machine- and human-readable descriptions of collections, applications and user profiles at the moment. None commands universal assent. Approaches may be embedded in particular application and/or professional domains. A review of some current approaches to collection and service descriptions has been prepared as part of the MODELS project.[21]

Brokers, islands and hybrid libraries

I have suggested that one way of looking at the hybrid library is to see it as an organized attempt to come to terms with the multiple islands that library services are increasingly becoming and to reduce the difference in patterns of access and management between those islands. Islands may be collections which have their own catalogues, organizational patterns or access mechanisms. They may be network or CD-ROM databases or repositories, or print or other material collections. And so on. There may also be service islands with different procedures and forms of interaction (Inter-Library Loan, for example).

Such islands will be material – a part of the physical library collections – or digital. Many, but not all, material collections will have digital catalogues. Digital resources – image and document repositories, catalogues, and so on – will be interfaced to the network in various ways, allowing different levels of interaction and data exchange.

Initial approaches to organizing such environments have focused on developing organized sets of links. Resource databases take this a step further, providing search and browse access to descriptions of collections and services. These might be seen as simple brokers which provide discovery services. However, they deliver us to the door of resources, rather than delivering the content of resources to us.

Broker services are emerging which support a complex of services. These operate in particular domains (library, museum) and so far have limited production use. Other domains are developing similar approaches. Brokers may have different business aims. A common requirement is to allow cross searching of heterogeneous metadata resources (e.g. library catalogues). Another is to automate end-to-end processes (e.g. Agora will attempt to automate the whole chain of document discovery, locate, request, deliver). Brokers may integrate access to other service components, terminology services, authentication services, user directories, and so on. A developing pattern seems to be where an 'information landscape' is presented which allows navigation, discovery and selection of collections and services, followed by resource specific interaction. Standards-based interaction between brokers and resources confers some benefits, but many resources are not made available through standard interfaces. The level of interaction possible between a broker and resources will vary. For this and other reasons the level of abstraction away from underlying resources the broker provides may not be very high in some cases. The ultimate ambition is to present a unified service over independently developed resources. Early experiences suggest that the construction of brokers is a complex undertaking, and it will be interesting to see how far they are developed. It should be noted that broker access to a resource is not incompatible with continued access direct to the resource itself. A fuller treatment of some of the problem issues that might be encountered in trying to build a system which brokers access to document discovery and delivery services is given elsewhere.[22]

Some final notes on brokers:

- Services and standards. As in other digital library areas standards work lags behind service requirements. This complicates development, as implementors may be unwilling to develop proprietary approaches in the knowledge that standards may shortly emerge. This is as true of general network information management issues as it is within the more specific library domain. The emergence of the structured web is a major factor here: 'will XML change everything?'
- Chicken and egg. The value of brokers increases where resources are available through standard interfaces. Without brokers there may be little value to an information provider in providing services through standard interfaces. This sets up a chicken and egg situation which is a further inhibitor to development. It is interesting to consider the widespread potential but little actual use of Z39.50 within the library management systems environment as an example here. Absence of a market means that there are few if any off the shelf products.

- Business models. A further inhibitor is the absence of clear business models for funding broker activity.
- Brokering access to heterogeneous legacy data is inherently complex. There is sometimes a culture clash between those developing new resource discovery systems in an Internet environment, and those looking to broker access to library, cultural and other legacy systems. There are a number of reasons for this. However, it is important to remember that it is just more difficult to broker access to data which is more richly structured, with different data schema, with different semantics for subject and name control, and with a history of development with accumulated inconsistency. The difficulties of working across different subject vocabularies, for example, are well known and unresolved.
- The broker will often provide less rich services than resources themselves do.

Conclusion

I began with some discussion of the catalogue, and moved on to a general discussion of brokers. They are different types of thing, and, indeed, one of the challenges for the library is to broker access to different catalogues, or to the catalogue alongside other resources. The association is for a different reason. Libraries add value by saving users' time and effort, by ensuring they are united with the resources most useful to them, and by releasing the value of resources over time. To continue to provide these services, libraries must move to a new level of activity which involves integration, not merely collocation, of services. In the current environment, how to do this is not straightforward and we are witnessing a range of interesting experiment and exploration. Users may not expect libraries to 'ordain the universe', but they do look to them to help them do useful things in a complicated network space. Thinking about how to do this brings us to the centre of what libraries are about.

References

1   Manguel, A., *A history of reading*, London, HarperCollins, 1996.
2   Norris, D. M., *A history of cataloguing and cataloguing methods 1100–1850: with an introductory survey of ancient times*, London, Grafton & Co, 1939.
3   Cutter, C., *Rules for a dictionary catalogue*, 4th edn, Washington, Government Printing Office, 1904.
4   This complementarity is discussed in: Oddy, P., *Future libraries: future catalogues*, London, Library Association Publishing, 1996.

5   These words are attributed to Sir Henry Ellis, Director of the British Museum in
    Pannizzi's time, in Norris, *op. cit.*, 204.

6   This relationship is further briefly discussed in: Dempsey, L., 'Afterword: places
    and spaces', in *Towards the digital library: the British Library's Initiatives for Access
    programme*, London, British Library, 1998.

7   Hanson, T., 'The access catalogue gateway to resources', *Ariadne*, **15**, 1998.
    Available at
    <URL:http://www.ariadne.ac.uk/issue15/main/>.

8   <URL:http://www.leeds.ac.uk/library/laser/>

9   Dempsey, L. and Russell, R., ' "Clumps" – or organized access to the scholarly
    record', *Program*, **31** (3), 1997, 239–49.

10 Bell, A., 'The impact of electronic information on the academic research commu-
    nity', *The new review of academic librarianship*, **3**, 1997, 1–24.

11 Winograd, T., 'From computing machinery to interaction design', in Denning,
    P. and Metcalfe, R. (eds.), *Beyond calculation: the next fifty years of computing*,
    Springer-Verlag, 1997, 149–62. Also available at
    <URL:http://hci.stanford.edu/~winograd/acm97.html>.

12 Blinco, K., 'LIDDAS – an Australian document delivery project'. Presentation at
    *Information Ecologies: the impact of new information 'species'. A conference orga-
    nized by the Electronic Libraries Programme and coordinated by UKOLN*. 2-4
    December 1998, Viking Moat House Hotel, York. Presentation is linked from
    conference report at
    <URL: http://www.ukoln.ac.uk/services/elib/events/information-ecologies/>.

13 Dempsey, L. and Russell, R., ' "Clumps" – or distributed access to scholarly
    material', *Program*, **31** (3), July 1997, 239–49.

14 The ROADS cross searching service is available at
    <URL: http://www.ukoln.ac.uk/metadata/roads/crossroads/>.

15 Valkenburg, P. (ed.), *Standards in a distributed indexing architecture*, draft version
    1, 24 February 1998.
    <URL:http://www.terena.nl/projects/chic-pilot/standards_v1.html>

16 Further information about MODELS can be found at
    <URL: http://www.ukoln.ac.uk/dlis/models/>.

17 The discussion here and elsewhere throughout this paper draws on: Dempsey,
    L., Russell, R. and Murray, R., 'A utopian place of criticism? Brokering access to
    network information', *Journal of documentation*, **55** (1), 1999, 33–70.

18 <URL:http://www.cdl.org>

19 Dempsey, L. and Heery, R., 'Metadata: a current view of practice and issues',
    Journal of documentation, **54** (2), 1998, 145–72.

20 Allen, J. and Mealling, M., *The architecture of the Common Indexing Protocol
    (CIP)*. Request for Comments draft version 1, 1997. Available at
    <URL:ftp://ftp.ietf.org/internet-drafts/draft-ietf-find-cip-arch-01.txt>.

21   The MODELS collection description study is available at:
     <URL: http://www.ukoln.ac.uk/dlis/models/studies/>.
22   Dempsey, L.; Russell, R. and Murray, R., 'A utopian place of criticism?
     Brokering access to network information', *Journal of documentation*, **55** (1), 1999,
     33–70.

2

Discovering resources across the humanities

AN APPLICATION OF THE DUBLIN CORE AND THE Z39.50 NETWORK
APPLICATION PROTOCOL

Daniel Greenstein

Introduction

The Arts and Humanities Data Service (AHDS) collects, preserves and encourages the re-use of digital resources which result from, or support, research and teaching in the arts and humanities.[1] Its collections are distributed across five service providers, each of which develops holdings of interest to a particular academic subject area. The AHDS collections also comprise a wide range of data types (for example, electronic texts, databases, digital images, geospatial information systems and time-based film data).

Given its mission, and the organization, nature and extent of its collections, the AHDS is forced to address issues of common concern to those interested in access to, and preservation of, our digital scholarly and cultural heritage. Those issues the AHDS has attempted to address through a mixture of research, broad consultation and practical application. In all cases it adopts internationally agreed standards and best practices where they exist, and uses its own research and development efforts to progress consensus where it is lacking. Integrating the users' online access to information about distributed, mixed-media, interdisciplinary holdings is one of the most significant problems confronting the AHDS and the broader community of information professionals.

This paper examines the AHDS work in this area, focusing on two major strands of activity: the development and deployment of Dublin Core resource discovery metadata, and the development of a suite of Z39.50-enabled information systems. It concludes with a number of screen shots demonstrating the systems' capabilities, and with comments about lessons learned and future directions.

Generalizing from the particular: resource discovery in distributed and deeply heterogeneous networked environments

The AHDS is a consortial organization comprising a managing executive and five service providers offering archival and other services on a subject basis. Its collections are managed on a distributed basis by:

- the Archaeology Data Service (ADS based at York University)
- the History Data Service (HDS – the Data Archive, University of Essex)
- the Oxford Text Archive (OTA – Oxford University Computing Service)
- the Performing Arts Data Service (PADS at Glasgow University)
- the Visual Arts Data Service (VADS at the Surrey Institute for Art and Design).

The collections are even further distributed insofar as several of the service providers have data-exchange and interoperability agreements with third-party data agencies. Thus the ADS integrates access to data resources maintained by itself and by the Council for British Archaeology, the Royal Commissions for the Historical Monuments of England and Scotland respectively, the Society of Antiquaries and others. Likewise, the HDS provides a gateway to data resources maintained by a wide range of social-science and history data archives worldwide.

Information about the service providers' holdings is also distributed – that is, service providers maintain their own online catalogues. Although early on the AHDS reviewed the possibility of creating a union catalogue, it rejected the option in favour of a more distributed approach, whereby users progressed queries in parallel against underlying catalogue systems. The distributed approach exploits better the developmental logic of network technologies, but also takes account of individual catalogues' dynamic development. It also complicates the resource discovery challenge, since service providers mount catalogues in very different hardware and software environments. ADS uses:

- Fretwell-Downing Informatics' SQL-based OLIB VDX
- HDS, the SGML-aware Cheshire system developed consortially by the Universities of Berkeley and Liverpool
- the OTA, Open-Text's SGML-aware PAT system
- PADS, an object-oriented product supplied by Hyperwave
- VADS, the Index+ system which is supplied by System Simulation.

The AHDS collections are also heterogeneous insofar as they comprise data in very different formats. Although any single collection is extensively mixed-media, the following concentration of data types evolves naturally from the service providers' subject focus:

1 The ADS's holdings extend to archaeological databases, excavation archives, and GIS (Geographic Information Systems).
2 The HDS's holdings extend to historical databases and statistical sets.
3 The OTA's holdings extend to text and linguistic corpora.
4 The PADS's holdings extend to digital film and sound as well as to performing arts databases.
5 The VADS's holdings extend to image banks and other related information objects.

The collections' heterogeneous data formats, and their interdisciplinarity, introduce additional challenges to resource discovery. Services must adopt very different cataloguing practices appropriate to the subject domains and data formats on which they concentrate. The diversity of practice is essential. A text corpus needs to be described and documented differently than, say, an archaeological GIS or an image bank. Archaeological databases need to be documented differently from historical ones, or those which comprise images of, and descriptive material about, art historical objects.

Further, no single cataloguing standard is sufficiently flexible to be applied across the services.[2] Thus, the ADS applies a catalogue record based upon the National Geospatial Data Framework.[3] The HDS uses the documentation standard agreed by an international community of history and social-science data archives, the Data Documentation Initiative's Codebook.[4] The OTA uses the TEI's (Text Encoding Initiative's) recommendations for SGML encoding of electronic texts, and thus the associated TEI header.[5] The PADS uses a proprietary format which reflects the lack of consensus within the performing arts community around any cataloguing standard.[6] The VADS employs another proprietary format, but in this case because standards proliferate within its particular domain. The VADS catalogue record maps onto any one of the major standards currently being applied within the visual arts.[7]

Of course, the challenge of resource discovery is principally shaped by users' needs, which were identified by the AHDS through a variety of consultation exercises. Most important amongst these was a workshop organized by the UK Office for Library and Information Networking (UKOLN) in the MODELS (MOving to Distributed Environments for Library Services) series, and a series of more broadly focused user-needs workshops hosted by the AHDS from January to May 1998.[8] Users' requirements that were identified may be specified as follows:

1   Integrated access to information resources irrespective of where they are located, or how or by whom they are documented, managed and stored. Users interested in the Crimean War, or in divergent trends in European and American Romanticism respectively, wish to discover relevant information objects irrespective of whether they are located in libraries, archives, museums or data services, or of whether they are catalogued according to MARC or any other standard.

2   Search and retrieval capabilities which become progressively richer as users refine their searches and home in more closely on information objects of interest. Users wish to translate the model used within traditional print-based and analogue environments into a networked digital one. First, they need to know where relevant information objects are located (in which collections); then they need to visit relevant collections, and search across their holdings according to a number of general criteria. Having identified a number of potentially relevant information objects, users wish to find out more about them, perhaps by browsing their contents, or where some data resources are concerned, the more richly detailed descriptions of their format and contents. Finally, from the same resource discovery environment, users wish to initiate a sequence of events which will result in their having access to the information object itself. Events may entail activity:

- on the part of the user (who, for example, goes to the stack or to the appropriate museum gallery to obtain access to a book or a painting);
- on the part of a third party (for example, where the user issues a stack or interlibrary loan request);
- or on the part of some automatic system (for example, where an online data resource is hyperlinked to the resource description located in an online catalogue).

3   The ability to configure the network environment according to their needs. Users do not wish to deal with all online information resources every time they seek to discover information via the network. Rather, they prefer to configure 'portals' which present only those information resources in which they are, or are likely to be, interested.

In sum, the cross-domain resource discovery challenge confronted by the AHDS, and arguably by a far broader range of information professionals, is one of meeting users' information requirements as set out above in a distributed and deeply heterogeneous networked environment. In order to confront the challenge, work was undertaken on two fronts: on a common mechanism for service providers to express descriptive information about their very differently described holdings (i.e. on common resource discovery metadata); and on a system architecture and tools to exploit any consensus and enable users to query a different AHDS catalogue as a virtual uniform database.

On metadata and network protocols: research and development on the common ground

The AHDS was encouraged in confronting this challenge by four promising developments:

1   The emergence of cataloguing standards in four of the five domains in which the AHDS service providers operate. Only the PADS was forced to develop a proprietary approach to describing its holdings.
2   The AHDS benefited from momentum behind the Dublin Core as a resource discovery metadata scheme which might support the kind of cross-domain resource discovery that the AHDS required.[9]
3   The growing experience with the Z39.50 network application protocol as a means of enabling users seemlessly to query multiple information systems as virtual uniform databases.[10]
4   The AHDS was not alone in trying to find a solution to cross-domain resource discovery problems, and benefited substantially from similar efforts undertaken by the Consortium for Computer Interchange of Museum Information (CIMI),[11] by UKOLN and by others.

AHDS work on metadata is well documented, and so requires only the briefest description here.[12] It began from two simple observations:

1   Where distributed information systems employed a common record structure, network application protocols existed which permitted users to query those systems in parallel. Thus, in the library community there was already experience with the Z39.50 network application protocol in integrating access to distributed MARC-conformant catalogues. Likewise, the archives community had some experience of creating integrated access systems with underlying finding aids conforming to the Encoded Archival Description (EAD) standard. The museums community, too, was beginning to develop integrated access systems which exploit the consensus emerging around the CIMI standard. Although there was an apparent desire on the part of users to integrate access to systems which conformed to different standards, and thus across collections in different curatorial domains, there was as yet no experience of, or mechanism for, doing so. Interoperability trials were constrained

fundamentally by agreement about underlying record structures, as can be seen from Figure 2.1.

2   Dublin Core was beginning to emerge as an interchange format of sorts, even though discussions surrounding its development were frequently clouded by a common misunderstanding that it might serve as a detailed resource description standard in its own right. In this regard, the Dublin Core might act as a lynchpin of cross-domain resource discovery, i.e. for integrating access to systems which conformed to various different standards, as shown in Figure 2.2. Evaluation of the Dublin Core was, however, limited to a small number of domains. Nor was there much in the way of guidance with regard to its implementation in any single domain. AHDS's work on resource discovery metadata therefore focused on a formal, cross-domain evaluation of the Dublin Core.

In conjunction with UKOLN, the AHDS sponsored a broadly consultative investigation involving a series of workshops where information specialists working in the domains represented by the AHDS Service providers brought their particular curatorial and subject-specific perspectives to bear on three common questions:

1   What cataloguing standards exist within your domain?
2   What are the most basic resource discovery requirements of users working within your domain – i.e. the requirements which enable them to locate appropriate information objects (but not necessarily to submit any particular information object to the additional level of scrutiny that may be required to

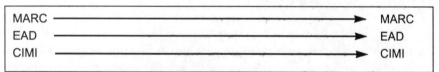

Fig. 2.1 *Interoperability within domains*

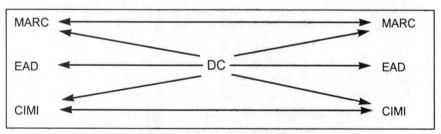

Fig. 2.2 *The Dublin Core and interoperability across domains*

determine whether or not the object was worth using – for example, in a particular investigation)?

3   Evaluate the Dublin Core in light of your domain's resource discovery requirements, suggesting possible amendments to it and methods for its use.

The workshop series resulted in five domain-specific reports and concluded with a further meeting at which workshop organizers ironed out discrepancies that had emerged when recommendations regarding the Dublin Core had been compared and assembled into a single cross-domain resource discovery metadata schema.[13] As a whole, the exercise produced both a formal evaluation and a practical implementation of the Dublin Core in the service providers' domains. The latter was agreed and adopted by the AHDS service providers, and service providers developed the detailed mappings needed to express their own catalogue records in a Dublin-Core-conformant fashion.[14]

AHDS research into information architectures and technical tools was also greatly assisted by UKOLN. It drew on and informed the development of the MODELS Information Architecture, which is amply described elsewhere.[15] Briefly, the architecture envisages a number of broker services which mediate between the user (situated at a network accessible machine) and a range of underlying information resources or targets (in the case of AHDS, the service providers' online catalogues). The brokering services, accessible from a client via the World Wide Web include:

1   Resource discovery services which enable users to select and simultaneously query a range of information systems, progressing queries using access points which are meaningful across the underlying services, and retrieving results in a unified format.

2   Registration services which enable users to become known not only to the broker but also to the underlying information services which may, for example, permit queries from registered users only, or may require some form of registration for users who wish to obtain access to selected resources once discovered.

3   Resource ordering services which enable users to obtain access to information objects which they discover by exercising the broker's search and retrieval services.

4   Authentication services which determine the bona fide of any users who requests access to a resource discovered via the broker.

5   User profiling services which allow users to configure the broker in a manner which suits their own needs – for example, to determine which information resources are included by default in any search, or how results are displayed and/or sorted.

After a review of appropriate enabling network application protocols, the AHDS adopted Z39.50 and undertook the development of a brokering client and Z39.50 capability for the service providers' own catalogues. The systems were procured from several suppliers selected through an open tender process. Although the involvement of multiple suppliers complicated the project management side of the procurement, it tested the robustness of the standards-based architecture. In all, five suppliers were involved:

1   Fretwell Downing Informatics supplied the client and the ADS's Target.
2   Index Data, working with Fretwell Downing, supplied target capability for the OTAs' and PADS' online catalogue systems.
3   The Cheshire project (from the Universities of Berkeley and Liverpool) supplied the HDS's Target.
4   NISS supplied the broker with its authentication function.
5   The VADS' system, procured through a separate tender process, was supplied by System Simulation.

From service environment to general information architecture?

The resource discovery and resource ordering capabilities which have resulted from the work described above are demonstrated in Figures 2.3–2.14. In order to emphasize the heterogeneity that exists across the services, Figures 2.3–2.10 demonstrate the native capabilities of the OTA and ADS catalogues respectively. The OTA's online catalogue is demonstrated in Figures 2.3–2.6.

Query capabilities appropriate to the OTA's literary and linguistic holdings are shown in Figure 2.3. Searches may be progressed against author or title, but also against genre, period or language.

Figure 2.4 shows the results of an author search for Dickens, and reveals 12 titles which, copyright status permitting, may be selected in any combination, either to download in a range of formats (including HTML, SGML and RTF), or to browse or search online.

Figures 2.5 and 2.6 demonstrate a simple linguistic content analysis on the text of Charles Dickens' *A Tale of Two Cities*, which produces what is effectively a concordance based upon the keyword 'French'.

The ADS's ArchSearch, is configured differently from the OTA catalogue in order to support the very different kinds of searches which are appropriate to the archaeological data resources to which it provides access. Figure 2.7 shows the search strategies supported by ArchSearch, and a simple search entered for the expression 'castle'.

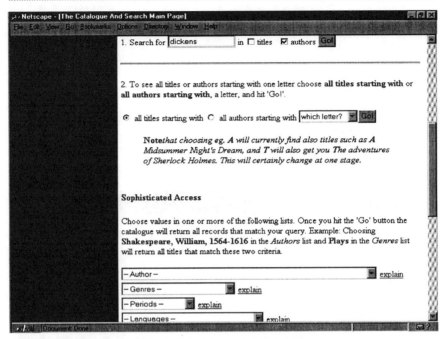

Fig. 2.3 *Author search for Dickens, OTA catalogue*

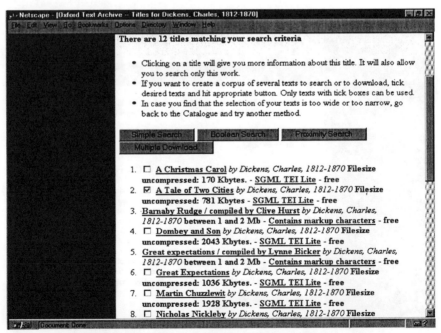

Fig. 2.4 *Results of an author search for Dickens, OTA catalogue*

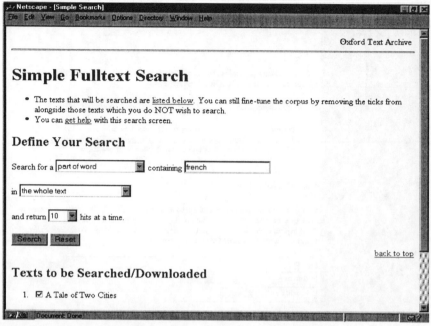

Fig. 2.5 *Simple linguistic content analysis, OTA catalogue*

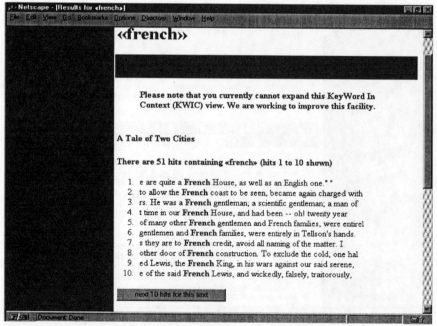

Fig. 2.6 *Results of the simple linguistic content analysis, OTA catalogue*

Fig. 2.7 *ArchSearch search strategies and a simple search for 'castle'*

The result set, a portion of which is shown in Figure 2.8, displays brief details about records drawn from two data resources, the National Monument Records of Scotland and England, maintained by the Royal Commission for the Ancient and Historic Monuments of Scotland and the Royal Commission for the Historical Monuments of England respectively.

A number of options confront the user from the initial results page: to get more detailed information about the site in question, about the district or unitary authority where the site is located (derived directly from the Getty Thesaurus of Geographical Names), or about the agency which maintains the record.[16] Some of the additional information that is available about the Dunimarle Castle site in Fife is displayed in Figure 2.9.

In the case of the Dunimarle Castle, still further information is available off site in a related data resource, and is available by clicking on the appropriate link as shown in Figure 2.10.

Whereas service provider catalogues offer research and retrieval capabilities appropriate to particular collections and their users, the AHDS Gateway assumes that, in some instances, scholars will wish to search generally across multiple collections. The Gateway's advanced search screen is shown in Figure 2.11. Here we see that users can select the AHDS services they wish to search. Other resources are also available. Although the resources shown in these figures are prototypes for demonstration purposes only, they will in time extend to actual data resources

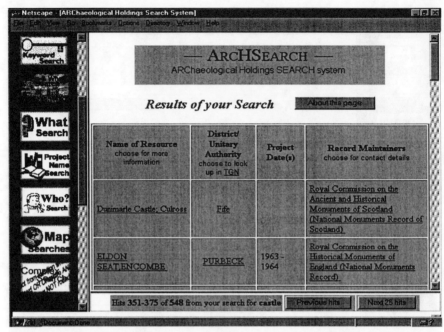

Fig. 2.8 *Partial result set from a simple search of ArchSearch for 'castle'*

Fig. 2.9 *Additional information supplied for a record returned in the ArchSearch catalogue*

maintained by third parties but still of interest to arts and humanities users. In this example, a third-party 'Books' database (in fact, the Library of Congress catalogue) has been included in the search.

Figure 2.11 also shows the Dublin Core access points available for searching. Those access points marked with an asterisk are supported by each of the selected underlying data resources. Those not marked are supported by some of the selected catalogues.

Figure 2.12 shows the search results. A hit list provides brief details about records maintained by the underlying services and matching the search criteria, while the status bar shows the progress of the search at each of the underlying services. Result lists may also be sorted from the hit list, by creator, title or returning service.

By clicking on a title in the hit list, the user can display fuller details about any result, as shown in Figure 2.13, and bona fide users may obtain access to the data resource to which the result refers (the screen also demonstrates that the Gateway is not yet complete – placeholders in the explanatory text permit some change in the resource ordering facility). Where data resources are maintained live and online, access to them will be via the web permit browsing and/or downloading. Where access to a resource requires some intervention – for example, where

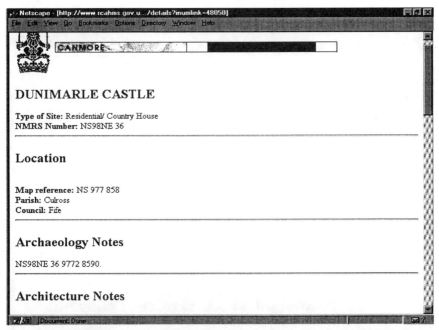

Fig. 2.10 *Additional information about Dunimarle Castle, available from the Royal Commission for the Ancient and Historic Monuments of Scotland's National Monunment Record for Scotland*

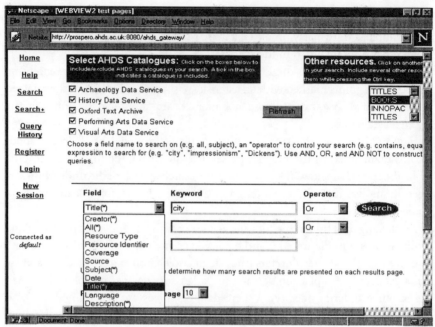

Fig. 2.11 *Advanced search, AHDS Gateway*

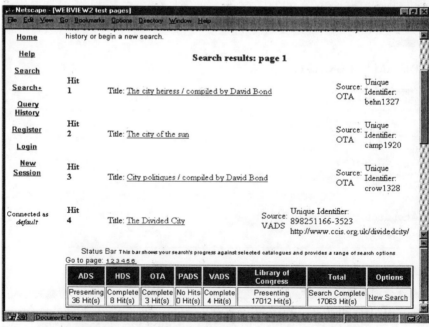

Fig. 2.12 *Search result, AHDS Gateway*

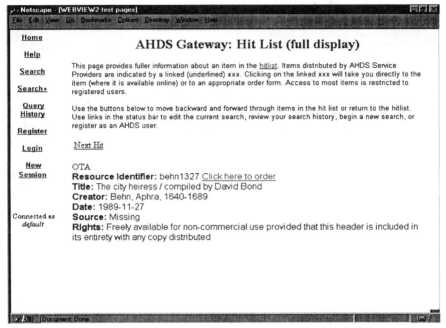

Fig. 2.13 *Fuller detail about a result returned to the ADHS Gateway*

resources are distributed on portable media or via private FTP sites – resource ordering entails the user's completion of an order form, which is submitted electronically to the appropriate service.

Because users may wish to configure the Gateway to suit their own resource discovery requirements, the Gateway permits registered users to set a limited number of preferences – for example, to select the catalogues presented to them by default for searching, or to select a preferred sorting order or hit list batch size. Registered users may also save queries across current sessions, recalling, rerunning or editing such queries as appropriate. Figure 2.14 shows the default advanced search screen presented to registered user 'zq4a0011'. In it, the user has configured the Gateway to include the ADS, HDS, OTA and Library of Congress catalogues, but to exclude others known to the system.

The Gateway offers a number of other services not demonstrated here. Users, for example, may register with the AHDS, supplying details about themselves and agreeing to the terms and conditions of data use as specified in the AHDS common access agreement. Such registered users will alone have access to the content of AHDS-maintained resources (although all users will be able to query the underlying service provider catalogues). Users may also amend whatever personal information they supply about themselves – for example, to notify the AHDS about a change of address. Such information that is maintained by the Gateway allows the AHDS to protect the copyright and other interests that are

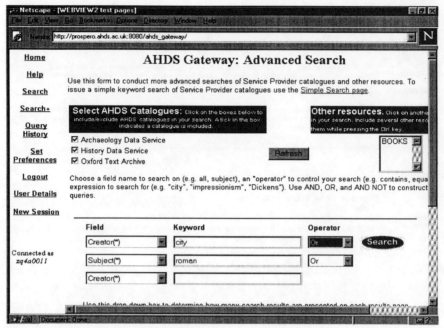

Fig. 2.14 *Gateway configured to a user's particular search requirements*

vested in its resource, and also to track how and by whom its data resources are being used. These performance indicators are critical to the service's collections development, which responds, at least in part, to users' specified needs. Where the AHDS can identify types of resources that are in particularly high demand, it may focus its collection's efforts accordingly.

Conclusion

Although it is too soon to give a critical assessment of the AHDS' various resource discovery systems – not all the services are completed or available to the public – some preliminary remarks are possible.

On metadata and cross-domain resource discovery

The AHDS experience suggests that highly generic and largely unqualified metadata schemes such as the Dublin Core do adequately support cross-domain discovery. At least on first brush, it appears that mappings to the Dublin Core from a variety of different cataloguing schema can support resource discovery both within and across domains.

Interdisciplinary and cross-sectoral activity

The experience also suggests that interdisciplinary and cross-sectoral activity is absolutely essential in solving the strategic and technical problems that commonly confront any who would exploit computer and network technologies for scholarly purposes. The AHDS work on metadata and resource discovery generally could not have been carried out by any one group of academic or information specialists, or strictly speaking within the scholarly sector.

Problems with resource discovery metadata and its use which are not addressed by the AHDS

Although service providers have reached agreement about the Dublin Core (an agreement which may yet anticipate broader agreement across the scholarly and heritage sector at large), no such agreement exists with regard to cataloguing practice. Thus, while the AHDS service providers can agree to the meaning and use of a common metadata element called 'creator', they each populate their own field in ways which reflect their user communities' particular resource-discovery interests. Where Anglo-American Cataloguing Rules are appropriate to, and used by, the OTA, for example, the Art and Architecture Thesaurus is used by the VADS. Even greater variation is apparent across the service in its use of date and coverage elements. Assisting users as they search across catalogues which are populated according to domain-specific controlled vocabularies is a challenge for the future.

Network application protocols

The AHDS experience with Z39.50 reflects the standard's relative immaturity. Simply, there are as yet few guidelines pertaining to the development of Z39.50-enabled systems in cross-domain environments. Accordingly, it remains possible (indeed likely) that independently supplied Z39.50-aware applications can conform to the standards and yet remain incompatible with one another, or at least interact in ways which are not necessarily meaningful nor helpful to the user. Within a bounded service environment such as the AHDS, interoperability can be achieved by communication and consensus amongst application suppliers. In a far wider and inevitably impersonal networked environment, other means will need to be developed.

User registration, authentication, and resource ordering

Here, too, the AHDS-circumscribed service environment obscures a problem of considerable moment within a wider networked arena. Through their organizational interworking, AHDS service providers have agreed the terms and conditions of data access, and apply these to data resources across the system through a bespoke user registration, authentication and resource ordering system bundled into the AHDS Gateway. Yet the Gateway also has the ability to present non-AHDS resources to its users – for example, as we have seen with the Library of Congress database. Should such third-party systems also permit online data access, then harmonization of registration, authentication and resource ordering procedures would be required before AHDS Gateway users would be able to take advantage of those facilities. Although such harmonization may be possible on an inter-organizational level, a more automated approach will be required to support scholarly and heritage users who wish to locate, scrutinize and acquire access to information objects of interest irrespective of their location, format, management etc.

Undoubtedly there are other constraints which will emerge through the extensive analysis of user behaviour which is envisaged for the AHDS Gateway and its supporting services. In the meantime, it would appear that those services do in fact integrate access to the AHDS holdings as intended, while pointing in a more general direction to interoperable information systems which work across curatorial, subject, regional and other domains.

Notes and references

1   More information about the AHDS may be found at
    <URL: http://ahds.ac.uk/>.
2   The MARC format makes claims for such flexibility, but these are reasonably contentious.
3   National Geospatial Data Framework World Wide Web home page. National Geospatial Data Framework available at
    <URL: http://www.ngdf.org.uk/>.
4   Data Documentation Initiative Committee, *The Data Documentation Initiative: proposal for an SGML document type definition for data documentation*. Available at
    <URL: http://www.icpsr.umich.edu/DDI/>.
5   Text Encoding Initiative, *Guidelines for electronic text encoding and interchange, P3*. Available at
    <URL: http://etext.virginia.edu/TEI.html>.
6   See Duffy, C. and Owen, C., *Resource discovery workshops: moving image resources* and *Resource discovery workshops: sound resources*. Both available at
    <URL: http://ahds.ac.uk/manage/metareps.html>.
7   The data structure documentation is forthcoming. For a survey of domain-specific standards, see Gill, T., Grout, C. and Smith, L., *Visual arts, museums and cultural heritage information standards: a domain-specific review of relevant standards for net-*

worked information discovery. Available at
<URL: http://vads.ahds.ac.uk/standards.html>.

8   For UKOLN see
<URL: http://www.ukoln.ac.uk/>.
For the MODELS workshop see Russell, R., *MODELS 4: integrating access to resources across domains*. Available at
<URL: http://www.ukoln.ac.uk/dlis/models/models4/>.
For a report on the MODELS 4 workshop see Porter, S. and Greenstein, D. (eds.), *Scholars' information requirements in a digital age: consultation draft*. Available at
<URL: http://ahds.ac.uk/public/uneeds/un0.html>.

9   See the Dublin Core web pages at
<URL: http://purl.oclc.org/metadata/dublin_core/>.

10 Library of Congress Web/Z39.50 Gateway. Available at
<URL: http://lcweb.loc.gov/z3950/gateway.html>.

11 See <URL: http://www.cimi.org/>.

12 See Miller, P. and Greenstein, D. (eds.), *Discovering online resources across the humanities: a practical implementation of the Dublin Core*, UKOLN, 1997.
Available at
<URL: http://ahds.ac.uk/public/metadata/discovery.html>.

13 Individual reports are available at
<URL: http://ahds.ac.uk/manage/meta.html>.

14 The mappings will shortly be available in Beagrie, N. and Greenstein, D., *Managing digital collections: AHDS standards and practices*. Available at
<URL: http://ahds.ac.uk/manage/manintro.html>.

15 See information about the MODELS 5 and MODELS 7 meetings, in *Managing access to a distributed library resource* and *The MODELS Information Architecture (MIA): deployment* respectively. Both available at
<URL: http://www.ukoln.ac.uk/dlis/models/>.
For a detailed statement of requirement for the AHDS suite of interoperating systems see Greenstein, D., *AHDS systems operational requirement*. Available at
<URL: http://ahds.ac.uk/public/ahds-or/ahds-or.html>.

16 Available at
<URL: http://www.gii.getty.edu/vocabulary/about_tgn.html>.

3

Networking the cultural heritage

Mike Stapleton

Introduction

Considerable effort is now being spent in museums in the UK and elsewhere in the creation of digital resources such as computer-based catalogues of objects, computer-based thesauri, interpretive text, digitized still images, 3-D photography, 3-D models and volumetric scans as well as time-based media such as audio, video and animation. Because of the costs involved in such activities it is important that the products have a long life time, that they are re-usable and, particularly where public money is footing the bill, that they are accessible from outside the institution that owns them. This paper describes some recent and ongoing projects aimed at creating such open, sustainable, resources for the cultural heritage and making them available to a greater or lesser extent on the public networks. The issues raised suggest requirements for the use of technology to provide the infrastructure for such projects.

Museum documentation

Many museums have a pressing need to have an online catalogue of all their objects. The number of objects may vary from a few hundred to several million. Natural history collections may run to many millions of objects depending on what is termed an object. Objects are seen largely as unique, each with its own provenance. Perhaps this is similar to libraries in the era before large-scale printing. Perhaps too, museum practices will change as collections increasingly include mass-produced and even digital objects.

Cataloguing sites and buildings introduces a different perspective from that applied to objects. Sites and buildings are unique, they tend to be large and they have many aspects of interest. They do not move around much but may change considerably over time, particularly in the case of archaeological sites. Sites and buildings may also be associated with the provenance of objects and may indeed contain the location of objects.

Whereas the popular interest may focus on valuable or 'priceless' objects, museum catalogues traditionally aim to meet curatorial and scholarly needs, with support for public access as a more recent requirement. Collection management systems also record information relating to the care and management of the collection, and this function requires some record for every item in the collection. Creating catalogues can be a very large data entry task extending over decades. Consequently attention has to be paid to minimizing the effort in recording information about large numbers of less 'important' objects for possible future research.

The history of online cataloguing in museums is relatively short, approximately 20 years. The earliest systems were batch systems. These were replaced by time-sharing systems with centralized computers and 'dumb' terminals. As personal computers became viable a range of systems emerged with similar functionality but operating on standalone DOS-based systems. These made computer-based catalogues affordable to a much larger range of museums but lacked the advantage of wide-spread shared access to a common catalogue. The current generation are networked-based, either using file-sharing or client-server technology. The database sits on a central server and is accessed by general-purpose desktop workstations. Collections catalogues have become just another application on the museum workers electronic desktop. This trend is likely to continue. The recent explosion in web-based technology is leading many institutions to adopt an intranet approach to information access and provide their information management services via web browsers over intranets. To illustrate this progression, the British Museum started using a time-sharing system, MAGUS, about ten years ago; prior to that they had a batch system known as *Gos*. In 1999 they will start migrating to System Simulation's MUSIMS with a client-server architecture, with the ability to deliver to both web browsers and Z39.50 clients as well as conventional clients on their Windows-NT workstations.

The Museum Documentation Association (now known as MDA) has been a major influence on cataloguing standards in the UK. Its Spectrum standard[1] for documentation is achieving international recognition. Spectrum is focused on objects, both natural and man-made, and does not currently address sites and buildings specifically. Other proposals (for instance the EU's recommendation on coordinating documentation methods and systems related to historic buildings and monuments[2]) specify additional fields for recording information relating to the built heritage.

The policy recommendations to the Heritage Lottery Fund[3] on the use of communications and information technology (CIT) in museums emphasized the importance of collections documentation. It recommended that funds be directed to the creation of information resources rather than independent interactive displays.

Current projects

The Victoria and Albert Museum CIS and Picture Library

The Victoria and Albert Museum (V&A) is implementing a collections information system (CIS) using MUSIMS. This provides a museum-wide catalogue of
the objects and also supports various museum procedures following the
Spectrum standard. It has replaced separate inventory catalogues for each department providing a common catalogue accessible via the network and supported by
centralized backup and operations.

System Simulation has also implemented a catalogue for the V&A Picture
Library. Although the majority of the pictures are of museum objects, the Picture
Library describes them as pictures rather than simply as illustrations of objects.
The same set of images are used for both the picture library and the CIS. They
are stored in an open fashion that makes them accessible to any software that can
access the file system, subject to the normal considerations of copyright permis-
sion.

Taking issues of open access further, the V&A is a partner in ELISE
(Electronic Library Image Service for Europe), an EU funded project to provide
remote access to high-quality images of objects between the participating partners. The ELISE server will have information automatically downloaded from
the CIS and will serve this, together with images, over the Internet to ELISE
clients.

In the past year the V&A has been reviewing its CIT strategy, aiming to establish common platforms wherever possible. It is expected that the systems
described will find a place in that strategy, either interoperating using open standards or migrating the data to new systems using open formats supported by the
sub-systems involved.

The London Transport Museum Total Access Project

The London Transport Museum (LTM) has outgrown its site in Covent Garden
and is developing a complementary site in Acton to house and present the majority of its large objects: buses, locomotives and rolling stock. This enterprise,
including the CIT infrastructure is called the Total Access Project (TAP).[4] The
TAP aims to provide a complete catalogue of the objects including digital representations of the objects as far as possible. The TAP information system integrates the descriptions of physical objects and traditional forms of reproduction
with their digital surrogates. The bulk of digital surrogates will be images but
increasing use will be made of audio, video, volumetric scans, models and interactive works.

The TAP digital resource will be used to provide virtual access to the entire collection both from inside the Museum and on the web. It will also be used to create exhibitions at the Covent Garden site relating to objects held at Acton and elsewhere.

The LTM has been cataloguing its objects and historical photographs since 1986. This experience has resulted in the specification for the TAP system. The first step in implementing the TAP system, currently underway, is to integrate the collections catalogue with the catalogue of the LTM Photograph Library using the new TAP structures. The TAP project aims to create at least one digital image for each object so that the collection can be viewed remotely. Where appropriate other forms of digital resources will be created. Having established standards for digital resources and documented the procedures for acquiring them, the LTM has now entered on a digitization programme to create them.

The British Museum COMPASS project

The British Museum is redeveloping its interior courtyard, creating a new public space called the Great Court. At the centre of the Great Court is the Reading Room recently vacated by the British Library. The Reading Room will be host to a number of public information services including COMPASS, a public access system providing information about a selection of objects from the galleries. The COMPASS (Collections Multimedia Public Access System) project[5] will build and make available a repository of information describing both individual objects and broader themes, complemented by digital resources ranging from simple images to complete interactive works.

COMPASS is not a collections management system. It does hold information about individual objects but using around 20 descriptive fields rather than the 200–400 fields used by typical collections management systems. The experience of a prototype project showed that object descriptions for public access systems need a different use of language from that typically used by curators cataloguing objects for scholarly purposes. The selection of objects to be included in COMPASS is made by curators from each department and then relevant data is exported from MAGUS, the British Museum's collection catalogue. The exported MAGUS data informs the people composing the COMPASS text but few MAGUS fields are presented directly.

As well as information about objects COMPASS stores glossary information explaining the background to topics such as materials, techniques, archaeological expeditions, historical periods and cultures. The glossary records can also link to representative object records or have pre-authored search specifications which will retrieve related information.

The COMPASS specification was developed out of a prototype project which showed the feasibility and advantages of basing such a large scale public access system on a database rather than a multi-media authoring system. The project will include a publishing facility to make datasets available for delivery in the Reading Room, on the web and elsewhere. It will implement an open system which can manage and present a wide range of digital content. The project is establishing standards for content that include image formats and resolutions as well as less usual forms of digital resources.

SCRAN

The Scottish Cultural Resources Access Network[6] is creating a online service providing access to a substantial collection of digital material describing the Scottish heritage. SCRAN is commissioning content from institutions from Scotland or with Scottish interests. These may be basic records describing an object, an image or a site or complete 'multimedia essays' covering a topic in an interpretive fashion. SCRAN's first target audience is pupils and teachers in Scotland's schools and it is also providing enabling technology to allow reuse of the digital assets in the schools.

SCRAN has established both technical standards for the digital resources and editorial guidelines for the supply of descriptive text. The digital resources used for the multimedia works are also added to the SCRAN repository as basic records. There are a variety of ways of in which the SCRAN resources can be accessed:

- HTML gateway. The primary way of accessing SCRAN is by using a web browser to provide a widely available method for public access.
- XML gateway. SCRAN also operates an XML gateway. SCRAN has commissioned an original authoring system, *Clipper*, from Electrum Multimedia Limited, to be distributed to schools. Clipper can be used to create original works using digital assets downloaded via the XML gateway.
- Z39.50 gateway. SCRAN is participating as a content provider in the Aquarelle project (see below). By adding a Z39.50 gateway, the SCRAN database appears as an Aquarelle archive, serving descriptions and images relating to the Scottish heritage.

Aquarelle, a resource discovery system

Aquarelle is a project funded under the EU Telematics Applications Programme.[7] It has created a distributed multimedia information system, offering a single point of access to interrelated multimedia reference documents and primary data that describe the cultural heritage of Europe. Unlike SCRAN, Aquarelle systems do not hold data about objects, instead they query a selection of registered databases across the Internet using the Z39.50 protocol with the CIMI/Aquarelle profile.

Aquarelle users access the system using a standard web browser. Once identified or registered they may access the information held by the Aquarelle data servers. The user interface provides facilities to select the databases to be queried and also to formulate queries in other than their native language. The user interface passes the queries to the Aquarelle central services module, the Access Server. There they are further processed and submitted to the selected data servers. The responses from the data servers are collated by the Access Server and passed back to the user.

Aquarelle supports two types of data servers, Archive Servers and Folder Servers. Archive Servers provide information about individual objects or sites, typically returning a record about each object or site. They follow a conventional information retrieval model for database access. The Archive Server model is designed so that existing museum documentation systems or data service systems could act as Aquarelle Archive Servers using the appropriate interface. Folder Servers provide access to 'folders' or hyper-texts, presented as SGML documents, and typically interpreting the primary object and site information held by Archive Servers. Folders may have conventional internal hyper-links and links between folders. They also support a more novel hyper-link to the information held in Archive Servers. This allows folders to reference the primary data held on Archive Servers. This capability allows all the information accessible to an Aquarelle system to be presented in a uniform fashion supporting both searching and hypertext browsing.

Open sustainable resources

The examples in the previous section clarify the implications of open, sustainable resources. To make digital resources available outside the context they were originally created for, the systems need to be capable of integration in an overall network architecture, and to deploy standard protocols or access and standard delivery formats.

Network architectures

- Point to point. The simplest approach is for each client to have information about the servers it wants to interoperate with and contact them directly. Figure 3.1 illustrates such point-to-point architecture, as seen in the Cultural Heritage Information Online (CHIO) project. More sophisticated clients

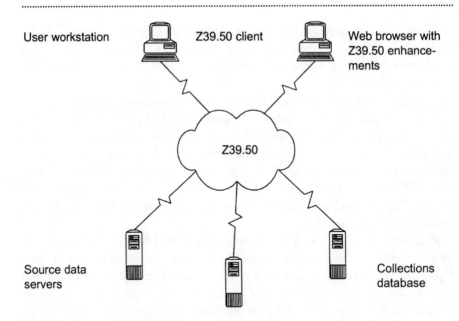

Fig. 3.1 *Point-to-Point model (CIMI/CHIO)*

have the ability to broadcast a query to more than one server and collate the responses. There is no possibility for any central services.

The LTM will allow network access to the TAP resources in this fashion. This model is also used in the initial phase of the SCRAN project. The SCRAN server provides a union catalogue of information and images of objects from the Scottish heritage, held at a single site. It allows access to registered users who contact it directly.

- Broker systems. Broker systems are based on a central component, the broker module, which can be operated independently of any primary content source. The broker provides access to multiple data sources and manages the community of users. It can provide centralized services such as user preferences, terminology facilities and intellectual property rights management. Importantly, in terms of the user interface at least, it provides a single mechanism for accessing a large number of different resources.

Aquarelle illustrates a broker architect, as in Figure 3.2. SCRAN acts as a data server to Aquarelle. A possible development for SCRAN is to become a broker system itself and to provide a gateway to some museums systems directly as well as holding surrogate data for others.

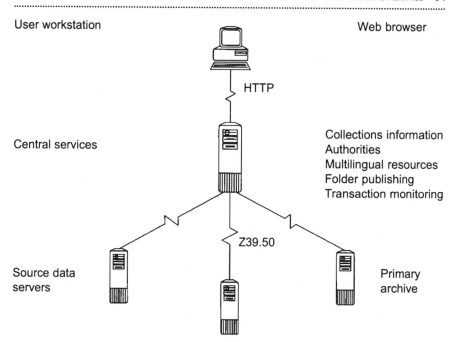

Fig. 3.2 *Broker model (Aquarelle)*

Protocols

The common protocols used on the Internet are Z39.50 for search and retrieval and HTTP and HTML for communication between the user's browser and a server. Another development from the SGML stable, XML, is a new contender which aims to avoid the limitations of HTML in describing information, thereby providing a mechanism for adding structure to information held as documents.

The Aquarelle system uses the Z39.50 protocol with the CIMI profile for search and retrieval. SCRAN were able to implement a Z39.50 gateway to their database and thus allow their data to be accessed through the Aquarelle single point of access. By virtue of using the common profiles, museum catalogues can be made available to web users via Aquarelle as well as directly to other museums operating Z39.50 clients.

SCRAN, Aquarelle and COMPASS all use HTTP and HTML for communication between the server and the user. This allows users to access the system using a standard web browser.

Standard Z39.50 browsers can access the SCRAN database using Z39.50. SCRAN also operate an XML gateway providing a further open interface that applications can use to access the SCRAN data.

Delivery formats

Formats for delivery change due to new technology across the whole consumer IT area resulting in new capabilities and raised expectations. This is out of the control of the institution owning the resources. The choice of format and resolution for delivering web resources will be determined by:

- Capabilities of the web browsers used by the intended audience. To ensure the widest potential audience, delivery formats for use on the web need to be those with the widest support. Although browsers can be augmented by 'plugins' to support additional media there can be obstacles to installing these. More recent developments tend to be less widely supported. How far behind the leading edge of the technology do you aim to support?
- Available bandwidth to the intended audience. The main bottleneck tends to be the connection between the user and the Internet service provider. Outside of academia and the larger corporations this connection will tend to be a modem. Although there have been significant improvements in modem performance in the last year or so the installed base of equipment is often not continually upgraded to the latest model.
- Fashion/user expectation. There are many technology developers who want to establish their technology as 'the next big thing'. There is also a very active and profitable computer games market. Both of these give rise to heighten expectations and the risk of technology that does not live up to its promise, particularly in the short term. Attention to bandwidth and browser capabilities will tend to curb the worst excesses.

Sustainability

To ensure the longevity of digital resources they need to be created to open standards and paying attention to possible future uses rather than solely the immediate purpose. The concept of 'data archiving' holds that digital resources should be stored in standard or published formats. This applies to both the software and the hardware involved.

Digital resources are created and used by software systems. Software may become unsupported due to the change in circumstances of its authors or due to changes in the host computer system. Although many systems, including most databases, hold the working version of the data in proprietary formats, they should be able to export it in an open format that preserves all the information. This should ensure that in the event of the associated software being no longer usable it will be relatively straightforward for the owning organization to change to use some other software. Databases can be exported in open formats such as

SGML or XML as well as collections of less well structured formats such as CSV tables.

Digital resources are held on some form of digital media. The medium itself will have a life, possibly dependent on storage and handling conditions. The type of medium will also have a life-cycle towards the end of which the equipment used to read and write it will become increasingly unsupportable. Even for a medium that gains a fair degree of acceptance this may be as little as five years. Archive copies should be stored on well established media according to the recommendations of the manufacturer and transcribed to new media of the same or a different type when necessary. An archiving strategy should include a periodic check of the actual recordings and a periodic review of the media types in use to see if they are obsolescent.

Common data model

Content owners may use a large number of fields to store the data in their respective databases. Typical museum documentation databases may use over two hundred different fields to store the information at the level of detail required by specific collections. Furthermore, different institutions, particularly when from different countries, have different approaches to structuring the data. Searching these databases using the native fields as access points provides the highest search precision possible but can lead to frustratingly low recall if the user is not familiar with the dataset.

Services affording access to multiple databases need to provide higher level access points for specifying queries. This approach improves the recall at the cost of reduced precision. The common set of access points are mapped to the target datasets to perform the actual query. Table 3.1 shows the generic levels of description that can be identified, characterized by the approximate number of access points.

Typically network access systems will support between ten and 30 access points. Although this sets a limit to the precision with which queries could be made, it represents a consensus as to the capability of typical users to formulate useful queries.

Repository approach

System Simulation's response is to advocate an approach based on repositories of resources adhering to open standards and decoupling the issues of resource creation and long term storage from those of delivery. Archive copies of the resources are created using the best affordable technology. These are converted to produce appropriate forms for the delivery platforms in use. By decoupling the primary assets from the more frequent changes in delivery platforms this approach provides a means for coping with change in the requirements for delivery.

Table 3.1 *Generic levels of description that can be identified, characterized by*
the approximate number of access points

1	'Just search', regardless of access points and data types. This is the classic free-text retrieval approach.
<10	E.g. Who, what, where, when; an appropriate starting point for low precision queries for public access or where the researcher has little knowledge of the subject domain.
20-30	Typical of general metadata schemes such as Dublin Core[8] and CIMI/CHIO.[9] Of use to researchers with a reasonable knowledge of the subject domain.
Approx. 100 >200	Typical of core data standards such as CIDOC and SPECTRUM Actual number of fields in use in full-scale collection documentation systems. Useful to researchers with detailed knowledge of the dataset.

Archive copies are created using the best available technology that can be afforded. The formats used should be reviewed from time to time as formats for long term storage change due to new technology, generally because it alters the cost/performance ratio and makes some formats affordable with the new technology. As long as the delivery format is of not capable of higher quality than the format of the archive copy there is no external technical reason to change. A museum may never re-digitize older material to a new format so any repository system needs to be multi-format.

Conclusion

The technological building blocks for networking the cultural heritage are thus:

- Databases. For creating and managing online catalogues and content repositories.
- Gateways. Provide interfaces to the repositories and deliver content in different forms.
- Brokers. Provide a common point of access to a range of repositories and data sources.

- Delivery platforms. Provide users with an interface appropriate for the task at hand. These may include web browsers and Z39.50 clients. They may also support authoring environments built round XML and SGML.
- Protocols. Connect it all together on the networks. It is crucial that open standards are adopted. Z39.50, HTTP, XML and SGML are frequently used as the basis of these systems.

Figure 3.3 illustrates a complete repository-based system.

This generation of projects have demonstrated the technological feasibility of creating systems for providing common access to multiple heritage information resources. They have exposed a series of issues that are being tackled in the next generation:

- Interpretation of access points. The first problem that arises when users are able to query multiple databases is that searches yield different results from different systems. The work to construct common data models represented by projects such as CIMI/CHIO and Dublin Core is just the start, at some point the common data model has to be mapped to the local data structures of the target database. Depending on the local structures this may be easy, difficult or almost impossible. It will probably be done differently from other data

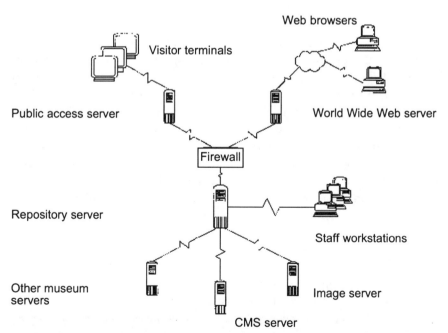

Fig. 3.3 *A complete repository-based system*

sources available to the network. These mappings and other issues of interpretation are the province of the community of users and content providers and not simple technical issues.

- Business models. The business models associated with the operation of distributed network-based information services are still unclear. The prevalence of 'free' information via the web makes it difficult to market the added value that broker services can offer. There are few if any examples to point at, the successful systems being either private or subscription based for a small group of users or public services with large numbers of users. Furthermore the success of the centralized access services depends on the existence of a sufficient number of data sources, and potential data source providers need to be encouraged by the availability of centralized access channels to make their information available. Further problems can be anticipated with interoperation between broker systems operating different business models.

- Large user communities. Content owners may well make their content available to third-party network access systems under conditions which mean the operator of the system has to register and identify the users. Doing this in an auditable fashion for a large number of users will impose a considerable burden on the operators of the system. There are third party authentication systems, for instance ATHENS[10] for UK academic users, but there are different models for their operation and as yet no emergent standard.

There is recognition in the museum area of a distinction between the care of the objects and the provision of access to the objects and their interpretation. Traditionally both activities have been carried out by museums although often by different departments. Increasingly broadcast television has taken on a role of providing access to objects in the form of interpretive programming placing objects in a wider context. Network systems such as described, as well as providing a technology to allow museums to afford wider access to the objects in their care or their surrogates, may encourage a trend to separate the activities of caring for the objects and their presentation to the public. This in turn raises questions about the importance of the physical presence of the object that will become more pressing as the technologies for creating surrogates improve.

References

1   Cowton, J. (ed.), *Spectrum, The UK museum documentation standard*, 2nd edn, London, Museum Documentation Association, 1997.

2   Council of Europe, Committee of Ministers, *On co-ordinating documentation methods and systems related to historic buildings and monuments of the architectural heritage*, Recommendation No. R (95) 3, 1995.

3   Humanities Advanced Technology and Information Institute, *Funding information and communications technology in the heritage sector*, Glasgow, University of Glasgow, 1998.

4   <URL: http://www.ltmuseum.co.uk/news/musfutur.htm>

5   <URL: http://www.british-museum.ac.uk/c_intro.html>

6   <URL: http://www.scran.ac.uk>

7   <URL: http://aquarelle.inia.fr>

8   Dublin Core Metadata Element Set: Reference Description, revision of January 15, 1997. Available at
    <URL: http://purl.org/metadata/dublin_core_elements>.

9   CIMI Profile Development Working Group (1996), *The CIMI Profile: Z39.50 Application Profile Specifications for Use in Project CHIO*. Available at
    <URL: http://lcweb.loc.gov/z3950/agency/profiles/> and
    <ftp://ftp.cimi.org/pub/cimi/CIMI_Profile/>.

10 <URL: http://www.athens.ac.uk>

4

Testing a general architecture
EXPERIENCES ACROSS APPLICATION DOMAINS

David Kay

MIA: model for a generic architecture

I shall begin with a brief resumé of the history of MODELS (MOving to Distributed Environments for Library Services) and MIA (the MODELS Information Architecture) within the context of the eLib (FIGIT Electronic Libraries) programme.

Since 1996, the MODELS project, led by UKOLN, has organized a series of workshops examining issues relating to MOving to Distributed Environments for Library Services. The participants have included a broad cross-section of practitioners from libraries and other curatorial domains, plus data service providers and system developers.

True to the MODELS title, the key themes have been *distribution* and *libraries* – with a view to the service models which libraries might adopt in the wired world to provide a common gateway bringing together information and consumers regardless of physical location.

MODELS is about the library as gatekeeper to the distributed (national) electronic resource.

Stuff – nice but messy

It was immediately apparent that the resource in question is the responsibility of a range of curatorial traditions, including libraries, archives, museums and data services, further segregated by subject specialization and media considerations.

As demonstrated in Figure 4.1, the information world to which libraries (or others) might provide one-stop access unavoidably involves a proliferation of *stuff*. To the user this stuff should be no more than a wealth of information resources, all equally available for discovery and subsequent delivery subject to rights and payment.

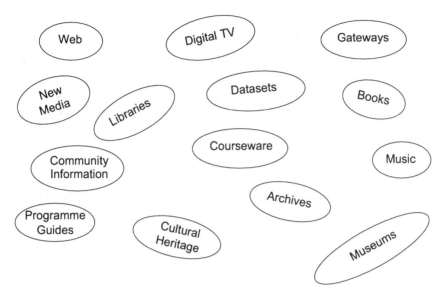

Fig. 4.1 *Stuff*

Theory into practice: MIA service examples

The primary responsibility of MODELS participants is to their current resource base and user community. Not surprisingly, therefore, early implementation forays have concentrated on a single domain:

- the eLib large-scale resource discovery projects, which are creating 'clumps' of bibliographic catalogues to support both regional resource sharing (CAIRNS, M25 and YHUA) and subject specialist demand (Music Libraries Online) and
- the National Networking Demonstrator Project initiated by the JISC (Joint Information Systems Committee) to determine the feasibility for a similar approach to archival finding aids involving university, public and special collections.

These projects are developing systems based initially on MIA to provide distributed retrieval services based on the Z39.50 protocol. They demonstrate already how a brokerage service, sitting between (on the one hand) distributed and diverse resources and (on the other) a widespread user base, can provide coherent and efficient access to catalogues or finding aids. Such a unified service is able to hide:

- physical distribution of resources

- diverse local search mechanisms
- heterogeneous classification schemas and data formats.

A further advantage of this architecture lies in the ease with which alternative user interfaces may be crafted using web technologies. This flexibility of presentation is already seen to include alternative branding, simple and advance query options, and flow of control options relating to functions like authentication. Figure 4.2 gives a representation of the MODELS Information Architecture, or MIA.

Further steps have been taken to validate the potential of this generalized architecture. Some service providers have a mandate requiring them to provide access within the same model to more diverse resources and data types regardless of heterogeneity in all respects. These hybrids may be regarded as second-generation MIA services:

1 The JISC Arts and Humanities Data Service (AHDS) serves as a common discipline-oriented gateway to a wide range of quality-assured digital collections. This implies heterogeneity of cataloguing traditions involving metadata descriptions and storage formats ranging from MARC to SGML to object database. The Dublin Core is adopted as a common denominator for cross-searching.

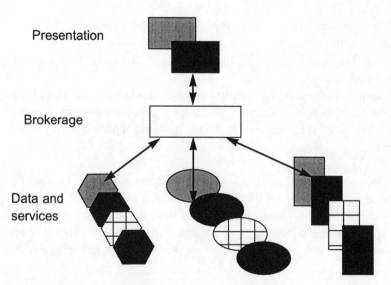

Fig. 4.2 *The MODELS Information Architecture*

2   The Essex Libraries' Seamless project, a one-stop distributed community information service (developed with BLRIC support) involves similar diversity in order to support the local data origination strategies of a wide range of government, community, educational and voluntary providers. Database, word-processing files and static web pages are the predominant formats. A subset of GILS attributes form the cross-searching profile.

3   The eLib Agora (i.e. marketplace) project plans to take on still further heterogeneity by dropping the mandate for the Dublin Core or GILS elements and the Z39.50 protocol as common denominators.

4   The EDUCOM-funded Instructional Management System project is facing similar issues in attempting to standardize the interface between online learning environments and the range of supporting content which must be accessed – sometimes online content, sometimes online metadata, sourced on publisher media servers, on CD-ROM, in electronic journals, in libraries, in museums, in archives.

In every dream home, a heartache: underlying issues

Beneath the veneer of establishing common search and retrieval environments, these projects have identified a number of alternative approaches to the management and presentation of the process and its results:

1   **Documents** versus **records**: there is a potential conflict in terms of presentation between resources that are described in a flat record format with little discursive text (for example, library holdings) and finding aids which take advantage of structured text to provide rich descriptions and multi-level representations (for example, museum and archival collections); the merits of a hybrid approach are emphasized in the online environment, where the transmission of an entire finding aid in response to a single keyword hit is clearly inefficient.

2   **Searching** versus **browsing**: the web has promoted serendipitous browsing using hyperlinks as an integral part of the discovery process alongside focused searching.

3   **Discovery** versus **disclosure**: the commercial world of the web is highlighting the potential for preemptive disclosure (information push, using what librarians would recognize as SDI) as opposed to the information pull of user-initiated discovery.

4   **Explicit** versus **implicit**: the breadth of users now encompassed by public access systems heightens the tension in user interface design between the explicit presentation of all options (an expert interface involving choice and training) and the guidance of the user through a more implicit search inter-

face where choice is limited and functions defaulted but where outcomes are guaranteed.

Furthermore, as implementers venture into the world of real services rather than demonstrators, they face common issues regarding connectivity, rights, authentication and sometimes payment.

The heart of the matter: metadata

Most critically, however, they have been confronted with decisions about the core metadata required to describe all information objects in their target area (typically beyond domain) to support a common retrieval framework.

To some extent, all classification schemas address this issue through the very task of defining attributes and sometimes pinpointing those which are mandatory. For example, the Dublin Core addresses this issue most generally, whilst ISAD(G) addresses this issue specifically for multi-level archival data. These schemas define core elements which should serve to ensure common ground across metadata descriptions – which could be catalogues, finding aids, web pages or any other well-organized resource – even when collections may optionally be described in much more depth using the full scope of MARC or EAD, for example.

However, the experience of adopters of such as Dublin Core and ISAD(G) for these purposes is that only a small sub-set of these core elements can be relied upon to appear consistently in metadata across domains and traditions. Only these key identifiers, illustrated in Figure 4.3, may be relied upon in a gateway application to provide:

- generic access points for searching
- attributes in collated displays of hit lists (brief details)

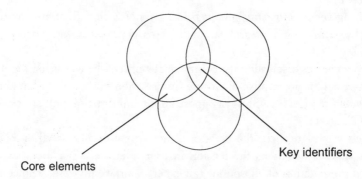

Fig. 4.3 *Common ground in information space*

- sorting criteria.

The development of cross-domain gateway services (like AHDS and Seamless) has served to highlight underlying conflicts and emergent metadata issues. Gateways handling multi-level metadata such as archival finding aids must address the implications in terms of searching – should all levels be searched and can levels be reliably represented across repositories? – retrieval – how much data should be returned to contextualize a hit list entry? – and navigation.

It may appear that these issues are just a special complication of the world of digital collections and SGML representation. A sideways look, however, at the trends in digital publishing and content purposing indicates that a multi-level representation will be required for an increasing number of collections and holdings. Here are some examples from 'out there':

1 The music industry is developing business models and technologies for personalized compilation of CDs, and also for the purchase of tracks on demand over the Internet; cataloguing at CD level will no longer be adequate.
2 The electronic publishing sector may take a view of digital objects that is even more granular than the journal article or the complete monograph; metadata will be required at the level of the unit of sale or licensing.
3 New teaching and learning strategies (online, distance, resource-based, personalized etc.) will inevitably require learning resources (i.e. any information object to be used by the student) to be classified and accessible if online at a level of granularity required by the course for purposes of book marking and charging.

These are examples of the market forces. As illustrated in Figure 4.4, atomic units of content are likely to become smaller, resulting in multilevel metadata require-

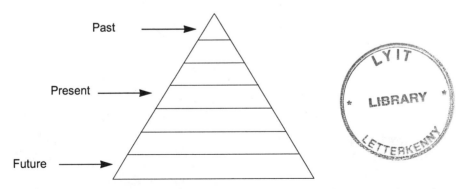

Fig. 4.4 *Metadata levels*

ments everywhere. Content should be accessible and saleable (and therefore cat-alogued) at an atomic level suited to the purposes of the users, the financial ben-efits of the owners and the constraints of transmission – not exclusively according to a curatorial schema.

Brave new world?: metadata beyond catalogues

The idea of metadata existing to serve a single purpose – essentially curatorial – may be seriously impacted by the same trends and market forces. If owners wish their data to be accessed and used in a variety of contexts, whether on account of their public remit or because of their commercial objectives, they must address the quality, flexibility, depth and breadth of its metadata description.

Figure 4.5 illustrates four aspects that might influence the enhancement of resource descriptions in the emergent research, learning and leisure market-places. In each case the implications for metadata might not be the direct respon-sibility of the owner or curator. It is, however, essential that structures and working practices are developed for catalogues and gateways to accommodate such requirements.

Packaging

Content often needs to be packaged into services. An additional layer of metadata is therefore required to describe the relationship of content to a particular service and its users. For example, a resource might be accessed and priced differently

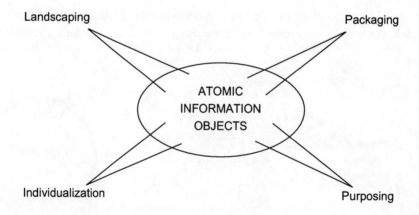

Fig. 4.5 *Metadata facets*

from within its originating institution than from the public domain, and there may be any number of such variants. Whilst access rights and price bands are handled by current library management and document delivery services, the solutions take little account of distributed brokerage models, which may require this information to be supplied as part of the search result set taking account of user status through a third-party authentication service.

Purposing

By offering access to distributed resources, the digital domain opens up the possibility of presenting access to 'virtual collections' in terms of metadata linked directly to delivery (both asynchronous and synchronous). This is most clearly appropriate for presenting study materials and associated secondary resource guidance to online learners. Content and metadata services should be capable of tight integration into specifically purposed cross-domain access mechanisms such as reading lists with access to catalogues and objects at the appropriate level of granularity – the right paper, chapter or diagram.

Individualization

The logical corollary of such services is that the users (for example, the learners) should be able to individualize their references to those resources. This might be in terms of adding further resources to a grouping or annotation of individual items. Whilst this can be achieved in user interface terms through browser facilities (for example folders, bookmarks), there are issues to be addressed regarding the persistence and for richness of those mechanisms. Information services should be active in such value-added developments around what are essentially their metadata.

Landscaping

Access to collections and across collections can generally be enhanced by providing a visual representation of the information space that resonates with the users, their interests and their concerns. Knowledge about collections, repositories and services can be provided in advance of searching or access in terms of subject specialty, subject mass, physical and electronic access terms and costs.

Figure 4.6 indicates a range of guides, advance knowledge and user tools that can be used within an everyday ICT framework to give meaning to information space by creating a landscape of value to all levels of user. The strategy of offering the means of target selection before queries are executed is increasingly seen as a key to addressing the problem of scaling the information world. Not only

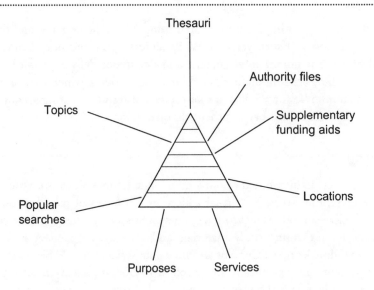

Fig. 4.6 *Landscape perspectives*

does it attempt to address the immediate (perhaps short-term) issue of the economic use of network resources and the user's waiting time; it also offers an approach (no doubt to be complemented by the use of reapers and other agentware) to the growing longer-term problem of finding out about what is available.

The presentation of advance knowledge is particularly powerful if devolved to gateways which might paint the landscape in a purposeful manner – to support a particular service or domain. Of the examples explored above, the Arts and Humanities (AHDS) or Music Libraries On-line might present a domain perspective, whilst YHUA might focus on the regional landscape.

The approaches set out in Figure 4.6 are not mutually exclusive – several may be used in the same interface. For example, the National Networking Demonstrator Project for Archives explored the value of guiding users to the most appropriate repositories through both a broad subject guide and location mapping. Some approaches are described briefly below simply to make the point that an information landscape need not involve artificial intelligence, virtual reality or other future technologies; the community has the information to do this stuff now:

1 **Topics**: broad subject-based descriptions of collections, perhaps limited to the number of -level terms that can be displayed on the screen at any one time.
2 **Thesauri**: the multi-level navigable structures that are so appealing professionally and yet perhaps prohibitive in terms of maintenance, user skills and

cross-domain consensus – but nevertheless an ideal tool to complement the topics list.

3 **Authority files**: different authority files will be particularly valued according to domain. Family historians may particularly benefit from location (place) and surname (person) listings. These will, for example, be prominent in the Internet gateway envisaged by the Church of Jesus Christ of the Latter-day Saints (Mormons).

4 **Supplementary finding aids**: documents which provide introductory knowledge, research guidance and even specific record links to add value to the researcher's initial forays. Both the Public Record Office and the Church of Jesus Christ of Latter-day Saints envisage these tools – typically word-processed document with hyperlinks, indexes and automated stored searches – as central to helping the naïve user to envision and traverse the landscape.

5 **Locations**: geographical and service information about physical (and possibly digital) service locations, including, for example, opening hours, prices or terms of access.

6 **Services**: presentation of the landscape with a service rather than a subject orientation. Such an interface, as prototyped by the eLib EDDIS project, might present the user successively with applicable choices of search, locate and delivery services.

7 **Purposes**: presentation of the landscape to meet the purposes of a particular service, a prime example being online learning. In this case the ability to discover and request resources would be tightly integrated with the presentation of the learning process, with particular resources and collections emphasized according to the coursework in hand. Such an adaptive landscape is a simple variant on the idea of reading lists.

8 **Popular searches**: gateway providers may present lists of searches that are proven and address popular issues (such as the search for 'Titanic' at the Public Record Office) or that illustrate search strategies. This landscape asset opens further opportunities allowing users to save their own useful searches for the personalization of the landscape and as an SDI tool.

We are not alone: real-world services

Current exemplars of distributed MIA-like services in the library community have focused on parts (or all) of the traditional service and supply chain from discovery (search and location) to fulfilment (request and delivery). This cascade of activity has in cases been encapsulated in methods that offer an end-to-end service, richer and more seamless than has been available through traditionally mediated interlending and document delivery; the eLib EDDIS and European Framework DALI and Universe projects offer clear signposts.

Nevertheless, we must beware of operating as if the complete supply chain can be operated within the confines of the information services community. The service architecture (see Figure 4.7) developed by the GAIA (Generic Architecture for Information Availability) project of the European ACTS (Advanced Communications Technologies and Services) programme focuses on the relationship of the 'vertical' supply chain with 'horizontal' services of a more generic nature such as authentication, payment and rights management. These services are likely to be needed at various stages in the end-to-end process, and are likely to be offered by external and powerful parties such as players in the banking sector.

As networked brokerage moves beyond trials to sustainable distributed (and often cross-institutional) services involving protection of rights, control of access and balancing of books, the integration of 'helper' applications from the wider world seems not only inevitable but also desirable in terms of economy, efficiency and effectiveness:

1 **Authentication**: externalization of authentication through the Athens service in UK higher education is just the tip of this iceberg; perhaps authentication will become closer to payment than to patron services.

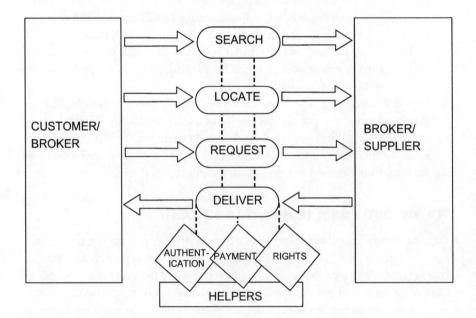

Fig. 4.7 *The GAIA service model*

2   **Payment**: global credit and debit services are evolving in a more open man-
    ner through standards such as SET (Secure Electronic Transactions).
3   **Rights**: rights management and the associated payments collection may
    become managed in a manner closer to the models in the music industry.

Regardless of which organizations own the particular elements, it is increasingly
apparent that they will be distributed.

Some services will become distributed within the traditional supply community – for example, the search gateways or federations for interlending and document delivery. As illustrated in Figure 4.8, the same resources will be presented in
apparently different manners, sometimes reflecting traditional boundaries (the
physical resource, such as a library, archive or museum), sometimes within a service model (such as LASER or AHDS), sometimes subsumed within a purpose
(such as an online learning module).

Some will be operated in a global dimension outside the information community – most notably payment, and perhaps therefore authentication and
aspects of rights management.

There is a potential conflict between each of these views of the information
world and the associated services required to deliver effectively in the digital
domain. In the network, economy branding, brokerage and repurposing are powerful forces, and traditional service providers may be justified in fearing not only
their immediate competitors but also the incursion of companies such as
Microsoft, Barclays, BT and Sky (to name a few).

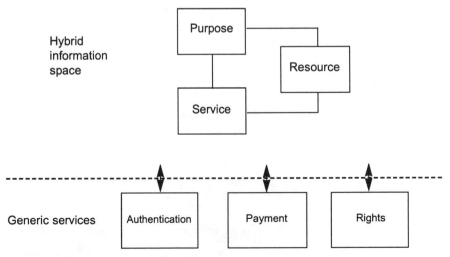

Fig. 4.8 *Competing paradigms?*

Whether these competing market forces and service paradigms will benefit our user communities is, it may be contended, a question that we do not have the luxury of asking.

Crossing Jordan: the learning challenge

The requirements of online resource-based distance and lifelong learning are most likely to raise the stakes relating to these issues. There has been debate throughout the 1990s regarding the types of online environments that will be required to support distance and lifelong learners ranging from postgraduates to those acquiring vocational skills. Whilst the web has simplified some aspects of this debate, major issues remain unresolved in the areas of cross-institutional services, wide-area resource access, authentication and payment.

Potentially, a number of these issues involve management of resources and repositories, with long-term implications for the role of librarians and other curatorially centred information professionals, both in our universities and in our public access centres (such as the library services proclaimed under *New library: the people's network*[1]).

With its beginnings in the USA EDUCOM (now EDUCAUSE) program, the Instructional Management System (IMS) is addressing these issues principally from the viewpoint of the learner and the delivery process, involving assessment and tracking.

The IMS model, as illustrated in Figure 4.9, does, however, recognize the interdependency of instruction, administration and content – a three-legged stool. IMS therefore sets out to specify formal interfaces between instructional management (the learner's purposed environment) and the core business processes of student management (known as 'MAC', 'MIS' or 'Back Office' and involving admissions, feeing etc.) and asset management (i.e. the future genera-

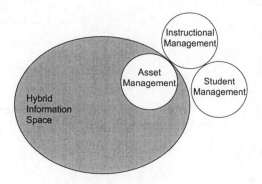

Fig. 4.9 *The learning environment challenge*

tions of content services and their proxies such as library management systems and networked information service portals).

It is contended that the ability of libraries (and other traditional curatorial bodies) to respond to the evolving needs of learning (UK National Grid for Learning, University for Industry and institutional initiatives) will cast a significant die in the determination of their future. Learning may not be the only agenda, but it is politically hot, it is a funding lever, it attracts other players into the market, *and* it is representative of the generic challenges facing traditional information brokerage services (not least the metadata issues set out above).

Put simply, libraries, archives and museums must determine as a matter of urgency whether they are in the business of representing the great wide world of hybrid information space to course developers and learners. Many potential benefits would be associated with such a stance:

- incorporation of traditional media and non-digital artefacts in the body of resources
- provision of guidance and standards for new media and metadata developers within their institutions
- economies of scale as places of deposit and management
- greater control for institutions and practitioners alike over their intellectual property and learning assets
- not least, a means of checking the imperialism of commercial brokers and content barons.

The battle for the interface between learners and content is already on. Even more than digital TV and web publishing, it presents challenges symptomatic of the key metadata and service issues outlined in this paper. It could provide a great opportunity for professional curators armed with systems predicated on the likes of MIA. It could trumpet the arrival of the 'New Library' or it could herald the slow death of us all.

References

1   Library and Information Commission, *New library: the people's network*, London, Library and Information Commission, 1997. Also available at <URL: http://www.ukoln.ac.uk/services/lic/newlibrary/>.

Part 2

Information landscapes: the accommodation of knowledge

5

Designing libraries to be learning communities

TOWARDS AN ECOLOGY OF PLACES FOR LEARNING

Peter Lyman

At their best, libraries are centres for learning that create and sustain a sense of community far beyond their walls – in towns, universities, cities and even nations. What is it about libraries as places that can create and sustain learning communities? How might digital libraries be designed to become such centres for learning – and if they can, what would be their relationship to physical libraries?

Given that we live in a time in which all institutions that create and manage information are changing rapidly – and indeed entirely new kinds of virtual institutions may emerge in the near future – these questions might well be posed in a more general way as well. What is it about *places* that are conducive to the formation of learning communities, whether physical places like library buildings or virtual places like computer networks?

To answer these questions we must try to link information technology to a social vision, just as we would have to when designing a landscape or the architecture of a building. Unfortunately, because professional discourse tends to gain status from technical terminology (the more technological, the more prestigious), discussion of libraries and networks as public places has often been hidden. Yet social visions and tacit assumptions about learning in libraries are latent somewhere within technical discussions of the structure of OPACs and catalogue record fields, and in information science within discussions of search engines, response time and user interfaces. When placing emphasis upon the social dimension, however, we need to be careful when using the technical term 'information' as a generic functional concept encompassing both physical and digital libraries, at least until far more research is conducted into the nature and use of digital information.[1] For now, it is as important to acknowledge and describe the *differences* in the way these two kinds of libraries may provide social contexts for learning, in order to discover the ways they might be designed to complement each other.

An ecology of learning places

When exploring the relationship between libraries and learning, one discovers a gap between the professional discourse about libraries among librarians (for example, in library facilities, collections, information and public service) and the professional discourse about learning among educators (for example, in the classroom or laboratory, teaching or research). This is an important gap, for it makes it difficult for libraries to describe the relationship between library services and collections, and the social utility of libraries for learning and other purposes. Within librarianship, one approach to this problem has been to describe and evaluate libraries in terms of outcomes or performance measures – that is, their impact upon users – rather than to evaluate the quality of libraries by assessing the number of books, the circulation of materials, the number of staff, and so forth.[2]

Another approach might be to explore the relationship between information itself, whether printed or digital, and learning. After all, the word 'information' was first used by the Scholastics as a term for learning, meaning 'to place form into the mind'. Yet the word 'information' alone does not solve the problem, for it means too many things. In information science and librarianship, discourse about information is most often about the management of things – the collection, organization, distribution and management of existing codified knowledge, information and data. Political discourse about information policy is generally focused upon the traditional institutions within which print has been managed – publishing, libraries and intellectual property law – and upon markets and international competition. Educational discourse about information and learning is often focused upon the places in which new knowledge is created: the social relations (for example, teacher/student, apprenticeship), the institutions (for example, schools, laboratories), and the tacit dimension of learning as it flows from person to person through speech and non-verbal communication. An ecology of learning places must find a way to combine these perspectives, not by shaping a new landscape, but by discovering a strategy for balancing the dynamics of human psychology and technological architecture into the design of learning places.

Libraries are not the only institutions facing these questions, for 'the library crisis' is only one instance of the impact of information technology upon all institutions dependent upon learning and research. For example, a conference on 'Knowledge and the Firm' asked how corporations can foster the social processes for the exchange of information between individuals that would promote learning, research and innovation.[3] This question suggests that libraries might best focus their attention upon the way that communities of learners might be fostered, as well as the traditional services which provide information to individuals.

Who uses libraries, and how are they used? Today we speak of people in the library as 'users'. The term 'user' suggests that it is the relationship to information technology that is central, just as the term 'reader' used to refer to a relationship to printed collections. While this is a valid perspective, there is a certain social isolation implicit in each of these terms, suggesting that a library is a public place where strangers might gather to work side by side in peace, but remain strangers. And clearly, the creation of a public place within which such peaceful strangers might dwell is a substantial achievement in an urban civilization. But while some people can learn some things alone by reading books or computers, much learning is collaborative and tacit, and requires a social dimension as much as it requires access to information. While individual people do indeed come to libraries in order to find answers to informational questions (or perhaps to be entertained, overcome loneliness or get out of the rain), information is often only a necessary yet insufficient condition for learning.

Beyond information alone, learning may require the exchange of information between individuals, and ultimately a sense of membership in a community of learners. How, then, does a library design and manage information to enhance communication among learners, to foster collaborative work and learning? While the epistemology of this question might best be explored by the discipline of cognitive psychology, an understanding of the political and social roles of libraries might best begin with an exploration of the nature and dynamics of public *places*.

Learning and a sense of place

Let us postulate, then, that information management alone cannot make a landscape for the accommodation of knowledge, but rather we must focus upon the use of information by individuals, and at a certain point upon the individual's sense of membership in a learning community. This implies a sense of place – simultaneously a sense of physical architecture and a sense of community. How do we construct such a sense of place?

On this subject, Japanese management theory offers the concept of *ba* – the equivalent of our term 'a sense of place'. This is useful when thinking about the future of libraries, because it extends the sense of place derived from geography and architecture to include other sources of a sense of place. *Ba* might reside in a physical place (such as a library or a classroom), or in a virtual place (such as a computer network), or in a cultural or intellectual place (such as that given by shared ideals or cultures), or in some combination of all of these kinds of places.[4]

Even more importantly, such a sense of place is thought to be the precondition for the creative life of any social group, and its design the ultimate creative act.

Therefore, print and digital libraries, however different they may be, should be judged by the same standard: their ability to sustain a sense of place. We should ask: what is it about these different kinds of places that are, or are not, conducive to various kinds of learning? Given these concepts and postulates – and admittedly they are somewhat foreign to the tradition of libraries – two important questions about the design of the library of the future may be posed. First, what determines the quality of physical libraries and virtual communities as learning places, and what is their relationship? Secondly, how might digital information be designed to support learning?

What is the utility of virtual communities as learning places?

If it is useful to think about the role of communities in learning, virtual community technology may be as important as digital library technology for the construction of the library of the future. Although virtual communities are still very young social experiments, and research on them is still incomplete, early findings pose very provocative questions for libraries.

For example, SeniorNet is an organization that uses digital network services to link together elderly people, many of whom live alone. Early studies of the use of SeniorNet network services suggests that it is not online information alone (such as bulletin boards and databases) that sustains a sense of community, but interactive services promoting communication (such as electronic mail and online discussion groups).[5] While the concept of *ba* suggests that shared information might provide a sense of place, the experience of SeniorNet suggests that person-to-person exchange of information is even more important. A digital library dedicated to the formation of learning communities must include both – providing the learner with both information and access to social networks which teach one how to use information. This strategy would resonate with Uri Treisman's findings about drop-outs from school, which suggest that a sense of social isolation is the major cause of academic failure.[6]

How can information resources be designed to foster a sense of place?

We do not yet know very much about the nature and use of digital information, and its implications for human understanding and organization, except that it may well be revolutionary. Yet the vocabulary with which we discuss digital information has been primarily derived from our experience with printed documents, including books, journals and newspapers, each of which includes numerous highly refined genres. But digital information is still in an early stage of innovation. In many ways it still imitates print genres (consider how little of the writing on the World Wide Web differs from writing in print), and only now is it beginning to develop genres that require the unique characteristics of digital information (for example, multimedia, collaborative writing and electronic mail).

Discussions of print may focus successfully upon the management of things or commodities, because the social arrangements for information management of print are well established and have become tacit knowledge. But it is too early to discuss digital information as a problem of the management of things, not least because it is dangerous to allow the discussion of political questions to be merely tacit within technical problems. Moreover, many of the traditional virtues of print are yet to be achieved by digital genres, such as quality, provenance, the organization of information, and preservation. Thus sociologist Manuel Castells[7] analyses digital documents as 'information flows', rather than as things or commodities, in order to place the focus upon social and political issues like equality, participation, free speech, privacy and confidentiality. These issues combine technical architecture with questions of social vision and political justice, thus they are among the constituent elements of a sense of place.

Although each of these questions is worthy of an extended theoretical discussion, given this early stage of innovation it is more practical to introduce them through brief case studies. Exploring the sociology of virtual communities will serve to introduce issues concerning the possibility of building digital libraries that include learning communities. The example of the World Wide Web (the web) will serve to introduce issues concerning the social nature, use and value of digital information.

Can virtual communities be places?

'Virtual community' is the term used to describe the feeling of intimacy and social solidarity felt by participants in computer-mediated communication (CMC) when using electronic mail, bulletin boards, Internet relay chat (IRC), MUDs and MOOs, computer games and other software. The first explorer of virtual communities, Howard Rheingold, says, 'IRC has enabled a global subculture to construct itself from three fundamental elements: artificial but stable identities, quick wit, and the use of words to construct an imagined shared context for conversation.'[8] He then poses the following questions about the architecture of virtual communities: 'What are the minimum elements of communication necessary for a group of people to cocreate a sense of community? What kinds of cultures emerge when you remove from human discourse all cultural artifacts except written words?' Although 'virtual' community is surely a very different experience from the traditional experiences of community, at this point it is clear that new forms of social solidarity are emerging in cyberspace, even though they are based solely upon the exchange of digital writing in real time.

Sociologists Mary Virnoche and Gary Marx have differentiated three kinds of virtual communities, each with its own quality as a place:[9]

1   Community networks

Community networks are geographical communities which use various kinds of digital communications to extend participation, such as electronic mail, Internet relay chat (IRC), bulletin boards and web pages. Examples of community networks include:

- municipal governments using networked communication to involve citizens in political deliberation such as the Boulder, Colorado Community Network at <http://bcn.boulder.co.us>
- corporations using electronic mail and teleconferencing
- scientists and engineers using software for collaborative work
- classrooms using web page and electronic mail to encourage discussion outside classroom hours.

Clearly the strongest sense of community requires physical proximity and frequent face-to-face interaction, but community networks may extend this sense of participation in useful ways by making information more accessible. One consequence of this is that digital libraries supporting community learning are more likely to complement physical libraries than to replace them.

2   Virtual extensions

Virtual extensions sustain a sense of community among a group of people separated by geographical distance but who have face-to-face interaction intermittently, by using shared information resources and computer-mediated communication (CMC). Librarians are an excellent example of a profession whose members meet often, but who also extend this sense of community through daily CMC. Biotechnology is an example of a scientific field in which the rapid advance of research and the technical complexity of the field requires that advances are often made by large teams using software for collaborative work, rather than geographical proximity, as their social glue. Sociologist Walter Powell says:

In the biotech industry, collaborative networks are becoming the 'places' where important intellectual activity occurs . . . These virtual teams point to the future shape of knowledge work in general, which some predict will be accomplished by widely dispersed groups and individuals woven into communities of practice by networks, groupware and a complex common task.[10]

Virtual extensions are a sense of place which may be created by collaborative work on a shared problem – one requiring occasional face-to-face meeting for the exchange of tacit knowledge, but which is sustained by a shared work governed by a sense of shared profession and problem-solving.[11]

3 Virtual communities

Virtual communities in the strict sense, then, are groups of strangers separated by geographical distance, but sharing a common interest expressed by an ongoing participation in CMC. Good examples of virtual communities are Usenet discussions,[12] Howard Rheingold's description of 'The Well' in *The virtual community*,[13] or the most famous example, Xerox Palo Alto Research Center's social experiment with MOO technology called Lambda Moo.[14] Virtual communities in this specific sense may have relatively little stability over time, and relatively more spectators than participants, and yet they are of interest because they are a new form of social group that is robust even if its members have never met, are separated by great distances, and possess significant cultural differences.

Virtual communities have an anonymous quality, perhaps, but this does not prevent them from forming a sense of belonging among strangers from around the world. They are dependent upon responsiveness and a shared interest in a sustained conversation on a topic of mutual interest, rather than upon physical proximity, shared work or common problems. They are most likely to be useful to those sharing interests or problems. Thus, many of the most successful sites provide scarce information and advice about very specialized topics, or perhaps simply a place to talk about a controversial topic without risk. For digital libraries they might be useful in linking citizens to those in other cities or nations.

How do virtual communities create and sustain a sense of place (when they do)? According to sociologists Barry Wellman and Milena Gulia, social relations in cyberspace have the following characteristics:[15]

1 They tend to be narrow and specialized, rather than general.
2 They have a social structure, based upon a sense of reciprocity, and social status in giving good answers.
3 Their anonymity fosters communication among a wider diversity of people than most face-to-face communities.

4   They tend to be responsive in an immediate manner.

On the other hand, unlike traditional communities, they are neither intimate nor long-term, do not require frequent contact, and lack depth with regard to many social contexts or concerns.

Despite this, Wellman and Gulia argue that few social collectives in the modern urban world can be said to be more communitarian than virtual communities. They estimate that the average North American has 1000 acquaintances, including six intimate relationships and perhaps only 50 strong friendships that might be described as constituting a community. Yet the other 950 acquaintances are important sources of information, support, companionship and a sense of belonging not unlike those in virtual communities. The social function of virtual communities might best be compared to the casual acquaintances of modern urban life, they argue, not to families or to the *Gemeinschaft* of medieval villages or even to social life in small towns.

Today digital libraries are designed for individual users, but they might well be designed for virtual communities in each of the three senses defined above. Thus far, however, the two technologies have not been linked. Yet if libraries are to foster learning, virtual community technology offers a new means of linking information resources to learning communities, and of linking libraries to civil society.

What are information landscapes?

Digital libraries are often described as 'information resources'. Yet it is difficult to use digital information, for it provides no sense of place. It has no boundaries, for in principle every networked information resource may be linked to every other, and indeed many encompass the globe. The structure of digital information is defined by technical standards, but unlike with print or other media, there is no authority in cyberspace that might determine the quality of information; even political regulation of cyberspace by national governments is very difficult, given its global scope, without international treaties. Information is not a landscape; it is a remarkable wilderness, needing the vision of a technological Capability Brown.

However, if digital information is a wilderness, we tend to judge it by the standard of printed information, which has evolved quality standards, genres, authority structures and institutional contexts over the past 500 years. Digital information is a new kind of resource, still in the early stages of innovation. The World Wide Web might serve to illustrate some of the remarkable properties of digital information, some of the problems in creating a sense of place in cyberspace, and some of the current attempts to create a landscape for it. Formally the web might be described in these terms:[16]

1 It is a medium for publishing, now equivalent in size to a library of one million volumes, and doubling in size yearly.
2 It uses a rhetorical structure based on HTML (Hypertext Markup Language), allowing any text to be linked to any other.
3 It accommodates multimedia text – now mostly words and numbers (some fixed and some dynamic) as well as images.
4 It is the largest information resource ever created, written by seven million authors.
5 It is accessible from any network node anywhere in the world, and mostly without charge.

A text written collaboratively by seven million authors is a remarkable, even historic event, but without structure it is no more a library than the sum of telephone calls or radio broadcasts made each year.

For this reason, digital libraries tend to include only citations, abstracts and indices of printed information, and digitized versions of printed documents. Yet more and more kinds of information are being invented each year which can only be created and used in digital form, such as scientific visualization, animation, collaborative data and analysis, simulations, digital arts, and the largest information resource ever created, the web itself. A true digital library would include the New World of digital information, if it contained the tools necessary to organize and search it. Four such projects are worthy of special mention here, if only to illustrate the scope of the problem of building digital libraries for learning:

1 XML (eXtensible Markup Language)

The most frequent prediction about the future of the web is that the problem of quality will be solved by electronic commerce: public information will be free but unstructured, and high-quality information will be provided fee-for-service only. But a sense of place is even more vital for electronic commerce than for libraries. Thus new software is being created to make it easier to search for information, to make the web more personal by creating a sense of virtual community, to make it less anonymous by recognizing each user and remembering his or her interests. One example is XML (eXtensible Markup Language), which is to be far more complex than HTML in supporting a sense of participation and community. XML will resemble SGML (Standard Generalized Markup Language) in providing complex and sophisticated editing capability for electronic publishing, yet will go beyond publishing to support a sense of personal contact between buyer and seller, often described as 'a shopping experience'. XML is only one example, but a telling one because electronic commerce software is required to link information to a sense of community. If commerce has set this as a requirement, can libraries do otherwise?

2   Searching and retrieval

Cyberspace is explored by search engines, yet librarians know that most people do not understand how to construct a logical search of online information, and that even if they did, no search engine could encompass all relevant information, and no two search engines would give the same response to the same query.[17] Search engine companies (for example, Yahoo! or AltaVista) attempt to catalogue the web, but unlike libraries they do not share catalogue structures, standards or records, and thus do not provide standard responses. Considerable effort is being made to improve search technologies, especially through pattern recognition and content analysis.

A second strategy is inductive and sociological: to discover the structure of the web by analysing its use. Unlike with a book, the structure of texts on the web is shaped by the actions of the reader, who links information in new patterns, thereby leaving traces which can be collected and archived. As in a wilderness, frequently used traces become trails, then roads; mapping these roads by 'link analysis' is the first attempt to create a social geography or roadmap of the web. Similarly, 'collaborative filtering' software indicates quality by allowing each reader to study the information preferences and choices of groups of people with the similar interests and backgrounds. Unlike cataloguing, these strategies seek to understand the social structures which guide the use of the web, rather than the intellectual structure of its content.

3   Archiving the web

Yet the web is also ephemeral, and cannot be treated as information unless it is archived.[18] Because the web is doubling yearly, the typical web page is only two months old. But only two-thirds of host machines are likely to be accessible on any given day, and most web pages disappear within a year. While paper is a relatively stable medium for the preservation of information, digital media are relatively unstable, less by virtue of their physical vulnerability (for example, ferro-magnetic tape) than because of the pace of technological change, and the obsolescence of both hardware and software. Alexa Internet has created an archival database of web pages that are no longer accessible, which now includes ten terabytes of data (see <URL: http://www.alexa.com>).

4 Genre

Anthropologist Eric Michaels pointed out that primitive art cannot be judged to be 'good' art unless it might also be judged to be 'bad'.[19] The same might be said of digital information, for it is always by definition innovative and new without necessarily being useful. In the world of print, there are a number of contexts within which information may be judged to be good or bad. Most importantly, the literate reader has been trained to recognize the genre of information and apply the relevant standards, while the provenance of the work is also defined by the reputation of the author, publisher and reviewers. But there are no such standards or contexts whereby to judge whether a web page is good or bad, well written or not, useful or not. This problem of genre is characteristic of all electronic media, but it is distinctly interesting in the case of digital information because (like print) it is *written* but (like television) it is *visual*.

Conclusion

This paper began with the goal of accommodating learning to the digital landscape, but noted that technical discourse, whether that of librarians or of information scientists, obscures the ground of such an accommodation. Moreover, the design of the digital library reflects the practice of print libraries in assuming that the learner is a self-sufficient individual. Many learners are self-sufficient, or come to the library looking for information ('When is the next bus to London?') or entertainment ('Where are the novels?') rather than learning. Many kinds of learning require participation in a learning community, particularly when one needs to discover the tacit dimension of a new field of knowledge. Moreover, much of modern intellectual life requires the participation of a relatively large number of people in cooperative learning and discovery, or collaborative work. On either ground, it seems reasonable to design a digital library for the use of communities of learners as well as individual users.

Based upon that assumption, the paper explored the early research on virtual communities. There are two important discoveries from that research that might have bearing upon the design of digital libraries for learning communities:

1 Virtual communities seem to be relatively promising places within which various kinds of learning relationships might grow.
2 Robust virtual communities will depend upon occasional face-to-face meetings within the physical library.

Equally important is the proposition that a sense of place might grow from a number of different kinds of shared experiences, and that every kind of learning place should be judged by its success in enabling those who live there to exchange information in a creative manner.

Finally, the paper briefly examined the early research on the nature of digital information itself, using the web as an example, and concluding that digital information is in a relatively early stage of evolution and is not well designed for group use. For this reason digital libraries have tended to be tools for the use of printed information, or digitized print, leaving the realm of information designed for new media in the hands of the entertainment industry and computer scientists. The information landscape within the digital library, like one of the early forts in the New World, is a secure foothold in the wilderness, but requires the presence of 'farmers' and 'agriculture' far more than that of landscapers.

Notes and references

1   In the UK, see, for example, the systematic research programme 'Virtual society? The social science of electronic technologies', sponsored by the Economic and Social Research Council (ESRC), directed by Prof. Steve Woolgar of Brunel University. In the USA, see the NSF workshop on the Social aspects of digital libraries, available at
    <URL: http://www.gslis.ucla.edu/DL/UCLA_DL_Report.html>.
    Note that this, and all web addresses in this paper, may be found at the Internet Archive if they are no longer available on the web, which in turn may be found at <URL: http://www.alexa.com>.

2   See, for example, the proceedings of the 2nd Northumbria International Conference on Performance Measurement in Libraries and Information Services, 7–11 September 1997.

3   Cole, R. E. (ed.), 'Knowledge and the firm', special issue of *California management review*, **40** (3), 1998.

4   Nonaka, I. and Konno, N., 'The concept of "ba": building a foundation for knowledge creation', *ibid*, 40–54.

5   Furlong, M. S., 'An electronic community for older adults: the SeniorNet network', *Journal of communication*, **39**, 1989, 145–53.

6   Treisman, U., *Developing the next generation of mathematicians*, Washington DC, Mathematical Association of America, 1991 [videocassette].

7   Castells, M., *The rise of the network society*, Oxford, Blackwell, 1996 (see especially 'The space of flows', 376–428.

8   Rheingold, H., *The virtual community: homesteading on the electronic frontier*, New York, HarperCollins, 1994, 176.

9   Virnoche, M. E. and Marx, G. T., '"Only connect" – E.M. Forster in an age of electronic communication: computer-mediated association and community networks', *Sociological inquiry*, **67** (1), 1997, 85–100.

10 Powell, W. W., 'Learning from collaboration: knowledge and networks in the biotechnology and pharmaceutical industries', Cole, R. E. (ed.), *op. cit.*, 228–40.

11 For a review of computer-supported collaborative work (CSCW), see Grudin, J., 'CSCW: its history and participation.' Available at
   <URL: http://www.ics.uci.edu/~grudin/CSCW.html>.
   A useful study of the use of CSCW in the sciences is Walsh, J. P., and Bayma, T., 'Computer networks and scientific work' in Kiesler, S. (ed.), *Culture of the Internet*, New Jersey, Lawrence Erlbaum Associates, Inc., 1997, 385–406.

12 Parks, M. R., 'Making friends in Cyberspace', *Journal of computer mediated communication*. Available at
   <URL: http://www.usc.edu/dept/annenberg/jcmc>.

13 Rheingold, H. *op. cit.*, 17–37.

14 See Dibble, J. A., 'Rape in cyberspace: how an evil clown, a Haitian trikster spirit, two wizards, and a cast of dozens turned a database into a society' in Stefik, M., *Internet dreams: archetypes, myths and metaphors*, Cambridge, The MIT Press, 1996, 293–316.
   Lambda Moo may be explored by Telnet at
   <telnet://Lambda.parc.xerox.com:8888>.

15 Wellman, B. and Gulia, M., 'Net-surfers don't ride alone: virtual communities as communities', in *Networks in the global village*, Boulder, Colorado, The Westview Press, 1999, 331–66.

16 A fuller version of this argument is in Lyman, P. and Kahle, B., 'Archiving digital cultural artifacts',. *D-Lib magazine*, July–August 1998. Available at
   <URL: http://www.dlib.org/dlib/july98/07lyman.html>.

17 Lawrence, S. and Giles, C. L., 'Searching the World Wide Web', *Science,* 280, April 1998, 98–100. See also
   <URL:
   http://www.research.digital.com/SRC/personal/Krishna_Bharat/estim/367.html>.

18 For a dialogue among technologists, librarians and museum professionals on the technical agenda for a digital archive, see the 'Time and Bits' web page and discussion at
   <URL: http://www.gii.getty.edu/timeandbits>.

19 Michaels, E., *Bad Aboriginal art: tradition, media and technological horizons*, Minneapolis, University of Minnesota Press, 1994, 143–62.

6

Very flat Norfolk
A BROAD HORIZON FOR AN INFORMATION LANDSCAPE IN THE NEXT CENTURY

David Baker and Hilary Hammond

Introduction and background

'Very flat, Norfolk', comments Amanda of the English county in Act I of Noel Coward's *Private lives* (1930). 'And difficult to get to', one might add. Certainly, motorists who have to endure the A47 or the A11 (to name but two of Norfolk's major, yet largely single-carriageway roads) or rail travellers delayed by unexpected accumulations of leaves, snow or even rats (who chewed through the signalling cables on one occasion) will be aware of the relative poverty of Norfolk's transport infrastructure. Indeed, newcomers to Norfolk have often been told that the paucity of good roads is deliberate: it stops too many people getting there and spoiling what has to be one of the loveliest and most varied counties in England.

Norfolk is a county with a rich heritage. In the Middle Ages, for example, Norwich was England's second city. Its wealth from wool and weaving is still evident in the several hundred medieval churches, including many of cathedral proportions, that almost litter this apparently flat landscape. There is one major advantage of a flat landscape, of course: you can see a long way.

It is a little depressing to think that it took a near-disaster to make Norfolk's libraries work together to develop an information landscape for the future. The event referred to is the destruction of the Norwich Central Library by fire in 1994. The basement of that building also contained the Norfolk Record Office (NRO) – one of the foremost regional archive repositories in Britain. Fortunately, the NRO was saved with only minimal damage.

In July 1994 the central library in Norwich had reached the stage in any building's life where its inadequacies to meet today's needs had been recognized, although thought to be 'plenty of life in the old dog yet'. This had resulted in the central courtyard being roofed over, both to expand the space for mainstream library work, and to improve the environmental conditions for the Norfolk Record Office, accommodated beneath a floor which had been designed to hold back a fire for two hours. This work had been completed about six months before the fire.

The fire itself and its consequences have been covered in many presentations, and also led to the British Library giving greater priority to a Loughborough University proposal for research on disaster planning. Its impact in Norfolk, apart from a raising of people's blood pressure and problem-solving abilities, was a political realization of the social and educational value of a library service. For six months the only central services were a quick-reference print-and electronic-based facility in a small city-centre office and the reference facilities of the UEA (University of East Anglia) library, for which Norwich Libraries were most grateful. The opening hours of the nearest branch libraries were extended, and a temporary mobile library service was provided for those living in the vicinity of the old building. However, it was very plain that a crucial support for education, the economy and the social fabric was missing.

It is fascinating to realize that there was not a single building in Norwich which could take the whole of the central library, even without the Norfolk Record Office. The lending service had to be split from the reference and local studies services: the former in an old furniture store, and the latter in the old CCTA (Central Computer and Telecommunications Agency) building.

The University of East Anglia (UEA) enjoys both an international reputation for excellence in research and a major regional role, the latter represented by the Centre of East Anglian Studies – a local history research centre awarded a grade 5 in the most recent Research Assessment Exercise. The University Library is by far the largest in the region, acting as the hub of the academic library and computing networks for Norfolk and neighbouring Suffolk. It is also the home of the East Anglian Film Archive (EAFA), the first and one of the largest of the UK's regional film archives. In recent years, the UEA Library has been heavily involved in the e-Lib programme of the Joint Information Systems Committee (JISC), with two major projects based at the UEA: EDDIS (Electronic Document Delivery: the Integrated Solution) and Agora, a major hybrid library demonstrator. The UEA Library are project managers for the JISC/BUFVC (British Universities Film and Video Council) Imaginations project to transmit moving images across JANET (the Joint Academic Network), and have also benefited from non-formula funding for the cataloguing and conservation of the archives held at the UEA, and in particular the EAFA.

The political and professional response to the fire was to ask the following questions:

1 Was a new central library necessary?
2 What was the role of electronic information access in its development?
3 Should it be a single-site building?

These questions were being addressed early in 1995. Desk research suggested that changes in the nature of publications themselves from print to electronic could be expected by around 2005 or 2010, but that until then print would remain the dominant medium. It was also clear that there would be more users of all ages making more complex demands than had previously been the case. The days of reducing the number of professional library staff were over. It is interesting to reflect that in 1998 the eLib programme forecast that the number of electronic journals would exceed 3000.

The result of a year's study into the nature and type of central library likely to be required for the next 25 to 50 years was the development of a subject department-based library, with the same stock level as the old building, but double the number of study spaces. Provision was also made for what at the time was a massive database, equivalent to 250 CD-ROM platters running concurrently, with 60 of the study spaces provided with on-desk devices, and all of them linked to the LAN (local area network).

To cut an exceedingly long and complex story very short, this became a 4500-m^2 library as the major part of one of the UK Millennium Commission's Landmark Projects. The total project received a grant of £30 million. The project is due to be completed around Christmas 2000. It will then be dedicated to the Millennium Commission for 125 years.

At the same time, a new home was required for the NRO, with its 11.5 million documents. This is sharing the old CCTA building at present. A bid to the HLF (Heritage Lottery Fund) was developed with the UEA for an exciting NRO co-located with the Centre for East Anglian Studies adjacent to the University Library. Unfortunately this was not accepted by the HLF because, in part, it was seen to benefit the academic work of the University. However, a new bid was developed for an NRO with EAFA at the County Hall site. This will continue to be in partnership with the UEA. This partnership is expected to include direct access to the digitized finding aids, as well as access to copies of the original documents as they become available.

Concurrently with these specific projects the libraries were working on what has since become known as the Information and Learning Network. This envisages some 18 to 20 locations across Norfolk, each provided with a range of PCs or other desktop devices, together with tutorial support and video conferencing facilities. They will be linked to the educational network for post-16 education, while those located in libraries will also be linked to the databases in the Millennium Library.

A further development is an agreement in principle from the HLF for a major development at the Norwich Castle Museum, which is of regional importance. Although primarily aimed at improving the facilities for the collections and for public access, this investment should also energize the Norfolk Museums

Service, as part of the new Department of Cultural Services, to build on its documentation project and to give added priority to the digitization of samples from its key collections.

Overarching objectives

Together, the UEA and Norfolk County Council have a number of overarching objectives which underpin the development of a Norfolk information landscape:

- the enhancement of the economic, cultural and social life of Norfolk
- the preservation and development of the region's heritage, for the long-term benefit and enjoyment of the population
- the provision of relevant, cost-effective training and education across Norfolk for its inhabitants of all ages
- the provision of leisure services
- the embracing of information technology for the future wellbeing of the region, its economy and its people
- the development of Norfolk as an information-rich society
- the stimulation of the regional economy through strategic investment, the development and retraining of the workforce, the inward attraction of new industries and spending power, and the development of a higher profile for Norfolk and Norwich.

The context in which we are developing our information landscape also includes the following key trends:

- an increase in the numbers of jobs requiring further or higher education qualifications, and with an IT base
- a continuing increase in the participation rate in further and higher education, among both school leavers and mature students
- an increase in non-traditional entry to university, often based on 'access' courses
- an increase in postgraduate-level studies (especially in the humanities), requiring access to primary source materials
- a recognition that UEA is one of the area's major employers and a significant contributor to the local economy
- a net 'export' of students to other parts of the country and an increasing reliance on international students and the high rating of research activity to bring funds to the University
- an ageing, longer-lived population with more leisure time
- increasing demands for learning resources

- a growing interest in the regional heritage and its conservation
- sustained expansion of the use of library and archive resources
- a substantial increase in network connectivity, teleworking and home owner-ship of powerful personal computers within the region
- a deterioration in the traditional Norfolk economy, coupled with a pressing need to attract money and business into the county
- a need to respond to the increasing pace of change in individual people's careers
- a need to provide access to an increasing amount of current data electroni-cally, wherever the data is held
- conversely, the increasing cost of accessing data at a time of increasing pres-sure on revenue budgets
- a recognition that Internet access is unlikely to be available to the majority of residents within a reasonable time-scale other than through public provision.

Developing the landscape

This, then, is the background for the development of an information landscape for Norfolk in the next century. UEA and Norfolk County Council are working towards the creation of a long-term, widely accessible resource of international repute for the collection, preservation, study, teaching and enjoyment of the doc-umentary heritage of Norwich, Norfolk and East Anglia. This ties in closely with the JISC's collections policy and its drive towards a Distributed National Electronic Resource (DNER) and the UK Library and Information Commission's vision for services in the next millennium. In particular, we sub-scribe to the widespread provision of access and the importance of creating a dig-ital library 'of the UK's intellectual heritage of culture and innovation', while the outreach and educational initiatives planned will help to equip 'individuals and organizations to play their full role in a learning and information society'.[1]

One of the other dominant factors is the Government's recognition of the importance of networked information sources, and the priority it is giving to developing both the content and networking facility for public libraries, through its response to *New library: the people's network*.[2] We will continually argue that this is a belated response, and that public libraries have a great deal of catching up to do before they can be equal players with universities. However, using a maritime metaphor, the ship is launched even if it is not yet properly fitted out.

We envisage that the process for developing the content accessible to the net-work will build significantly on the work we have been developing together. One test we expect to use in assessing the priorities for bidding for funds to support this area of activity is the usefulness of the content to a wide range of 'viewers' (who used to be called 'readers'). We think that there is a significant commonality of interests amongst academic researchers and interested amateurs for what has been called 'the national library – locally held'. For instance, digitizing mid-19th century photographs will provide a full range of resources, from illustrations for a school project to the study of the development of an aspect of behaviour in that period.

We are envisaging a hybrid approach. No diminution in demand for traditional paper- or parchment-based resources is foreseen. Indeed, we forecast an increase in demand for access to originals stimulated by better-quality catalogues.

The availability of the UEA's advanced network infrastructure, and the development of Norfolk's Millennium Library equivalent, will allow remote users access to information about the various collections, whether singly or together, and eventually to images of the materials themselves. The network infrastructure will also offer the opportunity to link with other relevant collections, both locally and nationally. The digitization of material from the NRO and the EAFA in particular will offer the convenience of immediate access to copies of records without compromising the security of the originals.

The partners intend to continue to work together to develop the significant outreach work already undertaken individually and collectively. Much of the perceived innovation and additional impetus comes from the expected collocation of the key archives and the associated technology-based developments. The potential for online instruction is already recognized, and this will be developed as part of a series of supporting projects associated with the development of the NRO and the EAFA.

Additionally, our partnership since 1994 has led to a number of supporting or parallel projects, including:

- the creation of a machine-readable version of the *Norfolk Bibliography,* which is being expanded to include holdings information as well as a broader range of subjects
- a pilot digitization project of Norfolk maps
- an image database project, based on still photographic materials housed in the central library and all the museums within the Norfolk Museums Service
- the creation of an East Anglian Sound Archive to complement the EAFA.

These projects are designed to fill major gaps in the information landscape – gaps identified as a result of our long-term partnership and the creation of an information topology for Norfolk and the region.

Document supply services are planned, using EDDIS-type technology. A balance will be struck between quality and speed of throughput in the case of heritage-type materials (e.g. manuscripts). Some material may be scanned and stored for future access; other items will be scanned and sent upon request but *not* stored.

Common standards will be applied wherever possible, building upon both local expertise and national trends and directives. In this context, emphasis is being based upon web-based developments, as the web can deliver the required information and material effectively and seamlessly. This will hopefully reduce the problem of using proprietary products and obviate the need for front-end interface developments locally. The use of SGML to enable data to be accessed from a variety of systems, and to be exchanged between them, is also being evaluated. In order to utilize network technology and to ensure maximum searchability in a networked environment, it is envisaged that all catalogues produced by our partnership will be Z39.50-compliant.

Conclusion

Norfolk's position, demography, heritage and background present challenges and opportunities. Our partnership is seen as being vital to the success of our information landscape in the next century. A full landscape must include *all* the key features, however shaped and whoever owns and maintains them. And the landscape must be enjoyable and usable by all, hence the need for a common approach and realistic approaches to the cost of development and maintenance of the core facilities.

References

1   'Millennium bid: second attempt for Norwich', *Library Association record,* **98** (10), 1996, 491.
2   Library and Information Commission, *New library: the people's network*, London, Library and Information Commission, 1997. Also available at <URL: http://www.ukoln.ac.uk/services/lic/newlibrary/>.

7
Who's in command?
DEFINING THE BOUNDARIES OF COMPETENCY AND ACTION FOR THE 'INFORMATIONAL SOCIETY'

Ray Lester

A micro-case study

The Natural History Museum,[1] like all large, diverse organizations, faces a number of challenges in using the Internet optimally to help make its resources available to users outside its walls. The museum's subject area is often described as 'the natural world', defined in a recent internal policy document as comprising:

> The Earth and its planetary environment; constituent minerals and organisms (including humans), living and past; human perspectives of, and interactions with, nature both living and material.

The notion of 'subject area' is important: it is the prime notion that we use to discover resources that we think that we might need.

The Natural History Museum contains the single largest and most important concentration of resources about 'the natural world', within that world, including:

* 68,000,000 biological/mineralogical specimens
* 1,000,000 library volumes
* 10,000 current serials
* 500,000 art and archive artefacts.

These resources are used by some 350 museum-based scientists, helped by about 50 library and information staff. However, access to the resources is required, not just by those internally – and externally – engaged in advanced scientific research, but also, at a less intellectually focused level, by those who wish to learn, or simply to enjoy themselves. As well as being designated earlier this year as a European Union 'large-scale facility' for taxonomically based scientific research, the museum has for many years been a pioneer in providing education about the natural world to schoolchildren and other learners. It is also now the fourth-most-visited paid-for visitor attraction in the UK.

Nevertheless, although the museum's 'real' exhibitions continue to draw in the crowds, the museum is also pushing ahead with designing a 'virtual' Natural History Museum. A report on 'exhibition policy' shortly to be presented to the museum's board of trustees pleasingly stated:

> While it is impossible to predict developments in information technology over the next 20 years, the policy for exhibitions can be based upon the Museum's intention to be fully integrated into a future information society, in which a significant and growing proportion of the population makes everyday use of IT. In developing its electronic exhibitions, the Museum will seek to take advantage of those opportunities created by an information society which complement its unique strengths.

Clearly, a key challenge, as with most other publicly funded UK bodies, is to balance the museum's public-good role – the institution is currently about 60% Government funded – with the need and desire to make money. For instance, the Natural History Museum Library mounted an exhibition of natural history art at Christies, the auctioneers, early in 1998:[2] not with the intention of selling items from the library's art collection, but to raise awareness of that important and extensive collection, and to generate the interest of benefactors in donating funds towards the collection's preservation. Many of the items in the collection are the best record the world now has of certain extinct species.

Taxonomy and systematics

The museum's unique selling point – its competitive advantage, if you will – is the quality of its specimen, library and art collections, together with the knowledge (often tacit knowledge), of its army of taxonomists and other scientists. *Taxonomy* is the 'science of identifying, naming, and classifying organisms. *Systematics* is 'the science of determining evolutionary relationships among organisms'.[3] Every preserved *specimen* is, by definition, a unique example of a particular. However, there is often a wish to focus on what is known as the *type specimen*. The *type* is the specimen from which the characterization of a species as being distinct from all other then known species was first written up and published in the taxonomic literature. The museum contains a very large number of *types*.

There is then a more than usually critical link between the objects of laboratory research and the objects of library research, with the species name potentially being the golden piece of metadata linking the two in a digital environment. Unfortunately, not only do some types known by different names sometimes eventually turn out to belong to the same species, but the taxonomists change their minds from time to time: for instance, previously distinct species may be 'lumped' into one single species, or what has been thought to be one single species is 'split' into two or more separate species. Further, the very basis for classifying species is fiercely argued. A recent article aimed at the non-specialist distinguished:[4]

- the biological species concept
- the morphological species definition
- the evolutionary species concept
- the genotype cluster definition.

Use of any or all of these potentially adds a yet further layer of complexity.

Thus, in this semantic domain, not only is there disagreement on what to call the object of study, the element of 'stuff'– not only do people have different views as to whether one particular object is for the necessary purposes needed the same or different from another object – there is also argument as to the techniques which should be used definitively to distinguish this object from that object. And then, if we add to all that the desire to plot evolutionary, host–parasite, environmental and other relationships between the different objects of study, it certainly becomes an extremely complex system to attempt to model and 'automate'.

Although the taxonomic and systematic navel-gazing can considerably complicate the task facing the designer of the information system in bringing together, for the user, different types of digital data (morphological, ecological, genetic, GIS, library, artistic, and so on) related to a particular species, for most people for most purposes, I would suggest that using a single agreed species name to reference the panoply of 'stuff' related to the specific species is good enough.

I shall repeat the phrase 'for most purposes for most people': it is one key theme of this paper. So it can be argued that we need a single agreed list of the names of all of the world's presently known 1.8 million or so species, which we can then all use, for instance, in our Dublin Core records. This policy is being pursued very actively at the moment. (Perhaps characteristically, people in the USA think that this list should be a single, centrally maintained file; most people outside the USA think that it should be a set of distributed datasets.)

Biodiversity networks

There is then a large amount of work taking place, aiming – via the use of global electronic networks – to bring together species-related data held, for instance, in the major specimen collection institutions of the world, such as the great natural history museum in Paris, the Smithsonian in Washington, the Natural History

Museum in London, and so on (see Figure 7.1). Much of this work is driven by the biodiversity imperative, which in turn gained a great boost from the signing of the Rio Convention by 154 nations in 1992.[5]

However, not only have a whole variety of funding agencies put forward proposals and funded exploration of information systems work within their jurisdictions (for example, the United Nations Environment Programme, the World Bank, several agencies in the EU, regional initiatives, national initiatives); but also, because no one is in overall command, a whole variety of network information architectures have been adopted. Two figures from a *Guide to information management*,[6] researched and compiled by the World Conservation Monitoring Centre with support from the Global Environment Facility through the United Nations Environment Programme, illustrate this point well. Figure 7.2 is conceptualized as a *fully distributed network* with minimal input from the centre: there are instead just a series of bilateral arrangements between stakeholders. Figure 7.3, by contrast, is designed as a *clearing-house network* with some sort of commander in the centre, or what I prefer to call the *middle* (cf. Figure 7.1).

But if we are to have some sort of commander in the middle, between those producers who generate biodiversity data and those who need to use that data, how is that commander to be chosen? Who chooses? What exactly is the commander's role? How can we be sure that the commander is competent to fulfil that role? Who decides that?

Meanwhile, there is an increasing and welcome desire amongst politicians and senior policy makers to get information presently 'sitting', as it were, in the vaults of institutions such as the Natural History Museum out to those who could profit from that information. The report of a recent meeting of the great and the good in Darwin, Australia (a symbolic venue indeed) solemnly asserted:[7]

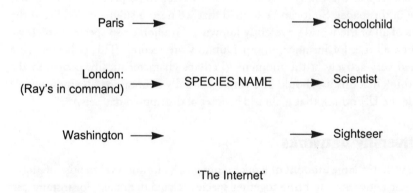

Fig. 7.1 *Who's in command?*

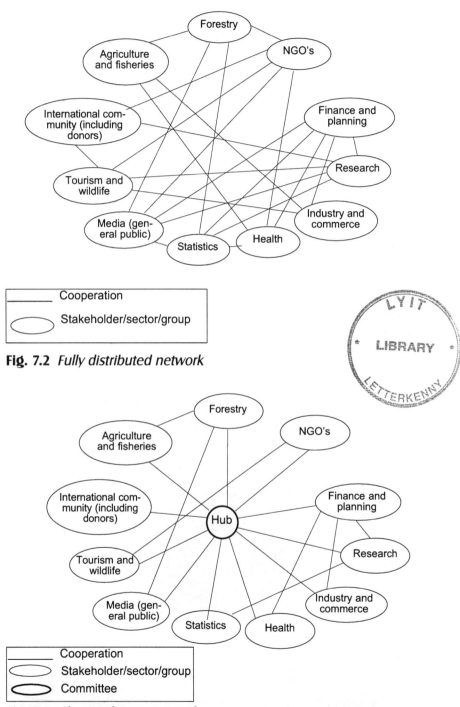

Cooperation

Stakeholder/sector/group

Fig. 7.2 *Fully distributed network*

Cooperation

Stakeholder/sector/group

Committee

Fig. 7.3 *Clearing-house network*

Taxonomy should be integrated at all levels of government into policies and programmes for sustainable development and biodiversity conservation. These include agriculture, forestry, fisheries, protection of threatened species, biological resources for medicine and human health, energy production, land use planning to accommodate human population growth, use of traditional knowledge, environmental education and training, print and electronic media, ecotourism and bioprospecting, as well as national and local programmes for inventory and monitoring of biological resources in ecosystems.

The report then goes on to say:

National governments and authorities should utilise information systems to maximum effect in taxonomic institutions. In developing priority-setting criteria for information products, taxonomic institutions should consider the needs of the wide range of users of that information, including biodiversity managers. In particular, taxonomic information, literature and checklists should be put into electronic form.

Within the UK, there are already laudable attempts to translate those sentiments into action. Figure 7.4 is a diagram taken from a brochure promoting the idea of a UK national biodiversity network.[8] As a final prelude to more generic consid-

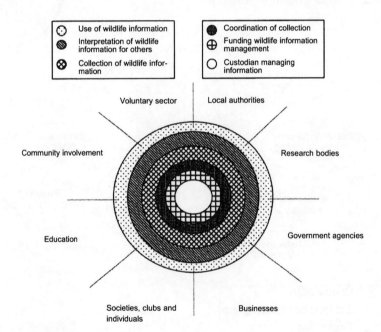

Fig. 7.4 *UK national biodiversity network*

erations, I wish to quote from the brochure itself. These words should ring many bells with those readers who have been grappling with proposals such as the National Resource Discovery Agency within the UK higher education community, the National Grid for Learning being promoted by the present UK Government, and similar collaborative initiatives:

> To help maximise the value of data, the Network will make 'best practice' guidelines available. These will not be prescriptive as the Network will have no power to direct the actions of any individual or group. However, membership of the Network will depend on meeting standards for access, service, quality, validation, survey and sampling, so that members can share information with confidence . . .
>
> The Network will establish common terms and conditions through which the owners of the data can offer different levels of access, with charges where appropriate. There will be no transfer of ownership of the data. Information, and the intellectual rights associated with its arrangement and interpretation, will remain with those who hold them at present. The Network will link these data sets into a coherent whole, enabling people to access the records. Ultimately, it will be possible to search for, arrange and interpret information on our wildlife, making use of the millions of hours which have gone into gathering and recording of the data. The Network will develop standards, such as those needed for species name, to improve our ability to share and integrate separately collected information.

The open-network society

Network or middle – whatever term we might use to designate the intermediating agency described above, there seems to be a tacit assumption that without any real thought 'it' will do all that is necessary to ensure digital connection between those who generate data for the public domain and those who desire to use that data – and what is more, do all that is necessary across some, and sometimes all, of these arenas of command:

- medium: data/text/image/moving image/voice
- institution: for example (within Kensington, London, UK), the Victoria and Albert Museum, Imperial College, Royal Borough of Kensington and Chelsea Public Library, Royal Geographical Society, Natural History Museum
- domain: museums/libraries/galleries/archives
- funding sector: for example (within the UK), DCMS, DfEE, DETR, DTI
- political jurisdiction: for example, OECD, EU, UK, Scotland.

But where there is a need for the user query to traverse the boundaries which exist between the various members of such different arenas of command, who is in *overall* command of the relevant members either side of the various boundaries so as to ensure that there is a single, coordinated, seamless and trouble-free matching of user query to desired resource?

Well, of course, almost always no one is in overall command, at least outside the private sector. And that, some will no doubt vehemently argue, is the whole point and great virtue of the Internet. It crosses all the arena boundaries listed above. It allows users to move seamlessly up and down the value-adding informational stack (see Figure 7.5).[9] The Internet is all about freeing information users and suppliers from the restrictions and inhibitions that have characterized societal communication to date; and moving that society into becoming a great 'informational' society. Any notion that any person or authority could, let alone should, try to 'command' who gets what information, when, where, how and so

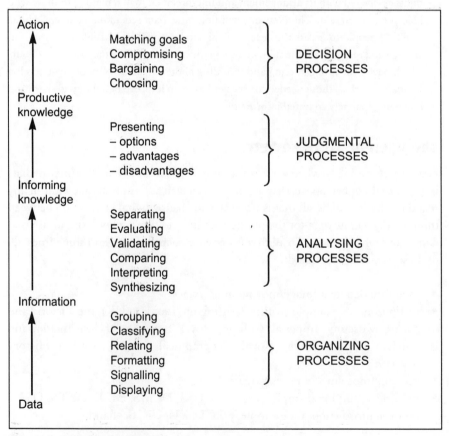

Fig. 7.5 *Value-adding information stack*

on is nonsense. Consider the immense number of fundamental variables external to any particular information system: economic, financial, commercial, industrial, political, legal, social, cultural, environmental etc. Movements of any one of these have the potential to scupper the best-laid command structure. We must know that from reading the relevant literature – and, indeed, from perusal of many of the papers given at this very conference. Any individual must concentrate on commanding that for which he or she is responsible and accountable for commanding, and leave the rest well alone.

Five difficulties

While this writer fully recognizes the force of that argument, nonetheless, as the manager of a significant publicly funded collection of information assets, he unfortunately finds himself presented with several difficulties.

First, there is the question of organizational mission. The Natural History Museum's mission is 'to maintain and develop its collections and use them to promote the discovery, understanding, responsible use and enjoyment of the natural world.[10] Within that brief, the museum's department of library and information services is concerned with 'organizing, preserving and communicating knowledge of the natural world.' When the director of the museum – or indeed the UK Department of Culture, Media and Sport, the museum's government funding agency – asks how the museum can ensure that all the money it is putting into networking, metadata creation, digitalization, website design and so on will lead to it being better able to fulfil its mission and goals, it does not sound very convincing to say: 'Well, we don't really know. We think that people outside the museum will be able to get at our information via the Internet. But it's all rather unstructured and disorganized out there . . .'

A second problem with an informational free-for-all is that the museum naturally does not want to be left out of any action that is being organized, leaving some other institution such as the Science Museum, the Smithsonian or the British Library, to profit from delivering services and products which the Natural History Museum could profit from delivering instead – after all, it needs the money too. So when the museum sees information system architectures published such as that for the PRIDE system,[11] whose development is being funded for two years by the European Commission, the museum wishes to find out who will be in overall command of such a system, so that it can make sure that it is one of the specified suppliers of the library, document delivery, publishing, information broking, services etc., and not some other (perhaps rival) institution.

When people at the Natural History Museum look around within the biodiversity arena, they find many different and overlapping mainly clearing-house-type command structures (i.e. with a middle) being promoted. They then wonder why so many such information networks and systems are needed: this is surely a rather inefficient use of scarce taxpayer funds. One particular system of this type which the Natural History Museum itself will most likely become involved with soon is being promoted by the USA-based Research Libraries Group. No doubt, museum staff will need to make a number of trips to the USA in order to become fully integrated into this particular network. Give that the taxpayers of the UK are supporting the museum financially, then they are the ones who should be asking the questions about inefficient use of funds.

The Internet is not exactly the uninhibited electronic highway available to everyone free that politicians and policymakers would have us believe. To take just one well-known small example from fairly low down the stack, there is the introduction by the Joint Information Systems Committee of the UK higher education community of transatlantic usage-related charges. This obviously has fundamental implications for those in the UK wishing to deliver to users specimen data located at the Smithsonian in Washington DC alongside complementary data located in the Natural History Museum.

Meanwhile, the commercial sector also has much to gain from the Internet. If we are committed to making at least some of our resources available free of charge via the Internet to at least some of our potential external users, then if we do not 'take command' of the appropriate elements of that Internet, then surely the commercial sector will. Once the commercial publishers are in a position to generate large profits from the delivery of our data, there will be a rerun of what happened, for instance, with scientific and scholarly journals. Intellectual property elements are for most purposes unique elements, so whoever controls them has the potential if so minded to make large profits from their exploitation, once they have acquired the relevant rights. Underneath the charm, the commercial players, whether concerned with hardware, software, data, people or processes, have to be commercially hard-nosed. Otherwise they will go out of business.

User needs and characteristics

What, then, is to be done? I have tentative recommendations for resource holders, for resource users, and for the middle as defined above – tentative because the whole business is rather complicated. However, before presenting these recommendations, let us first summarize the key needs and characteristics of the users of publicly accessible information resources:

1   Advanced researchers make their own arrangements for accessing the information resources they need – very much with the assistance of the appropriate 'invisible colleges'. The researchers are highly motivated to retrieve the information they need. They do not need societal resources devoted to the

middle, at least at the *content* level (although they do at the *conduit* level). These users will go straight to the 'rich' data they need. They know where it is; they know how to extract and use it. They do not, for instance, need the paraphernalia of the MODELS Information Architecture developed by UKOLN.

2   All other users – the bulk – have limited time/energy for resource discovery, location, retrieval, and use. This is the arena highlighted earlier as 'for most purposes for most people'.

3   These other users do not wish to be comprehensive in the resources they use. They simply want access to the 'best' resources. So someone has to value-add between resource cornucopia and user.

4   The users to do not expect to pay to decide whether a particular resource is suitable for the task in hand. That has fundamental implications for system design. The users do not pay to browse in bookstores and libraries, so why should they pay to browse online?

5   The users want structure and transparency in the portions of the global information system they choose to use. They do not trust people who seem to have something that they wish to hide.

6   Finally, the users want to feel that they are 'in command' of their own information destiny. For instance, they *do* want to use keyword access when they want to use keyword access; they *do* want to browse when they want to browse.

Resource-holder priorities

With those precepts in mind, I would suggest that the priorities for resource holders are:

- to preserve the original artefacts they hold in stock (that is most critical, especially where the artefact is unique or rare)
- to safeguard the internal IT infrastructure: the 'conduit' (we cannot deliver without that)
- to create resource metadata for their user communities – many different types of metadata for many types of clients and customers
- to capture tacit knowledge (this potentially gives competitive advantage)
- to form strategic alliances with resource-use *agents* (the term is defined below), to do deals, by-pass the middle
- to 'balance the books' in order to remain solvent in the long term (this is not about working out where the next grant is coming from: this is for real).

Some of the above is actually quite complex to specify, organize and manage, especially in an institution such as the Natural History Museum, which has traditionally operated very much as a series of individual departments, rather than as a corporate body. This in turn makes it relatively difficult to present a holistic view to the outside world of the resources held throughout the organization.

Resource-user priorities

It is implied above that strategic links between resource holders and those who wish to use the relevant resources might best be developed via *agents* – or brokers – who would act on the collective behalf of the users. These agents would locate information, barter, retrieve and refine it, against notified specifications. This is quite a good idea – and if it really took off, we might then try to find an acronym for the agents which we could use based on the overall job objective captured above.

Librarians are not the only professionals who might be considered as candidates for the role of agent. A recently published paper[12] hypothesized that there might be a similar shift across the professional boundary between librarians and researchers regarding content, as happened some years ago between centrally located computer officers and researchers regarding conduit. However, librarians potentially still have the edge over other professionals to play the role of agent for non-highly specialist information.

Middle priorities

In a recently published book from the business arena,[13] Weill and Broadbent report on some detailed empirical research carried out over a number of years. The question addressed was: how is that some large multinational enterprises succeed in leveraging IT, whilst others fail? What are the secrets of providing free-standing companies, albeit those belonging to the same corporate conglomerate (and librarians do not even have that sanction), to work together and use IT networks to deliver real cost/benefit?

In this context here, Weill and Broadbent discovered the following criteria of success:

1 There must be a commitment at the level of CEO/the Board within the stakeholder's parent organization to supporting each networked information-system stakeholder.
2 The participative requirement must relate to strong maxims within each stakeholder, which in turn must relate to the core rules of their organization.
3 The information system must focus on 'have to' rather than 'nice to have'.

4 The system must be able to display demonstrable benefits.
5 The system must be organized as a long-term sustainable operation.
6 Most importantly, someone must have a remit to command the whole information system.

We might then try to apply these success factors – to the extent that they are agreed to be applicable outside the business arena – to a gathering of middle stakeholders. There is a difference, not only in that such stakeholders do not have the umbrella provided by a holding company, but also, in that the success factors must ideally be applied within a rather vague collective arena whose only common defining feature is that each stakeholder is concerned with a particular *subject*. Non-specialist users wish to use the Internet to retrieve resources, and details of resources, of relevance to aspects of specific subject fields, and to do this irrespective of medium, institution, domain, funding sector or political jurisdiction. But who, overall, is in command of the subjects? How do we get long-term buy-in of the type indicated in Weill and Broadbent's research from (overlapping) collections of subject-based middle stakeholders?

Those of us with resources to manage, and those of us who have responsibility for resource users, face an immense challenge if we are to work together properly to exploit the Internet and deliver sustained benefit, irrespective of whether there is nothing in the middle or everything of importance in the middle. For the wide-area networked information systems that we would wish to have a long-term role, we have to take organizational strategy, management, design and culture seriously. If we are intent on running Internet-based non-commercial middle organizations which transcend resource-holder and resource-user organizations, they have to be managed. The panoply of issues which arise when dealing with information as a resource will not just resolve themselves of their own accord – or if they do, they will do so in a way that fails to deliver individual missions.

Optimal cost-beneficial use of inevitably finite economic and other resources within mixed-economy global information systems, whether taxonomically based or based on any other potentially unifying feature, will not just happen of its own accord. The constituent stakeholders, all necessarily with their own private agendas, need to be *commanded* (with all that implies) if we are truly to achieve the greatest good for the greatest number.

Meanwhile, if you are a holder of some worthwhile resources, or if you are a user with a potential interest in accessing such resources, wherever in the world they or you are located, my advice is to get yourself a good librarian.

But let us not get all this out of perspective. Alain de Botton, at the very end of his book *How Proust can change your life*,[14] cautions us against becoming obsessed with the places Proust visited. He suggests that a genuine homage to

Proust would be to look at our world through his eyes, and not look at his world through our eyes. De Botton writes:

> There is no greater homage we can pay Proust than to end up passing the same verdict on him as he passed on Ruskin, namely that for all its qualities, his work must eventually also prove silly, maniacal, constraining, false and ridiculous to those who spend too long on it.
>
> To make reading into a discipline is to give too large a role to what is only an incitement. Reading is on the threshold of the spiritual life; it can introduce us to it: it does not constitute it.
>
> Even the finest books deserve to be thrown aside.

Even the finest information systems deserve similarly.

References

1   See <URL: http://www.nhm.ac.uk>.
2   *Images from nature: drawings and paintings from the Library of the Natural History Museum*, London, The Natural History Museum, 1998.
3   Wallace, R. A., Sanders, G. P. and Ferl, R. F., *Biology: the science of life*, New York, HarperCollins, 1996.
4   Brookes, M., 'The species enigma', *New scientist*, section 111.
5   See the work of the Natural History Museum in relation to the Convention on Biological Diversity. Available at
    <URL: http://www.nhm.ac.uk/biu/cbd&nhm.html>.
6   World Conservation Monitoring Centre, *Guide to information management: in the context of the Convention on Biological Diversity*, Nairobi, Kenya, United Nations Environment Programme, 1996.
7   *The Darwin Declaration*, Canberra, Australia Biological Resources Study, Environment Australia, 1998.
8   'National biodiversity network: building knowledge by sharing information', National Biodiversity Network. Further information available at
    <URL: http://www.nbn.org.uk>.
9   Taylor, R. S., *Value-adding processes in information systems*, Norwood, NJ, Ablex, 1986, 6.
10 The mission statement is available at
    <URL: http://www.nhm.ac.uk/museum/info/mission.html>.
11 Colleran, A., 'PRIDE: People and Resource Identification for Distributed Environments', *LaserLink*, Spring–Summer 1998, 20–3.

12 Corrall, S. and Lester, R., 'Professors and professionals: on changing boundaries' in Cuthbert, R., *Working in higher education*. Buckingham. SRHE/Open University Press, 1996, 84–100.

13 Weill, P. and Broadbent, M., *Leveraging the NEW infrastructure*, Boston, MA, Harvard Business School Press, 1998.

14 De Botton, A., *How Proust can change your life*, London, Picador, 1997, 215.

8

Information landscapes
SECRET GARDEN OR WONDERLAND?

Cris Woolston

Introduction

First let me point out that I am neither a librarian nor an information professional, nor even a computing specialist. I am approaching the developing discussion about information landscapes as an academic with a science background
who is now involved in supporting and developing the processes of teaching and
learning.

This paper uses the Alice theme which runs through a number of the other
papers presented at this conference (see **Opening keynote address**). This not only
allows us to reflect back on the Alice of the Follett Report (see also **Opening
keynote address**) and her experiences and expectations of what is now called
C&IT, but also enables us to look at learning through the eyes of the Alice of
Lewis Carroll. In this paper I would like to explore some essential issues to be
considered when discussing the construction of learning landscapes. In exploring
these issues I will be drawing on my experience with learning technology – in
particular, through involvement with TLTP (Teaching and Learning Technology
Programme) projects – and also my experience with educational development
and investigation of learning processes.

For those not from the UK I should first explain that the learning institute I
represent is the University of Hull in the North East of England. In the past, the
city of Hull it was a prosperous fishing and trade port, but both of these traditional industries are largely gone. The result is that the city, and also the subre-
gion, has significant problems with unemployment, low aspiration, low
educational attainment and inadequate workforce skill sets. Whilst this paper has
a higher education focus, it should be noted that the University of Hull is playing a role in the wider educational context, and that much of what is said below
is influenced by an awareness of the needs of a broader community of learners.
In fact, very few universities can allow themselves the luxury of only considering
the needs of 19-year-old grammar-school-educated students.

In the **Introduction**, Lorcan Dempsey stated: 'If emerging network places are to support *rich learning experiences* they must be designed, organised and supported in ways that make users comfortable there.' This statement acknowledges that learners have needs which must be met in order to facilitate learning, and it also identifies the users and their learning experiences as central to the design of learning landscapes. In this paper, I will explore these needs in terms of the ways in which learners, particularly younger students, approach learning and learning technology. The use of the word 'comfortable' in the above statement is an interesting point which is not addressed directly below, but which we might need to think about: people can become *too* comfortable and need a certain level of challenge in order to learn effectively.

Overview

This paper covers three overlapping areas. First, I plan to discuss some ideas concerning the learning place and the ways in which our preconceptions and assumptions lead to the construction of online learning environments.

Second, I will offer some observations on learners – not just those we have in our institutions at the moment but also those who will be studying there in the future. In doing this I will be picking up on the issues discussed by Richard Heseltine in his opening keynote paper.

Thirdly, I want us to look at the process of learning – in particular, some of the more dominant theories of learning which involve the definition of learning styles. The idea of learning styles being individual and personal is important to us in the creation of learning landscapes.

Finally, I hope to draw together the ideas articulated during the course of the paper in order to synthesize the questions we should now be asking ourselves in the context of information architectures and learning landscapes. Please note that I don't necessarily have the answers to these questions. However, as library professionals are discussing issues which overlap with the teaching and learning debate being conducted elsewhere, I wish to tempt librarians into this area of overlap where much of the interesting work has yet to be done.

The learning place

It was the Roman theorist Vitruvius who first articulated the principle of architectural decorum: that the architecture, design and structure of a building should reflect its purpose and status. Institutional buildings, particularly public buildings, have therefore tended to reflect the structures of the institutions, and the physical structure has, in turn, determined the pattern and mode of usage of the spaces within the building. There is thus a complementarity between life and the bricks and mortar. This correspondence between buildings and institutions enabled people to determine value factors such as the importance and status of the institution in society. An issue which is beyond the scope of this paper, but which needs to be addressed as we begin to represent institutions online, is how we represent institutional quality and status in a digital world.

The role architecture played in the representation and functioning of the institution was therefore central and indispensable. This is no longer the case. As telecommunications and digital devices come to play an increasingly essential role in the functioning of our institutions, and as our personal use of computers and networks expands, there is a concomitant reduction in the need for the physical proximity of people and institutional services. A simple example of this is the 'hole-in-the-wall' ATM (Automated Teller Machine) cash dispenser.

This machine was first introduced into banks in order to ease pressure at the tellers' windows. As much of the tellers' work involved the dispensing of cash, the automation of these transactions was an effective way of freeing up the tellers for other tasks. Once users became accustomed to the use of the ATMs, the banks realized that they could effectively improve services to their customers and extend banking hours by pushing the ATMs through the wall, thus making them accessible from the outside of the building. The need for the bank as a physical presence on the high street began to diminish once ATMs were installed in the locations where users wanted access to cash: supermarkets, shopping malls, airports, railway stations and other public places. All of a sudden the banks have become distributed and less reliant on a physical building. The logical extension of this is to abandon the high street building altogether – a development that is already happening. FirstDirect is a bank with no high street presence in which all banking business is carried out online via modem and PC, over the telephone, or through any convenient ATM.

This story of transition from physical to digital is one that not only applies to banks. Telecottaging and teleworking are happening now, adding to the physical distribution of institutions and the workforce which once needed an iconic company building in which to work. How do people now interact with the institution? For libraries and for higher education this is an important question, because what has happened with banking is starting to happen to universities.

Winston Churchill once said: 'We shape our buildings and our buildings shape us.' William Mitchell in his book, *City of bits*,[1] recasts this statement in the light of our emerging information society: 'We make our networks and our networks make us.' Mitchell is right, except to the extent that people now have much more freedom to structure their online environment for themselves. In a circular manner, the way in which they structure this environment will determine how they use it. Mitchell's words should therefore be seen as referring to individuals, not society as a whole – in which case it is vitally important that we understand all of the issues outlined above if we are to stand any chance of creating effective online learning environments. What, we should ask, are the Vitruvian principles for cyberspace?

As some universities begin to understand the direction society is taking in the information age, they are starting to make this transition from the physical to the digital. At this early stage many don't see this as a replacement exercise: for them the digital is an addition to the physical. But in the same way as the banks are discovering that there is little need for tellers now that ATMs are ubiquitous, it would be naïve to think that, if the digital university is successful, the physical version will continue to have any role. Unless we see significant changes to funding regimes, physical universities will become economically unsustainable – a point already made by Richard Heseltine in his opening keynote address.

What is interesting to reflect upon is that the transition for banks was made possible by the technology but was not driven by this technology. The transition occurred, and is still occurring, because it is what people want that is driving change. The same will be true for universities: those parts of the physical university which people want to keep will survive; those parts which people would rather interact with in a different, more flexible way, will be the parts to be lost first. Perhaps the most immediate message here is that, if there is nothing in a teacher's lectures that makes the students want to come to them, then that teacher must start planning for when there is no longer an audience.

Virtual university sites are cropping up on the web now. These vary in the extent to which they implement online learning environments. At the simplest level we see the conversion of lecture notes to web pages. As people seek to promote the use of such resources, they start to engage with the andragogy and begin to understand that an online learning environment is more than a collection of electronic lecture hand-outs. Specialist environments are becoming available, either locally produced or authored by established software companies, which integrate electronic resources, assessment, course guidance, course structure, learning tasks, one-to-one and one-to-many e-mail and conferencing, and user tracking and evaluation. These environments are far from mature – partly because the implementation of the approach is still fairly crude, partly because the software companies do not really understand the nature of higher education, but mainly because we really do not know enough about how people learn, let alone learn online. We do, however, know enough to understand that any university that thinks a virtual university is created by putting course notes on the web is missing the point.

It is also important for universities to understand that their virtual manifestation must be an institutional endeavour supported by strategic and operational policy at the highest levels. While this sort of activity is left in the hands of small groups of enthusiasts and there is no sense of institutional ownership, the opportunity to make the transition from physical to digital will be missed.

Returning for a moment to Vitruvius, it is interesting to see that the interface universities put onto their virtual sites commonly uses an architectural metaphor, often with the buildings of the physical campus being reproduced in digital form. The University of Leeds, for instance, must take top marks for their Nathan Boddington Building, which is a cleverly constructed but totally virtual campus building. Apparently, the institution in this case does recognize and own this project, to the extent that the naming of the virtual building had to go through the same processes as the naming of a new physical campus building. However, we should question whether Vitruvian principles should be reimposed on digital environments. Virtual environments allow us to break free from the constraints imposed by physical buildings, creating opportunities for users to construct their own, personalized learning spaces.

Some may find this lack of imposed structure discomforting, whilst others may relish the opportunity to take control. Either way, we should ensure that the constraints are removed, thus giving people the choice.

The learners

Discussing the nature of the learning place leads on to a necessary discussion about the learners themselves. In the past, higher education has been guilty of focusing more on producing graduates than on recognizing individual needs. This approach worked when the (comparatively small), input to universities was an academic elite selected and trained in grammar schools to be able to categorize, analyse and construct hierarchies of information. Now that we operate in a 'massified' higher education system, we must finally acknowledge diversity and recognize the need to change the way in which we conduct the processes of teaching and learning. For this paper I will put the Dearing Report[2] on one side, since it acknowledges this point but does not in itself help us to develop a strategic response.

Learners entering higher education in the 1990s bring with them different skill sets. Mature 'returners to learning' often have experience of work and family life which translate into much better time management and personal discipline skills than are usually held by school leavers. These learners are also more demanding of the institution – a factor which will only increase as they are compelled to fund their own education.

The digital kids of Don Tapscott's book *Growing up digital*[3] will force us to take this debate to another level. Today's younger generation is growing up accustomed to an increasingly digital environment. They are comfortable with the use of Walkmans, mobile phones, Sega and Nintendo games consoles, calculators,

PDAs (Personal Digital Assistants) and whatever gadget comes out in time for next Christmas. These devices make their users independent of time and place and give them 24-hour access to information. American adolescents parting at the end of a holiday are more likely to exchange e-mail addresses with their exhortations to 'keep in touch' than phone numbers or postal addresses. The loss of conventional grammar-school training linked to this familiarity with access to information and entertainment through a digital interface will present significant challenges to higher education.

I can illustrate this by reference to my three-year-old daughter. In her use of an educational software package, *The logical journey of the Zoombinis* produced by Broderbund, a number of things can be deduced:

1 She is comfortable with the technology: she has learnt to use the mouse, she knows how to start the computer by pressing one button, and she is presented with a palette of applications, each of which she can launch with a single mouse click on the appropriate icon.
2 She is engaged by the software: the design of the interface encourages participation and interaction; it looks interesting and exciting.
3 She is learning: the software enables her to develop her logical and reasoning skills by setting challenges to solve in order to move her band of Zoombinis along the path towards the land they want to colonize.
4 She is happy and keen to go back for more. No one is forcing her to use this bit of learning software: she wants to use it, and to continue using it. Hence she is in charge of her own learning.

The process of learning

Digital kids will bring new approaches to learning into the formal education process, thus challenging conventional practice. The potential for these new approaches to unleash the creativity and intellectual ability of future generations is only just starting to become apparent. In order to understand how best to unleash the learning potential of the digital generation, we need to understand how we, and they, learn.

Despite a substantial amount of literature which has been accumulating from the earlier part of this century, we really don't know enough about how people learn. However, the work of psychologists and educationalists such as Piaget, Gagné, Pask and Kolb has allowed us to recognize and articulate certain basic principles.

For example, we are aware that people have different learning styles. Kolb[4] defines four main types of learning style depending on the way in which individuals respond to different forms of learning. If you look at Table 8.1, you will see that someone who prefers their information to be gained from a concrete experience, rather than an abstract one, and who likes to make active use of such concrete information, would fall into the Type 4 category. Such a learner would be characterized by the use of such phrases as 'What if . . . ?'. The best teacher for such an individual would be one who enabled the student to ask, and find the answer to, such questions. Another look at Table 8.1 would suggest that traditional university teaching in a lecture theatre, because it involves abstract information with no possibility of active investigation, caters for Type 2 learners only. We should be able to use new technologies to broaden our scope. Digital kids are more likely to belong to Types 1 and 4.

Table 8.1   *Kolb learning styles*

	Type 1	Type 4
Concrete	*Why?*	*What if?*
	Motivator	Enabler
	Type 2	Type 3
Abstract	*What?*	*How?*
	Expert	Coach
	Reflective	**Active**

Honey and Mumford[5] have taken the learning styles research and reapplied it in a business context, producing definitions and a profiling tool to enable people to determine their own particular learning style. Table 8.2 summarizes the styles and definitions given by Honey and Mumford.

The thinking behind this theory is that being able to recognize your own learning style is an essential step towards optimizing your learning. Application of the same thinking to university students is equally valid. Helping students, when they join the university, to identify their personal learning style will greatly enhance their ability to make full use of the learning opportunities offered them by higher education. Of course, paper-based profiling tools translate easily into an online environment. A consortium of universities, through the TLTP3-funded ELEN project, will be using a software tool which enables students to profile their learning styles, and also provides action planning to help them develop their approach to learning. My personal learning style is represented by the software-generated diagram shown in Figure 8.1. I will leave you to draw your own conclusions about what I need to do to develop my approaches to learning opportunities.

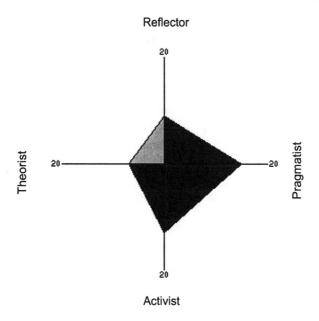

Fig. 8.1 *A learning style profile*

Table 8.2   *Learning styles*

Activists	Open-minded and enthusiastic learners; throw themselves in; live for the here and now; ready to try anything; thrive on challenge but soon become bored with routine.
Reflectors	Learn by collecting all the data they can and then considering it from different perspectives before reaching a conclusion; cautious, thoughtful; listen, act only when confident.
Pragmatists	Down-to-earth and practical people; they learn by putting theories and techniques into practice; like to get on with things and act confidently; impatient with long-winded and woolly discussion; enjoy problem-solving.
Theorists	Like to learn in a logical step-by-step manner; they collect and organize data, then devise their own theories for how it all fits together.

It may be that librarianship attracts people with a particular learning style. The problem here is that people will tend to develop teaching approaches and materials that favour their own style, thus alienating learners with the other styles. It is important not to overlook this point.

I can illustrate this with reference to David Kay's presentation (see **Chapter 4**). Early in his paper he introduced a number of paradigm conflicts, which are summarized in Table 8.3. I would contend that these are not paradigm conflicts but simply a manifestation of different learning styles (and hence approaches) to the location of information.

Despite all this, we cling to old methods of teaching and learning which address only one subset of the students by addressing only one of the main learning styles.

Table 8.3   *Paradigm conflicts/manifestation of different learning styles*

Discovery	versus	Disclosure
Documents	versus	Records
Searching	versus	Browsing
Explicit interface	versus	Implicit interface

The questions

We must challenge our existing metaphors when we design information architectures.

Creating virtual universities and learning landscapes is not about re-creating the physical online. Digital kids do not bring our preconceptions to their learning places. Richard Heseltine's garden, presented in his opening keynote, is an organic, adaptive and responsive environment which is user-configurable and is another metaphor worthy of consideration. We should of course think of it as containing fauna as well as flora.

The argument about learning styles is central to our creation of learning landscapes. Different users, with their different approaches to learning, will want to be able to create and customize their virtual environment. We should design the underlying architecture so that this process is enabled and not prevented. Our problem is that we, because of our upbringing and education, may not understand how the next generation will want to use our architecture. However, there is a tension between user configurability and learning style which is an extension of the match/mismatch argument. In this it is argued that matching a teaching style to a learning style creates a sense of complacency and comfort – an environment where the learner is not being challenged to look at doing things differently.

This reinforcement of one particular learning style is as bad, perhaps, as the lack of diversity in teaching styles currently found in higher education.

If learners have the ability to create and customize their own learning environment, then they might, without realizing it, limit the usefulness of that environment by favouring comfort over challenge. Alice's wonderland was a constant source of challenge and stimulation. A walled 'secret garden' in comparison, without wishing to examine the metaphor too deeply in relation to Frances Hodgson Burnett's book,[6] is self-limiting and enclosed. An activist would enjoy and thus create a wonderland. A reflector might be inclined to create a secret, walled garden – potentially very rich and structured inside, but isolated and limited by self-imposed barriers.

What we need are people who understand these issues and who can therefore frame and ask the right questions as we move from the physical to the digital. The rewards include a generation with minds liberated from the structures which conventional education imposes. The risks are equally great and include a generation for whom learning is an uncomfortable and difficult experience.

References

1   Mitchell, W., *City of bits: space, place and the infobahn*, Cambridge, MIT Press, 1995.

2   Dearing, R., *Higher education in the learning society: report of the National Committee of Inquiry into Higher Education*, London, HMSO, 1997.

3   Tapscott, D., *Growing up digital: the rise of the net generation*, London, McGraw-Hill, 1998.

4   Kolb, D. A., *Experiential learning: experience as the source of learning development*, Englewood Cliffs, NJ, Prentice-Hall, 1984.

5   Honey, P. and Mumford, A., *The manual of learning opportunities*, P. Honey, Maidenhead, 1989.

6   Burnett, F. H., *The secret garden*, 1911 (several editions).

Part 3

Information and the public space: an informed citizenry

9

Floods don't build bridges

RICH NETWORKS, POOR CITIZENS, AND THE ROLE OF PUBLIC LIBRARIES

Andrew Blau

This paper will deal with many things that might seem to have little to do with libraries – the history of medicine, American political reformers, and turn-of-the-century tenors, to name just three – but the purpose of this is to demonstrate how rich networks can create poor citizens, and to identify the role (or roles) that public libraries might play in reversing that effect.

There is in fact a great deal of excitement about a richly networked world, and about how networking might be the Viagra® which our declining public sphere seems to need. The ability to retrieve information quickly, share opinions broadly, and communicate easily with officials, is seen by many as the key feature of how networking will improve the politics of daily life in networked communities and strengthen the public sphere. But the relationship between the Internet and the public sphere is often understood as if networking simply eased, accelerated and amplified existing political and social information flows. It certainly does all those things, but the widespread adoption of networking will have a more complicated effect: it will fundamentally undermine the traditional, stable relationships between information authorities, information conduits and information consumers that have evolved to organize our experience of the public sphere since the end of the 19th century in the USA and many of the Western industrial democracies.

The resulting chaos in the political 'information space' of our society will change the shape of the public sphere, but not in uniformly positive ways, as new types of authorities, and new types of social organizations, emerge to reorder the newly chaotic relationships.

Realizing the potential benefit of the Internet for an informed citizenry engaged in democratic self-governance will depend in part, of course, on how networks are built – getting the technology right is a critical threshold for all that comes later. But even if we make the right choices on the technical issues, we must consider the possible forms of non-network institutions that will be negotiated over the coming decade – institutions such as journalism or other mechanisms to organize and assess information, as well as the institutions of elective or voluntary associations. We must also consider the effects of these changes on the role of the citizen and the possibility of deliberation.

We need to examine the logic of information relations in richly networked societies, to examine the resulting challenges within the public sphere, and speculate as to the roles the public library might play against that background.

The Internet and the practice of democracy

Let me begin with a simple proposition: participation in the public sphere turns on information and communication. Anything that changes our ability to distribute or retrieve information and communicate with others will alter the environment for public discourse. In particular, the Internet, which combines information and communication features, makes the key components for participation in the public sphere easier for its users. Such components include:

- gathering information (data retrieval)
- assessing information (through comparison with multiple sources, and dialogue with subject experts, officials or other interested people)
- deliberating preferences (discussions among citizens)
- expressing preferences (electronic publishing, or e-mail to elected representatives)
- organizing constituencies (both new and preexisting)
- coordinating political interventions.

All of these processes can to an extent be carried out across distances – and even across national borders –and with an ease for the individual that is unprecedented. In the case of the last three components, the individual or group is enabled to break through the traditional economics and barriers dictated by the mass-media and to create communities defined by common information.

More broadly, networked computer-based tools:

- will improve the availability and expand the quantity of information for those who choose to seek it
- will lower the barriers to exchange imposed by the traditional limits of time and physical proximity
- will moderate (if only temporarily) differences of power and status for entrants to the marketplace of ideas
- will enable functional responses to many of the broad social or demographic trends that have been identified with the loss of a stable community (increased physical mobility; fear of street crime; loss of leisure time; land

development based on the ubiquity of automobiles and high-speed freeways; the rise of air conditioning and the loss of the front porch).

The deep logic of these practices

All that suggests that we ought to think carefully about how the growth in networking will affect our experience of the public sphere.

The simple hope for those who advocate using networking to build community participation and political engagement is that these tools will accelerate and amplify existing relationships. Put differently, the underlying belief is that high-speed computers attached to fast networks and rich databases will take the basic relationships necessary for a successful public sphere and improve them by adding more information, more debate and more perspectives to the traditional public culture. This excitement is based in part on a fallacy, unique to the types of well-educated people who gravitate to computer networking and policy analysis, that most people want more information, and its correlate, that since information is good, then more information is better.

What is more likely, though, is something very different: the addition of widely accessible and widely used networking will act like a solvent on existing bonds of political experience, and will reorganize the sources, channels and relationships that have organized the public sphere for the last century.

To illuminate that possibility, we could consider the end of the 19th century, when efforts towards the professionalization of areas such as medicine, law, architecture and journalism were, in important respects, efforts to organize information. That is to say, questions such as:

- What counts as 'real' or 'credible' information?
- Where does credible information come from?
- What are reliable vehicles for transmitting information?
- What is the socially sanctioned relationship between the provider and the receiver of the information?

were settled at that time in the political realm as well as in many others. This is perhaps best seen in the ascendancy of the allopathic medical model (i.e. the official, illness-focused model of Western medicine) built around doctors, nurses, hospitals and specific types of medical interventions, as well as in the dominance of the medical field in the USA by the American Medical Association.[1]

The efforts to create guild-type structures to regulate legal practice can be interpreted in similar ways: to put the stamp of approval where 'real' legal information came from, who was sanctioned to practise in this field (and thus provide real information), and what the relationship of lay people to professionals should be. Similar scenarios can be played out for architecture, librarianship and other professional spheres, which organized themselves in similar ways in the late 19th and early 20th centuries. Some of this history has been traced by Van Slyck, who comments:

> By the late 1890s, however, the professions of librarianship and architecture began to move in parallel directions as each group independently began to adopt aspects of the culture of professionalism that had been pioneered in law and medicine.[2]

The effects of a richly networked environment are also best seen in the medical sphere. Instead of more sanctioned health care information from accredited sources flowing to consumers who retain their place in the social order, networking allows health-related information to arise from multiple sources, to be propagated along unregulated multiple channels, and to arrive on the receiver's desktop untested as to efficacy except for the claims of the provider (who may be unknown, and who appears without other well-understood social cues as to authority). While for some people the opportunity to sift, weigh and consider various options may be a boon, for others the division of labour implicit in the previously organized model was in fact more helpful. But, most importantly, the addition of more networking results not in more information flowing to the needy, but in the 'rechaoticization' of the information space so that it resembles more closely the conditions that prevailed before the ascendancy of the allopathic medical model, when various models of health-related practice competed for attention (and dollars) through unarbitrated competing claims as to efficacy.

To see what happens when we use that lens to look at politics; let us consider the organization of the political information space in 1880s.[3]

The efforts in the USA of the Progressives (and earlier proto-progressive reformers, the Mugwumps) to organize political information relied on establishing new relationships between parties, officials, the press and the public. Progressives strove to insulate their vision of the independent, rational citizen from the 'distorting enthusiasms' of party. At the same time, the rise of journalism covering and interpreting political events resulted in newspapers becoming the main printed source of political information. Campaigns became 'educational' and pamphlets replaced parades.

Broadly, this was an effort to make political participation more 'rational' and to put sanctioned information in stable vehicles that 'users' (voters, citizens) would consider in the private space of their living room.

This set of relations, which we live with today, has been 'rechaoticized' by the current flow of tremendous quantities of information through multiple channels from non-traditional sources. What is a source? What is a reliable conduit? What is the citizen's relationship to political activity? The answers to all these questions have become fluid, and newly subject to individual negotiation.

Under this microscope, it turns out that parts of this are the 'Ebola virus' infecting the body of politics as it has been practised, and causing massive 'haemorrhaging' among the 'organs'. This may not be a bad thing: political practice in the USA appears to many observers as moribund, alienating and increasingly irrelevant for millions of Americans of voting age. The steady decline in voter participation, even in national presidential elections, has continued until barely half of those eligible to vote do so, and even those who do vote appear increasingly cynical and contemptuous of current political practice.

As information tools and communications networks destabilize the traditional information relationships of the public sphere today, the challenge for democratic practice and fruitful deliberation – for a functioning public sphere – will be in the social formations that form to reorganize the information space. And there should be no doubt that such formations will appear: the division of labour will demand it. Few of us can manage the information that flows to us today. As Paul Evan Peters, former Director of the Coalition for Networked Information, put it:

> . . . we no longer can enjoy the relationship to information where we are the predators and the information we seek is the prey. For many of us on the Internet today, information is the predator; we are the prey.[4]

Reflections on the public sphere under successive stages of networking

To understand better this destabilizing process, so as to envision better the appropriate responses to it, it is necessary to examine more closely how this destabilization is set in motion by the very tools that appear to have so much positive promise. To do so requires three broad assumptions:

1 Technology deployment in large-scale social systems takes place over time.
2 Systems are by definition dynamic and responsive, which is to say that they accommodate the introduction of new pressures and adapt to new stimuli. A social system is not a static monolith, simply being acted upon by new external forces, but a complex, adaptive setting that responds to new forces and, by so doing, modifies the conditions under which these forces operate.
3 The effects of a technology are different at different stages of its widespread deployment (this is, of course, little more than a logical outgrowth of the two previous assumptions).

With these assumptions in place, the successive stages of networking become clearer.

Stage 1: arbitrage between more and less efficient information 'markets'

Early adopters take competitive advantage of the disparity between those who have new information and communications tools and those who don't have them. The early adopters exploit the fact that they can collect and share information, mobilize their constituencies, and disseminate their messages faster, more widely and more cheaply, than their competitors who don't use those tools. As such, strategies based on this approach are a bet placed against scaling, growing or expanding use of similar systems. Utopian scenarios of better living through networking assume that the dynamics of Stage 1 reflect the benefits of networking at all stages of technology adoption. Instead, once networking becomes widely used, the effects of networking move to the next stage.

Stage 2: the information space becomes flooded and chaotic

As more information, delivered faster, outside the bounds of traditional vehicles, enters the political sphere, so people experience the well-known effect of *information overload,* or flooding. Flooding the information space produces the same effect as flooding any other market: the currency becomes devalued. Compare, for example, the experience of using electronic media to lobby Congress: the flood of e-mail, faxes etc. to Congress led quite predictably to a steady devaluation of this 'currency'. A corollary proof is that what remains important or valuable in political communication is what remains difficult and hard to simulate by digital means: face-to-face meetings, hand-written letters etc.

There is another effect, though, and one that begins to bring us back towards the library. To understand it we need to consider Robert Bellah's observation that institutions are 'socially organized forms of paying attention'.[5] Yet to situate that insight in the digital age, we need to pair it with the conclusion drawn nearly 30 years ago by the Nobel-prize winning economist Herbert Simon, who noted that to understand the key dynamics of the digital age, it was important to understand that information consumes attention:[6]

> What information consumes is rather obvious: it consumes the attention of its recipients. Hence a wealth of information creates a poverty of attention, and a need to allocate that attention efficiently among the overabundance of information sources that might consume it.

In one sense, then, this flood of information will consume the very institutions organized to broker our attention. In order to survive, those institutions must adapt to this new information environment, one of the key features of which appears in Stage 3.

Stage 3: community formation, deformation, and dissolution become promiscuous and thus without consequence

There have been many strong claims about the Internet allowing electronic communities to form without regard for distance, geography, social status, physical appearance etc. The availability of low-cost networking poses extremely low barriers to community formation, which is good for political (as well as social and cultural) vigour, especially in Stage 1 described above. But low barriers to entry also entail low barriers to exit. If community is to have meaning, it needs a form and functional boundaries. In that sense, it is like poetry or marriage in that barriers to exit exist for various reasons, not the least of which is that they provide incentives to work out difficult problems.[7] The same applies to community. If one can leave at will, without even the burden of moving away from a keyboard, it is not a community in any meaningful sense.

Yet a key question for those of us who believe in the importance of a vigorous public sphere in the digital age is this: what keeps people within the form of a deliberating community, when, as in the electronic sphere, association is increasingly elective, not ascriptive (i.e. you choose your neighbours), escape is easy, and the creation of new separate forums is easy? What kind of true public sphere is possible under those conditions?

Clearly, the Internet has benefits: it reduces the cycle time for social invention and offers the temporary uncoupling of political voice from financial strength; it enables quickly forming, responsive, non-traditional entities to channel public attention; it extends the voices of traditionally marginalized groups or ideas, and may break the high costs imposed by mass media on political participation and association.

Yet, despite the appearance of ever more advanced information technologies, cheap global communications tools, and the prospect for computer-assisted politics and community-building, the real work to establish a public sphere that will be any better than what we have today will turn on meeting the need for institutions to be trusted guides and evaluators amid the information flows. These new entities will fill the need to reorganize the division of labour in the information sphere, and help us pay attention.

The public library: new roles, new options

So, we turn towards the library. Given that a richly networked society is likely to feature promiscuous community formation and dissolution, a tendency towards flooding of the information markets, and the erosion of previously stable information relationships, the problem of the public sphere comes into sharper focus. In particular, a working (or workable) public sphere requires:

* stability of attention among its participants
* manageable information flows
* legible, comprehensible, and accountable relationships.

We are undergoing a transition in which we will see the diminution of traditional institutions that organize our attention, but not without them being replaced by some new ones. The current fascination with 'portal' sites on the web suggests a flavour of this. Can content organizers such as Yahoo! play this role? Or will it be browser developers such as Netscape; or other firms such as Citibank? The issue for us here is how we might think of the public library under these conditions from different angles. I would like to offer three notions.

First, the research undertaken at the Benton Foundation on public attitudes towards libraries that adopt technology[8] suggests some useful assets – first and foremost, the librarian. Initial findings suggest that, while most library users have little or no understanding of what librarians do or what skills they have, these same users respond quite positively to the notion of the librarian as 'information navigator'. Indeed, one fear that surfaced among all the groups researched is that technology adoption among libraries may have similar effects on libraries as it has had on other workplaces such as banks and government offices: that the valued human relationship may disappear. The asset that users felt very strongly that they wanted to retain in the information society was the information navigator.

This is more than simply a question of providing adequate customer services. It is essential to a vital public sphere to the degree that there will be trained information specialists who command the trust of local community members. One issue that the networked society forces on us is the tension created when personal choice or freedom in the information marketplace resolves to poorer data sets. There are cases of students using the web to create personal libraries. Often there are even experienced students for whom, if an item doesn't appear on the web, it simply doesn't exist. The danger is that students become practitioners of information-age 'cargo cults', worshipping novel formations that they don't understand and which are meagre stand-ins for what we would understand as the real thing.

One possibly fruitful way to think of libraries and their communities is to consider the relationship between radio stations and the recording industry. It is hard
to imagine a recording industry with anything like its current size, diversity and
profitability without radio. Radio stations emerged shortly after the commercialization of recordings and, in large measure, structure the field. Radio broadcasts
are an essential component that makes the products of the recording industry
viable. The ability to generate CDs is now reasonably inexpensive, and one could
easily imagine a similar flooding problem with no way for cultural consumers to
navigate the choices offered to them. Can local public libraries play similar roles
amid the welter of networked information? As Greenhalgh *et al.* have pointed
out, the library operates as a network of cultural distribution, rather than cultural
production.[9] In that regard, it is like radio already. It tends to be community-
based, as radio often is. What libraries don't tend to do that radio stations do is to
cultivate communities of common information.

Lastly, we need to consider how high-speed networks promote 'winner takes
all' economies, or what we might call in the cultural realm the 'Caruso effect'.
When sound recording was in its infancy, there was a fair bit of excitement that
the ability to capture and distribute local talent would lead to bigger audiences for
those performers, much as the web makes every man, woman and child an international publisher. But in fact, once people could hear Caruso as easily and
cheaply as they could hear the tenor from the next town, they opted for Caruso.
Caruso became the first star of the recording age, to the detriment of lesser performers who found themselves competing with Caruso, which they had never
had to do before. Is it possible to set up the library as the bulwark of local culture
(not necessarily of local artists, but of local *interests*)? Is it possible to posit the
library as the 'friction' in an increasingly 'friction-free' setting, designed to slow
the loss of local texture? Might it be possible that the reason for getting public
support won't be that one can't get information elsewhere, but rather because the
library serves the community as a brake on those 'winner takes all' economics
which are likely to be detrimental to communities?

Conclusion

So rich networks can make poor citizens, and we haven't even begun to discuss
the issues facing households that face economic difficulties. The consideration I
would offer is that technological change happens within a system where elements
of the system push back. The question, then, is how shall we push? Libraries
surely have options here, although these may mean lifting the public library from
the fabric of community infrastructure and creating a role based on *making* the
community rather than simply *serving* the community. There are likely to be
many other options as well, but the first step is to acknowledge that the floods of

information we are already seeing are unlikely to build the bridges which a public sphere needs. Libraries can do that, and many will. The main challenge is to find ways to secure the support of the public that will need those bridges to cross information flood and survey the information landscape.

Notes and references

1   Starr, P., *The social transformation of American medicine*, New York, Basic Books, 1984.

2   Some of this history can be found in Van Slyck, A., *Free to all: Carnegie Libraries and American culture 1890–1920*, Chicago, University of Chicago Press, 1995, 46.

3   This interpretation finds support in the current work of American sociologist Prof. Michael Schudson, and some of what follows is based on materials found in two as yet unpublished papers: Schudson, M., 'The second transformation of American citizenship: 1865–1920' and 'The social construction of the "informed citizen" '.

4   Peters, P. E., Keynote address, *Digital libraries '94:The First Annual Conference on the Theory and Practice of Digital Libraries*, June 19–21 1994, College Station, Texas, USA. Notes available at
   <URL: http://csdl.tamu.edu/DL94/peters.keynote.html>.

5   Bellah, R. *et al.*, *The good society*, New York, Alfred A. Knopf, 1991, 252.

6   Simon, H., 'Designing organizations for an information-rich world', in Greenberger, M. (ed.), *Computers, communications, and the public interest*, Baltimore, The Johns Hopkins Press, 1971, 40–1.

7   For an extended discussion of this notion, see Berry, W., 'Poetry and marriage: the use of old forms', in *Standing by words*, Berkeley, CA, North Point Press, 1983,.

8   *Buildings, books, and bytes*, Benton Foundation, 1996. Available at
   <URL: http://www.benton.org/Library/Kellogg/buildings.html>.
   and *The future's in the balance*, Benton Foundation, 1998.

9   Greenhalgh, L. *et al.*, *Libraries in a world of cultural change*, London, UCL Press, 1995.

10

Uphill and down dale

CITIZENS, GOVERNMENT AND THE PUBLIC LIBRARY

John Dolan

Anyone who read Julie Sabaratnam's paper to the UKOLN conference of 1995 must have been taken by its vision and enthusiasm. Here she projected a vision of the needs and potential of the public library service in Singapore in the 21st century:

> The Singapore Library 2000 vision aims at 'continuously expanding the nation's capacity to learn through a national network of libraries and information resource centres providing services and learning opportunities to support the advancement of Singapore.' Library 2000 will provide Singaporeans with access to the right information at the right time and in the right form. Similarly libraries and librarians worldwide need to respond to the challenges of the twenty-first century.[1]

Lessons from an earlier era

Over the last couple of years we have recalled, at times, the aspirations of public librarians in the 1980s when we were freshly and enthusiastically promoting the concepts and opportunities associated with community information and a new grassroots role for the local library. In local communities the apparently declining 'academic' and reference role of the library was being shifted to make room for the new proactive responsibility of informing people and communities, giving access and a voice to the disadvantaged in particular and to citizens in general.

This brought new challenges to the librarian, who wrestled with the notion of being active rather than passive in the dissemination of information. Librarians seemed to struggle with the implication that they would have to 'take sides', that the service might appear to favour one party over another. This was particularly difficult when helping community organizations in contact and dispute with the local authority, which is, after all, the library's parent and funding body.

This was nowhere more evident than in the Library Association's publication *Community information: what libraries can do*, in which the working group had to spell out the variations on 'information-giving' which would be the task of the library worker in this early era of proactive community librarianship. This term itself seemed to carry within it a combative culture which ran counter to the assumed passive image and culture of the public library environment. Interactivity, as we might now call it, was broken down into a spectrum of service choices including:

* straightforward information
* explanation
* advice
* practical aid
* active referral
* mediation
* advocacy and campaigns.[2]

Unfortunately, a mix of internal and circumstantial factors – political, financial, cultural, social – prevented the public library from going very far down this route. The public library changed, advanced and modernized in other ways than those implied in the early thinking around the roll-out of community information/action/development services.

In the intervening period things have changed in many ways. The development of technology, the change in industrial and economic infrastructures, the emergence of 'leisure', lifelong learning, and the growth in service industries, have created a society with a different composition and character. Public libraries like other services have been through a period characterized by budget decline, cuts in the scale and depth of service and a review of roles based if anything on the pursuit of greater value for less money.

Now we approach not just the ideas of a new decade but, it is said, of a new era in the evolution of our civilization. The information society, albeit in its infancy, is here and now; it is not something in the future for which we have to prepare. We are now in the position of developing and managing it.

Exclusion, inclusive government and the new technology

Most significantly, the last ten years have seen a growth in media and communications technologies and the new services they are generating. Combined with secularization, the new 'relativism' – a negative reaction to centralization and the traditional hierarchies and authorities (monarchy, government, church, the law and so on) – there is a culture emerging in which everyone's view and the community perspective has taken on a new validity. Without the widest ownership of both problem and solution, we will progress further towards an unhappy state of exclusion, alienation and violence culminating in individual isolation and communal insecurity and misery.

The emergence of such scenarios, informed by this dark vision, is currently expressed in the concern about the lack of interest in politics and community affairs. For the UK, in the changed atmosphere which followed the general election in 1997, this has brought about a new concern to improve the quality of life. Part of this need will be fulfilled by pursuing economic and social wellbeing through the best exploitation of the new technologies per se and, implicitly, by combating the very threats that those technologies bring with them.

In the meantime the concerns are illustrated by analysis of participation in elections. Lord Bassam (Steven Bassam, leader of Brighton and Hove Council) addresses in a recent article the threat to the Labour Party in particular and democracy in general, drawing on the results of the local government elections in May 1998:

> The big message from these elections is not so much the results but the turnout. Many commentators will focus on these figures. The conclusion I draw is that they highlight the need for the pace of modernisation and democratic renewal to be speeded up, not slowed down. Local government needs to look more at itself and ask why it is that it registers so poorly in the esteem of voters that turnout can fall to levels below 28%, in some areas even lower than that. The forthcoming local government white paper needs to address the legitimacy deficit left by low turnouts and poor-quality and unaccountable services.[3]

Measuring the 'turnout factor' has lately become the easiest way of exposing the myth of government and is also a threat to democracy. Witness the concerns around the turnout for the vote on an elected mayor for London. While 72% supported the policy, only 34% had bothered to vote. In contrast, but to the same effect, there was elation at the 81% turnout for the vote in Northern Ireland on the Good Friday peace agreement.

The Government's consultation paper, *Modernising local government*[4] is founded on these concerns. This is especially so in relation to local government. There is a basic premise that democracy is the most valuable form of government and vital for peace and security. This is the sine qua non of the argument. In addition, local government matters 'because it is the one government institution which through its democratic mandate can empower citizens locally.' It brings home to us the scale of the issue by reminding us that 'in the United Kingdom today it is spending some £75 billion each year from taxes and charges, around a quarter of all Government expenditure.' Unfortunately, however, 'there is a culture of apathy about local democracy.'

The consultation paper proposes four broad areas of improvement:

- modernizing electoral arrangements to improve the accountability of councils and to increase participation in local elections
- developing new ways in which councils can listen to their communities and involve local people in their decisions, and in their policy planning and review
- devising new ways of working for councils, giving them clearer political and management structures
- strengthening councils' role as leaders of their local communities, by reinforcing their existing potential for local leadership.

A new role for the library

It is certainly the case that the vision for public libraries which has emerged over the last year in particular includes the part it can play in the transformation of local government. It will change from an aged and feeble offspring of Victorian aspirations to the bright and energetic child of a new, inclusive and vibrant democracy.

The report to Government, *New library: the people's network* by the Library and Information Commission[5] proposed the transformation of the public library service in the UK so that it can play a central role in the information society. The debate which has ensued since its publication has been primarily around the library's role in two key areas:

- as a centre and resource for lifelong learning
- as a community base for citizen information, involvement and participation.

These two strands are frequently reiterated as the most significant aspects of the information society in terms of its impact on the ordinary citizen. Increasingly, in fact, they are seen as the two inextricably linked halves of the model of interaction between citizen and government in the 'informed' society.

For example, learning is traditionally seen as an activity limited by time, age, location and circumstance. Now it is an essential activity that will continue in different forms throughout life – informing and supporting the individual in all areas of personal, family, social and economic endeavour. Citizens' information and participation is the counterpoint to the convention of voting every five years and leaving the rest to someone else. The notion that good government must increasingly be government both of *and* with the people is widely recognized as the prerequisite of civilized living and the survival of democracy. Thus, active citizenship is informed citizenship; learning is essential to taking an active part.

The consultation paper on modernizing local government identifies several approaches to involvement, including:

- seeking the views of citizens
- recognizing communities by increasing their involvement in direct decision-making
- enabling the electorate to determine and influence policy on a specific issue
- a citizen's watchdog or scrutiny role
- opening up the authority
- using technology as a vehicle for communication and interaction
- developing education for citizenship.

Under the latter heading the paper continues:

> . . . a wider acceptance of the need to be active as a citizen is likely to mean greater interest in local government. Authorities therefore have an interest in promoting citizenship and a number are already taking steps within schools and by other means to encourage greater involvement and interest . . .

In the paragraph outlining the potential of technology to improve the quality of government and citizen participation, the paper notes:

> Its main uses so far are in the provision of information, but as technology develops, its potential is huge. Interactive technology will offer new ways to work with individuals and groups, even to sound out opinions 'on line'. Local authorities should attempt to harness this potential, and make the benefits widely available, possibly even providing access at shopping centres and *libraries*.

The statement and proposals seem hesitant, even under-informed, but they reflect nonetheless the role which even the least-likely partners are beginning to recognize for the public library.

Meanwhile, in April of 1998 the British Prime Minister visited Croydon Library to launch *Our information age*,[6] the Government's response to *New library: the people's network*. Together with the document launch, the event included the announcement that lottery funding (from the New Opportunities Fund) would be available for the creation of digital content for the public library network (£50 million) and for the training of library staff (£20 million). Interestingly, the content funding is for 'lifelong learning and education in the broadest sense'. It is yet to be seen if this can be tested against the interrelationship of learning and citizenship outlined earlier; the guidelines for the deployment of the funding are still being composed. The implication, however, is that the use of the funding is limited to what is feasible within the legal remit of the lottery – education and healthy living.

The Government's response makes no direct reference to the need to fund other content. This would, notably, be new information for citizens that might not be eligible under the lifelong learning/education umbrella: content purchased from a commercial supplier, and content on the web for which payment is required. Moreover, the infrastructure for a public library network is only addressed at this stage by the £6 million DCMS/Wolfson fund and a third Library and Information Commission task group. This group is working on a specification for the network technology which will be seen as a means of attracting private-sector funding partnership.

Even so, with these uncertainties in mind the Government's response to *New library: the people's network* represents the most significant boost to the image and morale of the public library community for some decades. *Our information age* says:

> The Government's response to the Library and Information Commission report is being published today. We recognise the public libraries' central role in ensuring that all members of society have access to ICT and can enjoy the benefits it brings. So the Government is setting the objective of ensuring that every public library should, where practicable, be connected to the National Grid for Learning by 2002. To encourage this, the Government will provide £50m from the national lottery . . . [6]

It seems that at last there is a partial, if not complete, recognition of the potential for the library in this environment of change, innovation and funding which is informing and energizing the movement to improve the partnership between the Government and the people.

New library: the people's network may be said to be partisan, favouring a key role for the library in the environment of participative democracy envisaged by Government and other commentators. However, the case has to be made when so many people of influence are articulating the potential for the various public, private, community and voluntary-sector agencies to play their part. The Library and Information Commission report outlines the library vision:

> In recent times disillusion with political, legal and social institutions has generated an atmosphere of cynicism and alienation. People – particularly young people – have distanced themselves from a system which they see as irrelevant to their circumstances. A public library network of access points, open to every citizen for the delivery of information on government and government services – both local and UK-wide – and especially for enabling interactive communications with govern-

ment and others, will help bring a sense of belonging and renew the potential for participation in society . . .

When citizens are openly and freely in communication with government, democracy can be said to have 'grown up'.[5]

Importantly, and we touch on this for the first time here, the report continues:

Those groups generally regarded as 'minorities' are, together, the majority; ensuring improved access for those with a minority or special interest will also enhance the quality of life for the whole of society.

Easier said than done: some barriers to progress

There is a widespread awareness of the barriers that will inhibit the realization of the central part the public library is envisaged to play. These are laid out in the EC report *Public libraries and the information society*:[7]

- policy framework and administration – lack of recognition of the library by the state and municipal government; lack of a central policy and difficulty of having a central initiative
- financial barriers – reduced budgets, reduced staffing; lack of capital resources and revenue funding for renewal and sustainability of initiatives; winning partnership funding; tension and uncertainty about provision/value-added services/charges etc.
- legal issues – especially copyright/intellectual property rights; free Internet access and the protection of children and other vulnerable groups
- low awareness, suspicion, rejection – the lack of ICT provision combined with low levels of training create uncertainty and resistance among staff who will be the keys to success; lack of access to IT support
- barriers caused by cultural, linguistic and personnel problems – there is a need to provide universally, including for those with disabilities or special needs; lack of language skills (particularly for non-English speakers); general illiteracy
- topographical barriers – a particular need to incorporate small and remote libraries in networks where provision and/or delivery is more difficult and costly; services which reach fewer people are inevitably seen as less cost-effective but rural communities are among the most disadvantaged
- barriers to cooperation – in some European countries there is less of a tradition of cooperation, although – the UK libraries (with regional systems and so on) are seen as having the advantage in this aspect

- competitive barriers – in the information society libraries are operating in an expanding, more complex, arena; commercial providers are moving more smoothly and quickly than a local authority service often can.

Libraries have to develop the service, not merely for their survival (a futile argument on its own), but for the benefit of the whole community, which will never be served, in all its needs, by the commercial sector alone or even by the vital but exclusive education sector. More commonly, as in *New library: the people's network*, the fundamental argument is made that the development of the information society must be based on a mixed economy of public and private services – sometimes together, sometimes in partnership, sometimes in competition or even just separately. There is still a case to be promoted that public services have to be supported to contribute to the inclusivity of the information society which cannot be guaranteed without them.

An earlier report of the Information Society Forum[8] paints a bleak picture of the consequences of failure to act in the provision of interactive public information and service systems:

> The costs to Europe of failing to adapt swiftly and efficiently will be very high. We shall not only see a growing competitive weakness in relation to the US and the leading Asian economies but also the threat of widespread social alienation . . . Those that have undergone profound changes in their social and working lives will feel betrayed if the expected economic and potential social benefits do not fully materialise. Their discontent will add itself to that of very large sections of our societies who either cannot or will not exploit the new technologies because we have failed to respond to their *needs*.

This brings us back to the *needs* of the people.

Not so much a solution, more a way forward

In the research recently undertaken and published by Project CIRCE[9] the views of library managers on the definition of community information are quoted. Mostly they are not unfamiliar and are reminiscent of the early days of community librarianship. Apart from a quote from the 1980 LA publication *Community information*[2] there is only one direct reference to needs:

> There does seem to be the beginnings of a move away, though, from the traditional structure of listing the information by the department it comes from towards structuring the information to the user's needs.

In the report from the Information Society Forum – in a chapter headed 'Putting people first' – we read that the hoped-for social inclusion of the information society will only be realized if people are included from the very start:

> No one should be excluded from the Information Society: we must not tolerate people becoming information have-nots or want-nots, in Europe and elsewhere . . . Governments should commit themselves to a broadly-based improvement of the quality of life for ordinary people assuring the electronic provision of public services . . . Much more effort should be devoted to raising people's awareness of the issues and opportunities raised by the Information Society and to involving them in the debate on how to respond to the challenges.[8]

There is still a low but growing awareness in the public library sector of the new technologies. The full potential is somewhere in the future but getting nearer. The library's role in exposing the nature and opportunities of the information society to the widest community is one of its most valuable features and one of the key elements in the case for its funding. In the UK, recognition of this role has begun to be evident in the response of Government and the invitation to libraries to participate in the national strategies to take us forward. These include the National Grid for Learning and the University for Industry. The success in libraries of the BBC's campaign, Computers Don't Bite, represents a foot in the door of the growing prospects for digital broadcast media. At local level, too, a number of library authorities are working with the media to roll out information services via cable television.

However, the power of the public library is not yet fully determined, nor is it widely owned. A recent survey of local authority electronic public information services by SOCITM (the Society of IT Managers in Local Government) showed that in only 8% of the authorities making a return was the library service a lead partner in the development. There is still much to be done.

In the industrial society we are leaving behind, the landscape is contoured by class, power, money and tradition. Currently, the library is in the valley – close to community life, accessible, safe and intimate. Government stands at the top of the hill – secure but remote. Participation is sporadic, intermittent and, often, incidental rather than instrumental to change. Information is rarely given but often asked for. Learning is limited to the few or, where widespread, it is functional, vocational and economically driven rather than socially or culturally driven. The new technologies have the potential to level the landscape, to lower the peaks of power and to give people the chance to elevate themselves to a higher level of democracy characterized by involvement.

This is an aspiration infused with rhetoric and not universally desired. Democracy is still accompanied by the free market, by competition, by winners and losers. There is much to be gained in the information society, not only by the many, but also by the few. Everyone may not espouse the concepts of participation and involvement, and indeed the consequences may not match the aspirations: it is likely that a referendum on capital punishment would support the return of hanging, in contrast to the outcomes of recent House of Commons votes on the issue.

Universal access to information, knowledge and decision-making may mean a loss of central control and discipline. Some may see it as a threat to community safety and wellbeing. Such concerns may seem cynical but they inform the case for a deliberate proactive development of new technologies, which is in the interests of an informed and inclusive society that is not merely tagged by the term 'information' because that is its dominant economic characteristic.

The thrust to modernize government will manifest itself in new structures for the Home Counties, London and the English regions. Transnationally, the British Isles as well as Europe will be further reshaping both democracy and the economy. For libraries to be a part of this, they must take up and press for more of the kind of challenge presented in the Government's response to *New library: the people's network*. This report has been widely acclaimed, but that is largely *within* the LIS community. Elsewhere, its value has been less intrinsic; it has been a platform for the persuasion of others. So far, it has begun the debate, initiated partnerships and generated some new money, but only in the specific areas of life-long learning and staff training. The next stages are vital. The case must continue to be made by the Government to further willing partnership with:

- the DETR (Department of the Environment, Transport and the Regions) in relation to regional government and the modernization of local government
- the DfEE (Department for Education and Employment) for partnership with schools in learning the skills of the new literacies, curriculum support and homework and in relation to employment, training and job creation
- the DTI (Department of Trade and Industry) in relation to commercial partnerships and strategies for telecommunications and related industries.

Also, local authorities, the Local Government Association and chief executives must place the role of the library service on the corporate agenda of each local authority in relation to structural change, communication with citizens and strategies for participation.

Twenty years on from the birth of community librarianship, the vision of the public library at the heart of the community must not be lost again. This means responding to a remarkable challenge for cultural, organizational, structural and budgetary change:

1   We must build up our capacity (in both time and skill) for campaigning and promoting the library's value. This might be done by individual library authorities, but will be more effective if undertaken by groups at regional and national level.

2   We must address, within our organizations, the issue of structural change – we will be less able to build a new future if we try to do it with the tools of today; organizational structures will have to be re-shaped to handle the tasks and responsibilities of the 'New Library' service.

3   We must acquire the new skills for LIS leaders which will allow them to articulate the vision so as to win status, partners and resources – the experience of 1998, both in the UK and in the wider European context, has demonstrated that, justified though we believe the case to be, low awareness of the global social and economic picture, the technology, and what might be achieved, is still a serious counter-force.

4   We must implement new training for strategic managers – this must not be overlooked in the rush to train front-line staff. Fundamentally, the move to the information society is a cultural move that will be achieved primarily by the people involved through vision, leadership, strategic planning and the development of new ideas and services.

5   We must build links with higher and further education – as they develop new approaches to community-based learning, we can be involved in the thinking and planning so that as 'new learning' emerges, the public library is already recognized as a vehicle for information and guidance, delivery, support and evaluation, and accreditation.

6   We must continue to put the case for investment, in infrastructure and content, for new needs which are not yet met by current and newly available funding – further development depends critically on the outcome of the Library and Information Commission task group on infrastructure.

7   We must create partnerships with the private and voluntary sectors, each of which has access to crucial resources and markets.

8   We must develop further our recently increased capacity for research and consultation, winning resources to fund development and marketing for expansion.

This is essential work still to be done to ensure that, in the levelled landscape of the information society, every city, town centre, neighbourhood and village high street enjoys the presence of the uniquely supportive and resourced venue that gives universal and equal access to the world of information, knowledge, opinion and decision. That place is the public library of the 21st century.

References

1   Sabaratnam, J. S., 'Transforming libraries to support change and growth' in Dempsey, L., Law, D. and Mowat, I. (eds.), *Networking and the future of libraries 3: managing the intellectual record*, London, Library Association Publishing, 1995, 74.

2   Library Association Working Party on Community Information, *Community information: what libraries can do*, London, Library Association, 1980.

3   Bassam, S., 'The discerning voter', *Municipal journal,* 15 May 1998.

4   Department of the Environment, Transport and the Regions, *Modernising local government: local democracy and community leadership* (consultation paper). Available at <URL: http://www.local.detr.gov.uk/sponsor/democrac.htm>.

5   Library and Information Commission, *New library: the people's network*, London, Library and Information Commission, 1997. Available at <URL: http://www.ukoln.ac.uk/services /lic/newlibrary/>.

6   Central Office of Information, *Our information age: the government's vision*, London, Central Office of Information, 1998. Available at <URL: http://www.number-10.gov.uk/public/info/index.html>.

7   Thorhauge, J. *et al.*, *Public libraries and the information society*, European Commission, DG XIII/ E.4, 1997.

8   Information Society Forum, *Networks for people and their communities: making the most of the information society in the European Union*, First annual report to the European Commission from the Information Society Forum, June 1996.

9   *Project CIRCE: networking community information.* Available at <URL: http://www.gloscc.gov.uk/circe/>.

11

Everybody's archives

Sarah Tyacke

Introduction

Within the cultural and informational landscape, UK archives have, until recently, had low visibility, regarded more as guardians and repositories of heritage artefacts than as major contributors to the textual and historical resource of the country and of the world. In part this derives from the archives sector's earlier inability to take advantage of technical and organizational development which other sectors, including libraries, have constructed. Now as a community, archives (together with their extensive readerships) need to recast their traditional roles, both in the democratic process of central and local government (records management and legal access to those records) and in the 'unlocking' of historical archives, not only for the benefit of traditional users but also for the public at large.

Why do we need to do this? In some areas of interest (family history, for example) the demand is already overwhelming conventional services, and if we are to meet and manage that demand we need to be innovative. At the same time the Government has made clear its wishes that archives should be more widely available.[1] This requires us to be more user-focused, not just in the sense of thinking how we might make our collections more accessible, but in partnership with the users, thinking with them about how to improve services. The opportunity which technology now offers us is the prospect of reaching potential users whom we were unable to consider in the book and telephone age. We can now take unique information (metadata) and items to millions of people simultaneously.

This can be done by using the new technology sensibly and cheaply, and by forging new alliances across sectors and localities, thus enabling users to find out what *they* want in archives, museums and libraries from wherever they are.

The archival landscape in the United Kingdom

The public record system in the United Kingdom is a distributed one. Public records are those government records which are selected and preserved for *public use* from the miles of government records produced each year. The system is run by the Keeper of Public Records, who is a statutory office holder reporting to the Lord Chancellor. The Lord Chancellor is advised on public records matters, including the closure of records beyond the 30-year period by his advisory council on public records chaired by the Master of the Rolls. The Keeper has a duty to 'guide, supervise and co-ordinate' record selection in government departments, and has recently been asked to take the lead in records management matters, including digital records, across central government. The white paper on freedom of information (FOI) also proposed that similar guidance be available to FOI bodies. Much of the Public Record Office's work, therefore, involves dealing with current record systems and records approaching 30 years old. Its public face, so to speak, is in its public services, making available archives from Domesday onwards.

The Public Record Office (PRO) is the de facto national archive of England and Wales and of the United Kingdom Government.

The records it holds centrally at Kew, London, date from the Domesday Book (1086) to the present day, and amount to 167 km of shelving; but public records are also held in 240 other places of deposit (PODs) across the country.[2] Local, private and government records of local significance are often held together, especially in local record offices, but also elsewhere, and this must be an economical solution for the general archival system of the country.

Scotland has a separate but similar archival system, as does Northern Ireland. The Welsh Devolution Act 1998 gives the Welsh Assembly the possibility of keeping Welsh public records in Wales in the future.

Not all places of deposit are local record offices: some are libraries, such as Cambridge University Library, which holds the records of the Royal Observatory; others are like the Hydrographic Department in Taunton, which holds its own historic records, manuscript charts etc. as a POD which is open to the public as if it were a record office. This distributed system, based on local and central repositories, inspected as to standards of care etc., but not run administratively by the PRO, has some bearing on how we might proceed in the digital age to provide network access to our archival heritage in collaboration with other government departments – for example, the Department of Culture, Media and Sport – and with supplier/user partners – for example, the higher education sector.

While the present distributed public record system is large, it is not archivally comprehensive. In the recasting of our world, we will also need to include links to the museum, library and higher education worlds where archival collections also reside. Those in private ownership will also need to be considered, in particular by the Royal Historical Manuscripts Commission, which lists all non-public records as they are notified to it via the National Register of Archives.

Thus it could be said that the present arrangements for archives outside government are a patchwork of jurisdictional, administrative, informational and cultural pieces, now over 40 years old, which will need to be altered if the archives are to be unlocked not only for present readers and users but for potential users in our society. This is not merely a matter of rearranging the pieces, bolting bits together and hoping things will happen, but of *repurposing* them to serve the public digitally. We will also need to run programmes to make the public aware of archives, what they hold and how they can be of use to the public. The public are only dimly aware of archives and have no idea what they hold.

In other countries, notably Australia and Canada, archives are just beginning to promote themselves beyond their record-keeping roles for government. In 1993, the Australians remarked that:

> . . . most archives maintain statistics about their users and about the types and frequency of records requested. However it is often acknowledged that not enough use is made of information gathered and collated about reference services. Still many archives bemoan the under-use of their materials and the lowliness of their public profiles. It is also often argued that archivists are ineffectual in selling their services and their value to their masters.[3]

This is a not unfamiliar view in the UK.

Changing this cannot all be achieved at once, but the archival community, together with both traditional and new partners, is embarking upon a fast evolutionary track which has as its focus the users themselves, both those who visit now and those who will visit in the future, digitally. This paper is therefore not concerned with the governmental records management side of archival work (although without it the future of archives will be in serious doubt as this is where the future accessions lie), nor is it concerned with the problems of preserving or migrating digitally created records safely for posterity. This paper will concentrate on the public face of archives, in particular examining what we think potential users will want and how we can best deliver it. Inevitably, as it involves work in progress, this paper can only be indicative of how we might proceed, rather than being in any sense prescriptive.

It is not a case of abandoning our traditional readers and partners, but rather of adding a new dimension to our services and thus demonstrating to our ultimate funders, the taxpayers, that we recognize that both the PRO and the country's archives have a contribution to make to the history of each person, of our society, of the British Isles and of the world. After all, the country's archives make up the foundation collections of the English-speaking world and are the nation's memory.

Present users

There are estimated to be about one million visits to archives across England in a year, of which 230,000 are to the Public Record Office at Kew and to the Family Records Centre in London.

In 1998, however, 450,000 visited the PRO website, and this number will increase exponentially. The fastest-growing leisure pursuit is thought to be 'looking up your ancestors', and as populations grow older and have more leisure time that trend looks set to continue. Although, therefore, we are constrained by the physical capacity of our sites, it seems that we may not be in the digital world. Because archives are by their nature unique, no more than a few people can see them in the 'real' world except when they appear in publications or on display. In the new digital world, there is a self-evident potential for making the indexes and guides to the archives, and to the unique 'stuff' itself, available to a wider audience.

Present users are composed of:

- 56% family and local historians (usually for personal interest)
- 18% students from schools, colleges and universities
- 14% professional researchers who make their living in this way
- 10% academics
- 2% others.[4]

These figures are similar to those in the USA and in local archives here.

In comparison with the 19th century, when the PRO was built to house the historic archives of the country and was called by the first Deputy Keeper of the Records the 'strong-box of empire', archives have become popular, and are no longer the sole preserve of the literary, legal and historical elite.

What are archives?

Archives, certainly in the English tradition, are assemblies of records, in any medium, of actions, thoughts or conversations, fixed in time. (Records, i.e. things that have been recorded, are not to be confused with the librarian's bibliographic record, so to avoid confusion I have used the term *metadata* for the latter form of descriptive or indexing 'record'.) The above definition includes recorded telephone conversations as well as written documents. The medium is not the message. If whatever it is can be recorded, in whatever way, it is a record. In government and elsewhere, records are already being produced in digital form and are being preserved by the PRO and the departments themselves. The same is true, in particular, of the banking and pharmaceutical worlds.

Archives or records are the residue of human, governmental and other organizations' activities in the broadest sense. In the case of government about 1–2% of the total produced is selected, which amounts to about 1.5 km of shelving a year. On top of that, the UK National Digital Archive of Datasets (UKNDAD) has just been established by the PRO in partnership with the University of London Computing Centre, where un-anonymized and unaggregated datasets of such informational content as recent hedgerow surveys and school-leavers' qualifications in the 1970s will be kept as part of the economic and social history of the country in the late 20th century.

Records or archives are more akin in type to archaeological deposits than to collections of papers, manuscripts etc., which have been carefully collected by someone as a collection and placed in libraries and other institutions. It was not until the mid to late 20th century that libraries began to distinguish between constructed collections and natural archives, and ceased 'arranging' the latter (the previous practice of arranging archives had effectively destroyed the record's context and the history of its accumulation or 'assembly'. This seemingly arcane difference between archives and manuscripts has some bearing again on how we should access the archives in the digital world. We need to provide a picture of the archives as they were accumulated as well as, for example, providing an easy keyword search. The more 'contextual' access which lets the readers know why, when, and by whom the archives were accumulated is essential to critical analysis of the evidence recorded in the documents.

In some cases we will need to do even more to explain what the 'stuff' is and how to use it to find the answers to the reader's question. A number of approaches are necessary: not merely searches, using, for example, Boolean logic, but a full range of searches and means of disclosure now available to us in present search engines and in the ones to come. We can answer people's questions now in ways they immediately understand, and we should be doing this whether we are librarians, archivists or museum curators.

As already mentioned, records answer questions or at least give clues to the answers. The normal enquiry is not about a particular reference work on a particular subject, but 'I want to know if Roger Casement was framed' or 'Why was Hess sent to England?' At a family history level it will be about a grandfather or an earlier ancestor: 'Did he get any campaign medals in the Boer War?' The questions are direct ones requiring either the exact answer or a way forward to finding the exact answer. The records need to be searched to find the answers and digital technology will help, provided the archives are not once again left out of the 'new technology loop and fail to climb aboard the content creation train which is leaving the station now.'[5]

How are we going to serve our new users?

Our new users are going to include everyone. They will come, as they already do in the conventional world, from the ranks of schoolchildren, from higher education, and from the working and retired population. They will be interested in their own family histories, women's history, children's history, colonial history, immigration history, black history, local history – indeed, many different histories, all of which are to be found in the archives.

The new users will not be confined to the British Isles because, quite simply, digital services are not so confined. Thus, certainly in English-speaking countries and in others with similarly shared pasts,[6] the digital world will propel us to open up our records to these users. The Commonwealth countries want to share our combined colonial pasts, and the UK's neighbours in Europe similarly want to have access to UK records which they value for their own histories. This is particularly true since the fall of the Soviet Union, when archives suddenly became more accessible in Eastern Europe for the first time since 1917. In this respect, Poland springs to mind because of the dispersed nature of its archives, and because of its present programme of bringing together microfilm and digital archives of records relevant to Polish history. We could of course ignore the service potential beckoning us, but in doing so we would consign archives to the margins of cultural and informational history, just at the time when technology makes it possible for millions to 'use' them.

Each sector, however defined for service purposes, needs the 'stuff' to be described in ways which are immediately recognizable to them. Sometimes this will be easy to do, sometimes difficult and different from our traditional ways of delivering the records.

The schools

Most record offices and archive services have education programmes and the PRO is no exception. Now, however, the National Grid for Learning (NGfL) gives the PRO the opportunity to take the archives into the classroom as well as inviting the children to come to Kew. The Department of Education has set up Virtual Teacher Centres (VTCs) and via these it is providing teaching products that can be accessed and downloaded to schools. To meet this challenge the PRO are constructing digital 'snapshots' of documents which directly relate to GCSE course work, so that the use and relevance of the 'stuff' is immediately obvious. Snapshots from the educational pages of the PRO website, showing the range of material and its direct relevance to particular key stages in the National Curriculum, can be seen in Figure 11.1.

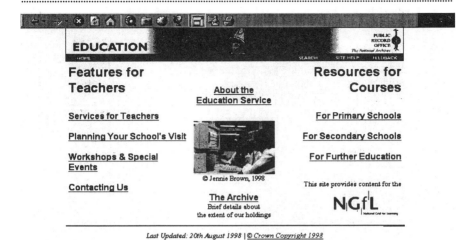

Fig. 11.1 *Snapshots from the educational pages of the PRO website*

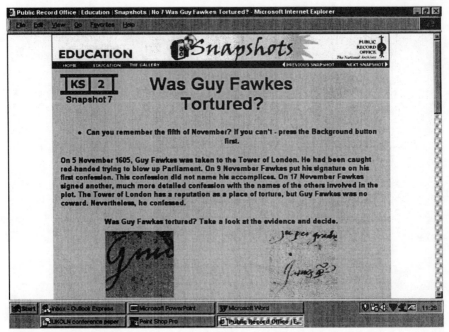

Fig. 11.1 *Continued*

This differs from conventional services not merely in the digital network and content but in the focus of the records towards what teachers and pupils need: the documents are tailor-made for the courses, not just resources.

The finished contribution to the NGfL will comprise the educational snapshots and also a series of galleries of interactive material designed to take the pupil through historical subjects for GCSEs and 'A' levels. This latter more ambitious programme is called The Learning Curve and begins in the first gallery with the study of the growth of political rights in the 19th century (see Figure 11.2).

Each gallery contributes to the study of history according to the relevant stages of the National Curriculum, and places emphasis on literacy and on the critical skills needed for dealing with documents. Thus the digital educational service is very focused and will be measured for its effectiveness by the teachers themselves.

General publics

There are a number of publics which we serve already, and these are likely to grow in size and in variety. In the non-digital world we are used to certain ways of organizing archival services: these may be by jurisdiction, by institutions etc. Archives may be in museums, libraries, universities, private houses, private businesses as well as in central and local government record offices. This has suited us in the past but hardly seems relevant to offering the public ready access to

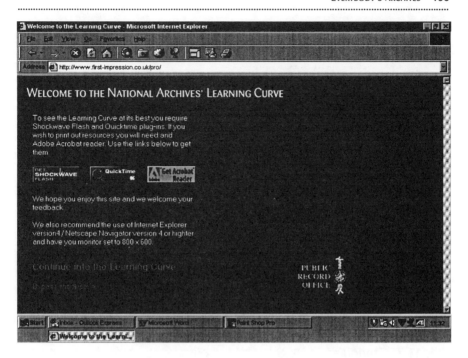

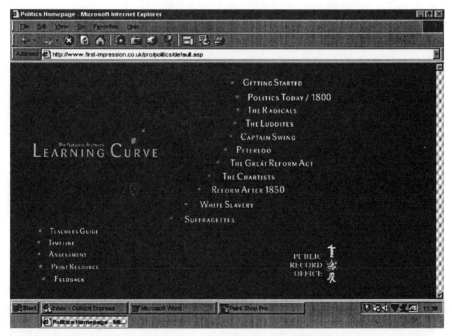

Fig. 11.2 *The Learning Curve: political rights in the 19th century and today*

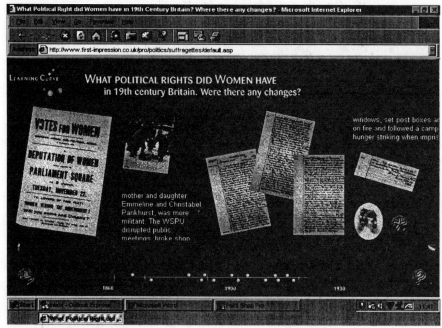

Fig. 11.2 *Continued*

answer their questions wherever the resource. Already, the case of the Family Record Centre, which brings together the records of births, marriages and deaths, and the census records, in one building but under the jurisdiction of two government departments (namely the PRO and the Office of National Statistics), illustrates the efficacy of what is known in the jargon as *one-stop shops*. How much easier it would be if seamless access in the digital world were available either to traditional providers or to new providers.

How to meet the demands of these publics

If we have a way of reaching the schools, how do we intend to reach the general publics beyond the present distributed conventional arrangements? The present system comprises the PRO at Kew and the local and other major repositories across the country. It may be called a rich patchwork of documentary resource, but it now needs to become a network. The archives are identifiable by the National Register of Archives and by whatever lists and card indexes the central and local repositories have made over the decades. In some cases the lists are automated, but this is by no means common. The PRO, for example, is about half-way through a retrospective conversion of its paper lists and will have finished the work in 2001. If the indexes and lists (metadata) are variable in quality, the original documents are also in varying states of preservation, as are the repositories themselves. Some records have been microfilmed, a few digitized. The absence of information and communications technologies (ICTs) beyond stand-alone PCs is painfully evident. The staff are knowledgeable about the records, or at least some of them, but while that may serve to run record offices and archives at their present levels of use, it will not suffice if the archives and their keepers are to be able to flourish in the digital world. Much still needs to be catalogued before archivists can join the 'content creation' train, but we cannot wait to finish that task if we are not to be left behind on the platform. We need to catalogue *and* provide the 'stuff' simultaneously in digital form. This does not have to mean every-thing, but it should mean the major part, however defined, of the documentary heritage of this country, wherever it is held.

Elsewhere in the world, especially in the USA via the Research Libraries Group (RLG), the cataloguing of archives and manuscripts has proceeded at a good pace and the catalogues are online. Elsewhere in the UK – for example, in the higher education sector – initiatives arising from the recommendations of the Follett Report have enabled the cataloguing of archives and manuscripts to be done for universities, and some major libraries like the Bodleian in Oxford and the British Library in London have automated their manuscript catalogues. However, this is all very ad hoc, and does not enable people to find out where archives are in an easy and consistent way, nor to see the 'real thing' digitally. In Europe, the Nordic countries and Spain in particular have begun to make 'stuff' and metadata available to their users, sometimes on internal systems but now more often via the Internet. Scotland has embarked on its own archival network (SCAN) and, together with Sweden and other partners, it also has a project to construct what may become the first phase of a European archival network (EUAN), with funding from the EU.

The archival community as a whole needs to learn from these projects. Two recent conferences have focused on access: one at the PRO in June 1998 acted as a showcase for European systems and discussion of the issues, and the pre-IFLA conference in Amsterdam in August 1998 looked at the possibilities of conver-gence of libraries, archives and museums, at least in respect of access agendas and potential access programs under the forthcoming EU Fifth Framework Programme (DGXIII).

Traditional and new partners

Archivists' traditional partners have been the historians in the higher education sector, and again we need to revamp our relationship to find new ways of work-ing: for example, delivering records not merely through graduate induction courses at Kew, or via presentations at universities or at particular seminars at the Institute of Historical Research and elsewhere, but also by exploring how to deliver relevant resources or coursework digitally to history departments in the universities. We have begun discussions with the JISC on the subject of content creation and the means of delivery. We have also contributed to the JISC-funded 'core executive' project, which has explored combining catalogues and searching them.

Similarly, if archivists are to reach the general public more easily than we can at present, then we need new partners on the high street. The obvious partner is the public library network, and we are exploring with, for example, the EARL consortium ways of delivering, amongst other things, family history records to their readerships.[7]

At the same time, the numbers of home owners of PCs grows, and for those who are interested in history, particularly family history, we need to give them information about 'how to get started', catalogues and indexes to the 'stuff', and in some cases images of the records themselves. While basic access will remain free, products of whatever sort will be charged for as the technology for micro-payments now allows. The challenge will be to let people actually know we are providing the service. Thus a public awareness programme is now essential as these new services become available, or else the archives will remain as invisible in the digital world as they are in the conventional.

The problem of balancing what may be a limitless demand in cyberspace with resources will require a marketing strategy and managing ingenuity of a new order.

Can we plug the gap between potential demand and where we are?

It is critical to begin to create the content, and both the metadata (digital descriptions, lists indexes etc.) and more 'natural language' guides to the records. The selling point of these records and metadata is quality: the records are unique, and need to be known to be reliable and authentic, or 'kite-marked' as being from the PRO or from part of the country's national online archives system. At the same time, in this digital world we need to be able to channel users towards what they want, to guide them to the resources effectively from wherever they start, be they in the local record office, museum, library, university department or a school, or sitting in front of their home PC exploring the Internet or visiting a popular website (for example, the BBC). They have to know the archivists are out there now. Otherwise other content providers will fill the vacuum and the opportunity will be lost to provide everyone with unique, authentic and reliable records kite-marked by archivists. For the schools and higher education in particular, this is a critical matter.

Next steps

The PRO has already converted three million pieces of metadata (its descriptions) retrospectively to digital form, and is exploring the best ways of searching these lists or finding aids.

This block of content, however critical, is only a part of what needs to be done, and the National Council on Archives report, *Archives on-line*,[8] provides a further basis for determining how best to organize and fund the cataloguing of archives, the digitizing of the descriptions and of the records themselves. The track or network on which the content will run has yet to be fully realized, but in view of the need to reach as many relevant users as possible, the system will need to be compatible with (or part of), for example, the NGfL and the public libraries network, as well as accessible via JANET for higher education users and, of course, well signposted on the Internet itself. The archives network may be distinct in aspect, but it cannot be standalone.

In furtherance of the network, the PRO will contribute to its setting-up, especially in the matter of assisting other archives which hold public records so that they can begin to convert their metadata to digital form. It will collaborate on helping other archives to catalogue collections of national significance according to international standards, and will help to find the funds to do this. As noted above, it is already seeking partners to network and distribute catalogues, services and the digital images of the records themselves, both via public-sector partners and via the private sector as appropriate. The PRO will also help construct or revamp organizations to carry the work forward, as existing arrangements are unlikely to be robust enough to do so.

Key benefits for the users

At the very least the programme should promote the wider use of archives both in the UK and elsewhere, make them available in the ways preferred by the particular categories of users, both now and in the future, and in the places where they want them. We may at last 'unlock' the unique documentary history of this country for ourselves and for our children. Perhaps then we may be able to overturn David Bearman's acid but accurate comment on the use of archives in 1986: 'Most people don't.'[9]

Acknowledgments

I would like to thank my colleagues for their help with the presentation of this paper, and in particular Dr David Thomas, Head of the Archives Direct 2001 programme at the PRO.

Notes and references

1   The Lord Chancellor, as the senior cabinet minister with archival responsibilities across Government, wrote (September 1998) to the President of the Society of Archivists welcoming their report, *An archives policy for the United Kingdom*, and reiterated the Government's views on access as follows: 'The Government attaches great importance to the development of information technology as a means of widening public access to information and heritage collections.' This relates to both the informational and cultural areas, including legal access matters.

2   The Public Records Act 1958.

3   Ellis, J., *Keeping archives*, 2nd edn, 1993, 304.

4   National Council on Archives, *Our shared past: an archival Domesday for England*, London, Public Record Office, 1998.

5   See in particular Horsman, P., 'From users to visitors?: information and communication technology strategies for archives', paper delivered to the International Council on Archives, Stockholm, 9 September 1998.

6   By 'shared pasts' I refer to those countries which share records in common, albeit through different histories, whether ex-colonial pasts or shared war pasts (for example, Poland, Russia etc.).

7   During the UKOLN Conference we established the 'Bath Accord' between public libraries and the Public Record Office with a view to determining what was the best way forward in subject areas like family history where we both have a common interest in serving the public.

8   National Council on Archives, *Archives online: the establishment of a United Kingdom Archival Network*, London, Public Record Office, 1998.

9   Bearman, D., cited in Wilson, I. E., *Strategies for communication*, Janus, 1995, 70–84.

12

Joined-up thinking
STRATEGIC PARTNERSHIPS FOR LIFELONG LEARNING

Andrew McDonald

Introduction

This paper will concentrate on learners, and in particular on the challenge of meeting the information needs of the new, lifelong learners referred to in the Government's green paper *The learning age: a renaissance for a new Britain*.[1] Some of the concepts in the green paper are challenging, particularly for those of us who work in 'traditional' educational institutions and who are the successful products of the 'traditional' education system. There are some who are dubious about lifelong learning and who regard it as 'New Labour' hype, but I can assure you that lifelong learners do exist and, furthermore, that there is tremendous potential for growth here. As I shall demonstrate later, almost 10,000 people of all ages have been brought back into learning in the last two years through various University of Sunderland initiatives in the North East of England.

Rather than contribute further to the stimulating if theoretical discussion about paradigms, metaphors and landscapes, I will present an interesting case study of 'joined-up', cross-sectoral library collaboration as a result of which the city of Sunderland is delivering library and information services to support lifelong learners. I must stress that these services are being delivered *now* and that this is not a planning paper for the next millennium.

Sunderland: the learning city

The context within which many of our cities aspire to be learning cities will be similar but I would like to point out some of the particular challenges and opportunities within the city of Sunderland.

The city has one of the lowest participation rates in further and higher education in the country, and there is a strong commitment to lifelong learning and to encouraging wider participation in learning in the broadest sense. It has been recognized that improving learning opportunities and skills training within the community as a whole is an important contribution to social and economic regeneration of the city.

There is a strong tradition of collaboration and partnership working in the city, and indeed in the North East generally. This, together with the University of Sunderland's commitment to community-wide lifelong learning, has enabled the city to launch two new 'lifestyle' learning initiatives for reaching these new life-long learners.

Learning World is a joint venture between the University of Sunderland and Gateshead College, providing a friendly, accessible and different kind of learning experience in the MetroCentre, Europe's largest shopping mall. The development has attracted a great deal of interest and is pictured on the front of the green paper. It is open at weekends and in the evenings and is based near where people work (6000 employees), shop (26 million visitors a year) and live. Learning World has recruited about 4000 new learners within two years onto business, computing, health and language courses, from basic to masters levels.

The University for Industry (UfI) pilot project, coordinated by the University of Sunderland and the Institute for Public Policy Research, has also attracted over 5000 new learners within just ten months in the North East.

Essentially, UfI is a one-stop-shop for education and training, a gateway to existing lifelong learning opportunities. By calling a freephone number, people gain easy access to information, advice and enrolment for a whole range of courses. UfI operates 12 hours a day, seven days a week. Staff at the call centre search their Internet database for suitable courses from a number of providers, including the University of Sunderland, a number of local further education colleges, the National Extension College, TECs in the region, the BBC and local companies. The courses can be studied at one of the 47 UfI learning centres around the region in places to suit people's lifestyles – in companies such as Vaux, in stores such as Sainsbury's, in health centres, in factories, in the local football club's Stadium of Light, and in libraries.

UfI is really a simple concept, but it is important to grasp that it is not a new university and is not really just for industry, although learning at work will become increasingly important. Experience suggests that the whole concept has been readily accepted in the 'marketplace', but that some traditional institutions seem to struggle with what they regard as an ambiguous piece of 'badging'. The success of the pilot project has indicated the huge potential of the UfI to make a real difference to lifelong learning when it is rolled out nationally. The project has included two very interesting features: cold telephone calling has resulted in a staggering 22% success rate in enrolment, and the analysis of demand for learning by postcode has provided the potential to respond to local requirements or even commission new courses.

Another significant influence is the City Partnership's 'Telematics Strategy' launched in 1996. Drawn up by local government, academia, business and the voluntary sector, it is a strategy to establish Sunderland at the forefront of telematics nationally and internationally, and to ensure everyone in the city benefits from developments in the use of computers and telecommunications. Engaging the voluntary sector has been extremely valuable since they have a particular understanding of the real needs of people in the city. The strategy concentrates on three main themes: the intelligent city, education and training, and business.

Enhancing access to library and information services throughout the city was a key objective within the intelligent city theme. Through a city-wide network, the ambition was to link online catalogues and enhance access to electronic information sources. Already, novel learning places had been established in the city libraries where the public could access electronic information and IT facilities and be trained in their use.

Libraries Access Sunderland Scheme

This innovative, open-access library scheme was launched in July 1997 and it promotes access to the wealth of libraries and learning resources in the city of Sunderland. Affectionately known as LASH, the Libraries Access Sunderland scHeme was planned by the City Library and Arts Centre, and the libraries of City of Sunderland College and the University of Sunderland. It is a fine example of cross-sectoral collaboration, or partnership between the public, further education and higher education libraries working closely together to support lifelong learning in the city.

Under the scheme, anyone who lives, works or studies in Sunderland has free access to all 29 libraries in the city. This includes the 21 public libraries, the four learning centres in the City College and the four libraries in the University. Learners can study at any of the 3000 reader places in these libraries spread around the city, and they can make use of the collections and services provided there. All the user needs is a current membership card for Sunderland City Libraries or a current library card for the City College or University. Users are simply asked to respect the regulations of the library they are using and to study in a responsible way with consideration for the needs of other learners.

The benefits

Promoting access to the network of libraries in the city encourages learners of all ages in the community to step on the 'ladder of learning.' Providing seamless access between libraries also enables learners to progress on this ladder of learning and to develop their interests without unnecessary institutional barriers. It is an important building block of the City Partnership's Telematics Strategy and an attribute distinguishing Sunderland as a learning city.

The scheme provides the following benefits:

1 It opens up the world of learning to people of all ages in Sunderland.
2 Learners can use the whole range of libraries in the city, not only the City Library, but also the college and university libraries.
3 People have somewhere to study and learn with free access to books, IT and services.
4 Learners can use the nearest or most convenient library, and this may be particularly attractive to part-time and disadvantaged students.
5 The public are encouraged to use academic libraries.
6 Members of the public may get their first taste of life on campus.
7 Registered staff and students of the City College and University have reciprocal access rights for the first time.
8 The academic institutions are reminded of the value of the public library for their work.
9 The public have access to information about courses and training opportunities in the city.
10 Sharing resources means that everyone can benefit from the investment in libraries in Sunderland.

How was it achieved?

A small working group drawn from the three institutions came together with a clear commitment to develop a scheme which had learners rather than institutions or libraries at its heart. In addition to the heads of library services in the City Council, the City College and the University, we also had the Vice-Principal of the City College, the IT Development Officer of the City Library and Arts Centre and, usefully, the Head of Adult Education in the City Council.

The focus was simply to open up the city's libraries to everyone in Sunderland. The working group carefully considered the opportunities and implications of an open-access library scheme both for learners and for the libraries and institutions concerned. They aimed to minimize bureaucracy and to share any costs involved.

Given the challenging nature of the task, they first of all identified all the positive benefits and potential of the scheme, and then went on to list their various concerns. These included:

• possible competition for study places, collections and IT, especially at busy times

- the need to restrict the use of certain collections and services, such as the student text collections in the academic libraries
- how to enforce the rules and regulations of each library
- responsibility for damage, loss or bad behaviour
- the security of the buildings, collections, computers and people
- the need to inform new users of health and safety regulations
- the risk of, and responsibility for, admitting very young people
- the difficulty posed when a library is located in a building to which access cannot be granted
- the possibility that the public might need a helpline in each library.

The working group considered each of these concerns and resolved them satisfactorily. For example, it was accepted that responsibility for dealing with cases of damage, loss or bad behaviour should lie with the host institution and that enrolled students should come first in the academic libraries. They were unanimous that the benefits heavily outweighed the perceived difficulties, and that the scheme had tremendous potential to enhance library and learning support throughout Sunderland.

Even at that early stage, a number of interesting possible future developments were identified, but because they all required further discussion and organization, it was decided to defer them and launch the simple access scheme.

Promotion

The scheme was actively promoted throughout the city, and learners were positively encouraged to use all the libraries in Sunderland. This is perhaps one feature that distinguishes Sunderland from other cities in which public access to academic libraries is offered 'in principle', or at least whilst there was a requirement to do so under the now defunct Net Book Agreement.

An attractive, professionally designed bookmark advertises the scheme and gives some clear messages: 'Our libraries are open to everyone'; 'Sunderland – The Learning City;' and 'Lifelong learning – all you need is a library card'. A colourful leaflet gives further details of how the scheme works and information about all the libraries in the city. The scheme was promoted in the local press and through displays in the libraries, adult education classes and various local interest groups. It was also advertised on the city's website on the Sunderland Host.

Progress and development

Since the scheme was launched in mid-1997 considerable progress has been made on a number of fronts, including:

- joint staff training and development
- sharing online catalogues
- delivering electronic journals
- supporting certain learning initiatives
- undertaking research projects.

Staff training

Joint staff training has been encouraged, not only to share the benefits but also to promote an understanding of the collections and services in each of the libraries in Sunderland. Well-informed staff throughout all the libraries are important in underpinning an effective scheme. The senior management teams, middle managers and library assistants from the three library systems have all held joint training and development events. In most cases this has been the first time staff from different libraries in the city have ever met, and certainly the first time they have visited each others' libraries. As well as providing an opportunity for an exchange of experience, this has also enabled useful ideas to emerge – and in particular from the library assistants. A web page has been designed and LASH packs have been put together which give details of the services in each library. The chief librarians of the City Library and the City College have been invited to the University Library staff conference.

Research

The University of Sunderland, together with its partners in the city, has successfully bid for a British Library Research and Innovation Centre research grant to investigate the staff training necessary to underpin successful local library collaboration and service development.

Sharing catalogues

It has proved difficult to share online catalogues because the three participating bodies have different systems at various stages of development. The University's online catalogue has been made available at the central public library and is, of course, available on the Internet. There is a scheme to pursue broadcast searching or some sort of catalogue clump, and a consultant is investigating the advantages, costs and savings of adopting the Dynix system currently used by the University Library in all the libraries in Sunderland.

Electronic journals

An exciting development is the fact that several thousand full-text electronic journals have been made available throughout the city's libraries on Internet terminals. The three libraries have jointly negotiated a city-wide license with EBSCO for their Masterfile service. The journals are just at the right level to be of interest to the public and users of the further and higher education libraries, and the new service has attracted considerable interest from the business community and other groups. This city-wide licence is apparently the first of its type in the UK.

Learning innovations

Because of their close links, the libraries in the city have been able to respond quickly to learning innovations. For example, they have all been designated UfI learning centres as part of the University of Sunderland's pilot project. Indeed, it is no surprise that the public libraries have proved to be amongst the most popular learning centres with these new, lifelong learners.

Outcomes

Experience suggests that many of the predicted difficulties about cross-sectoral library collaboration, which would arise mainly from those who have not tried it, have turned out to be unfounded. None of the three libraries has been overwhelmed by new users, and those who have been attracted have not presented any major difficulties. The only reported problem so far has been where university students have made increased use of the free interlibrary loans service at the public library when their free allowance in the university has been used up. The costs have been minimal: the modest costs of publicity, and subsequently the cost of the subscription to the EBSCO Masterfile service, have simply been shared. The considerable benefits and huge potential of the scheme far outweigh any minor difficulties and costs.

No systematic evaluation of the uptake or benefits of the scheme has yet been undertaken, not least because there would be certain costs involved. However, anecdotal evidence suggests that women returners are now making greater use of the University's libraries, and this is just the sort of group who, it was thought, might appreciate the use of a high-quality learning environment, and who should be welcomed into higher education.

It is reassuring that the achievements of the libraries in Sunderland are regarded as one of the most successful aspects the City Partnership's Telematics Strategy. As a result, the librarians of all three institutions are now closely involved in planning the next five-year Telematics Strategy for the city of Sunderland. This will revolve around three main issues:

- business and industry
- the digital citizen
- education and training.

LASH has attracted considerable interest in the profession and this has been a welcome endorsement of the city's brave efforts in developing the scheme. There is a certain pride in the city and its libraries in the scheme. While that this sort of open access policy may not be high on the agenda for libraries in other cities, it may nonetheless be appreciated by the learners themselves. It is interesting to speculate where Government might invest resources in order to implement its lifelong learning policies. There were some messages for higher education from Kim Howells, the Minister for Lifelong Learning, when he addressed a recent SCONUL meeting. He likened libraries to 'lighthouses' and spoke of 'fortress higher education'.[2]

Plans and developments

There are plans to extend the successful joint staff training and development programme, to investigate further city-wide licenses for electronic information, and even to consider collaborative purchases. In view of the interest of the business community in city-wide electronic information services, there is a move towards exploring similar services for the health, legal and community information sectors. They would very much like to hear from vendors with relevant products, particularly full-text services.

The working group have discussed the feasibility of a city-wide document delivery service using manual and electronic means, believing it to be easier to lend to each other than for the academic libraries to lend to the public. They have even discussed using university minibuses to transport readers and, more realistically, books around the city.

A common library card might be attractive but, in a way, this is already provided by the City Library card. For the moment, it is easier to have the particular cards necessary for the different issue systems in all three libraries, but the introduction of a city smart card might give further food for thought.

There is a need to make more course and careers information available in each library, and to enable users to enroll directly with courses whilst they are in the libraries.

Other libraries in the surrounding areas in the North East Region are interested in joining the scheme for access and electronic services. It would also be desirable to involve the schools of Sunderland, particularly as progress is made in connecting them up as part of the National Grid for Learning. At a time when the concept of 'a learning centre' is broadening, it should somehow be possible to involve the electronic village halls and the UfI learning centres in the region.

There is tremendous scope for delivering ICT training locally, and for developing digital content and local archives with the resources made available as a result of *New library: the people's network*.[3]

There is a need to evaluate the scheme and, in particular, to collect some statistics about who is using the libraries, and to assess the benefits to them and the responsible institutions. It would be interesting to find out how many people have been encouraged to use the academic libraries and enroll on courses as a result of the scheme. Indeed, the scheme could prove to be a powerful recruitment tool for the academic institutions. Similarly, the City Library would like to know about the take-up of local authority courses as a result of publicity in the libraries. Further research might consider the economics of cross-sectoral partnerships, and the service standards or the explicit service entitlement of lifelong learners in the city, and could identify some performance indicators against which a learning city might be assessed.

It is worth mentioning some other partnerships achieved within the city. The University Library, for example, has collaborative relationships with a number of health trusts, Learning World, the European Education and Information Centre at the MEPs Office, the UfI pilot project, some local schools, electronic village halls, the new National Glass Centre, the BBC and Blackwell's Bookshops. It is important that we look beyond building strategic partnerships with libraries and collaborate with the other organizations involved in learning in both the public and private sector.

Some lessons and observations

Many librarians suggest that cross-sectoral collaboration and an open-door policy can be both expensive and problematic, and are particularly concerned about being overwhelmed by new readers. The experience in Sunderland suggests this is not the case. None of the three libraries has been overwhelmed and the new users attracted have not presented any major difficulties. The costs have been minimal and have simply been shared equally. It seems that many librarians overestimate the problems involved, and it is surprising that so many of the enquiries made about LASH focus on the problems rather than the benefits. While it is true to say that the planning group did identify a number of potential problems, they only did this *after* considering the benefits of the scheme, and none of these apparent problems has caused any difficulty in practice.

The Sunderland approach has been pragmatic and very much along the 'just do it' lines. Care was taken to introduce a simple scheme which could be communicated and delivered immediately, rather than attempt an elaborate scheme which might be ultimately self-defeating. For example, discussions about introducing borrowing raised a number of difficulties, so it was decided to introduce the simple access scheme without borrowing. In any case, the planning team were not at all sure about the real demand for borrowing or whether a city-wide document delivery system might be preferable. They have chosen to introduce new services and developments as the need arose, always with a clear focus upon the needs of the learner in the city, rather than upon the particular interests or idiosyncrasies of the various libraries and institutions.

This is not to say that 'joined-up' cross-sectoral thinking is not challenging or without difficulty or even disagreement. Everyone has preconceived ideas which often arise from prevalent attitudes and funding arrangements in their particular sector. The steering group were reminded during the planning of publicity material of how misleading and even threatening the term 'academic library' could be to members of the public.

Successful cross-sectoral collaboration in Sunderland is underpinned by effective 'human networking' amongst the librarians. A number of factors have contributed to this success:

- a culture of cooperation rather than competition in the city
- the political will in the various institutions for lifelong learning
- the framework provided by the Telematics Strategy
- the lack of any significant costs
- good cooperative attitudes amongst the library managers and staff
- effective communication between the libraries.

In cities where there is more than one of a particular type of institution, there may be a greater feeling of competitiveness, but Sunderland was fortunate in having just one university, one further education college and one public library. As with many new developments, there was a need for a catalyst or someone to take a leading role.

Indeed, the scheme has generated considerable enthusiasm in many quarters of the city. Even those designing the publicity material grasped the concept enthusiastically and were pleased to be involved in a simple but cutting-edge development.

Conclusion

I have described how the libraries in Sunderland have worked together across traditional sectoral boundaries to create a unique open-access library scheme which is playing a significant role in facilitating and supporting community-wide, lifelong learning within the city. The Libraries Access Sunderland scHeme is an important achievement and one which distinguishes Sunderland as a learning city. The promotional bookmark proclaims a simple but important message: 'Our libraries are open to everyone' and 'Libraries for lifelong learning – all you need is a library card.'

It is not common for university, further education and public libraries to work together in this way, and LASH is apparently amongst the first, if not *the* first, cross-sectoral open-access scheme of its type in the UK. However, the scheme has gone well beyond actively promoting broader access. Jointly, the libraries concerned have introduced several new services, including electronic information services and support for new learning initiatives, and have developed collaborative staff training and research projects. This 'joined-up' thinking in the library community in the city is just another example of the partnership working for which Sunderland has become justifiably renowned.

As a nation, we are lurching towards a rather different education system with an emphasis on mass further and higher education and lifelong learning, and one which will be led more by customer needs than by the interests of traditional providers. Lifelong learners really do exist and we must find ways of supporting this new learning, which will not only be delivered in educational institutions, but will also, increasingly, be delivered to the home, to communities, to the workplace, and to learning centres in all sorts of places convenient for people's lifestyles.

The challenge for library and information services is how to respond to these changes. As experience in Sunderland indicates, we must develop a system with learners at the centre rather than libraries and parent institutions. We must think across traditional sectors, and develop partnerships between libraries and other bodies in order to deliver a network of learning opportunities to people when, where and how they need it. We need 'joined-up' thinking. As The Library Association's *Declaration from the library and information community* so beautifully put it:

> The Library and Information Community will break down barriers and create the new alliances necessary to realise the vision of a Learning Society and attain the objectives of the National Grid for Learning and the People's Network.[4]

If we fail to grasp the nettle and deliver the support required in the new learning age, other organizations are well placed to so – the BBC and Microsoft to name but two. We can speculate where resources may be invested or redirected in the learning age, but higher education should not underestimate the importance of further education, and no one should underestimate the importance of schools and public libraries in delivering the Government's agenda for lifelong learning.

There seem to be several barriers to greater collaboration and partnership working in the library world:

* the funding, politics and culture of the various sectors
* institutional competitiveness
* inequalities in funding.

Indeed, some librarians receive little encouragement to develop strategic partnerships, and certainly do not receive any additional resources in order to promote new cross-sectoral initiatives. They often refer to poor vision and direction at institutional level. However, in some cases it may be the attitudes of librarians themselves which are the barrier to change. Developing partnerships need not be a costly exercise, and the allocation of library resources is always a matter of priorities. What is clear is that the learner in any city can face a bewildering range of libraries and some formidable barriers to gaining access to the library and information services necessary to support their learning.

During this conference a great deal has been said about building digital databases, but it would be a tragedy if the learners in our communities could not have access to this information, either because it is locked up in selected academic and research libraries, or because of prohibitive licensing costs or restrictive copyright legislation.

It is regrettable that the contribution of libraries to lifelong learning continues to be underestimated in some circles. Many learning cities are planned without the crucial role of libraries being taken into account. Several conferences on learning cities in recent years have failed to address the importance of libraries in distributing and supporting learning in the communities they serve.

However, there is a tremendous future for libraries in the information age. Indeed, the learning age could lead to the rediscovery or a renaissance of libraries. The various libraries in any city or community form an accessible, trusted network of places where learners can study, access information of all types, use IT and benefit from the support of trained information professionals. Libraries also form the hub for distributing networked electronic or virtual services to the community. Sunderland's experience with Learning World and UfI confirms the central importance of libraries in supporting innovation in the delivery of learning. The network of libraries is used by millions of people a year, and already makes a tremendous contribution to community-wide lifelong learning. Our contribution could be enhanced by developing new strategic partnerships with other libraries and with the other organizations involved in learning. All that is needed is some 'joined-up' thinking.

References

1   *The learning age: a renaissance for a new Britain*, London, DfEE, Cm 3780, HMSO, 1998.
2   The SCONUL Conference, Manchester, 31 March–2 April 1998.
3   Library and Information Commission, *New library: the people's network*, London, Library and Information Commission, 1997. Also available at <URL: http://www.ukoln.ac.uk/services/lic/newlibrary/>.
4   The Library Association, *Declaration from the library and information community*, The Library Association, 1998.

Part 4

Information exchanges: the library, the network and the future

The future: organizations and people

13

The electronic library

JOB DESIGN, WORK PROCESSES AND QUALIFICATIONS IN ELECTRONIC INFORMATION SERVICES – THE JULIA PROJECT

Lars Bjørnshauge

Institutional context

The Technical Knowledge Centre and Library of Denmark (DTV) is the library of the Technical University of Denmark (DTU) as well as the national centre for scientific technical information in Denmark.

DTV has always been in the forefront in implementing technology in library and information services. For instance, the DTV was a development partner for the Exlibris ALEPH library system and has participated in several EU and Nordic-funded development projects. The first WWW-server in Denmark was in operation at DTV in the summer of 1993, but at that time the web was thought of as a strange toy for freaks, and none of the researchers, decision-makers or library directors had any idea of what was on the move!

Strategic plan

Until the summer of 1997, the DTV operated under a strategic plan with the primary objective of implementing the electronic library at a steady pace, as well as to be active in the development of the primary university activities:

- developing personal information services for researchers and research groups by implementing new technology in these services
- implementing IT in teaching and learning processes
- supporting the university knowledge management in operating the university CWIS (campus-wide information service) etc.

The JULIA project (human resource development in the transition towards the hybrid library)

Developing and implementing services based on electronic information and being a partner in the development of new teaching and learning environments, means that a whole new set of skills has to be available in the library. Besides operating the 'old' paper-based library, new services have to be invented, and available technological solutions have to be implemented and applied in the daily operations. A comprehensive programme for continuous education and in-house training has to be established.

On the basis of a project description, an application to the Danish Ministry of Labour Relations was made. The Ministry was offering funding for projects designed to contribute to the development, change and growth of public institutions towards more customer-oriented services, as well as designing attractive jobs for the staff employed by those institutions. The project, hereafter labelled the JULIA project, was granted £50,000 from these funds. The DTV's own financial contribution was calculated to be £100,000.

The JULIA project was scheduled to last from 1 July 1997 until 30 June 1998. The primary objective of the project was to ensure that the transition to the hybrid library would be a direct process in which the design of new jobs, new work processes, qualifications and on-the-job training was carefully worked out so as to reduce the feelings of insecurity that would naturally be engendered by drastic changes in the work environment.

A further objective was to utilize the new technological opportunities to create more comprehensive jobs for employees, and in particular to explore the possibility of creating secure jobs for qualified non-library staff.

It was a condition of the funding that the project should be established on the basis of mutual understanding between the management, the liaison committee and the shop stewards, and that there should be a continuous flow of information to the liaison committee and the staff in general.

A project team was formed, consisting of four managers and six staff members from different departments and with different educational backgrounds, and the project work took off in August 1997.

Re-engineering plan for library services: changing conditions for the project

At the same time the library management was preparing the budget for 1998 and the 'normal' round of journal cancellations. Libraries worldwide have problems keeping pace with the ever-increasing body of scientific information, and the escalating prices result in journal subscriptions continually being cancelled.

For the DTV this has meant a 40% reduction of subscriptions from 1990 to 1997, with another 700 cancellations in prospect for 1998. This brought the concept of a comprehensive academic library to mind. The library management raised this issue with the library board, and it was unanimously agreed that the trend of annual cancellations could not be continued. Unless more funding for library services became available for 1998, something radical had to be done in order to stop the negative trend and move more decisively towards the electronic, or more precisely the hybrid library.

Informal discussions between the university and library managements made it clear that no additional funding for 1998 was possible so, on the basis of these facts, the library management drew up a plan which was agreed upon by the library board. The plan consisted of four main actions:

1 Staff reductions: 13 staff were to be made redundant, which would bring yearly savings of £275,000.
2 Additional funds for the purchasing of information: £200,000 was needed to maintain subscriptions for 1999 and buy electronic licenses and technology for the development of electronic information resources.
3 A policy to minimize the handling of printed material wherever possible.
4 Investment in continuous education, new qualifications and on-the-job training.

The plan was approved by the university board in September 1997 and library funds for 1998 were increased by 5%. The staff reductions took effect from 1 November 1997, which meant that 13 staff were made redundant by 1 May 1998.

The overall objective of the plan was to meet the information needs of researchers and students. The researchers (especially in the science, technology and medicine disciplines) want *one* point of access to everything – databases and electronic journals – and they want it on their desktops *now*. Unless libraries can make significant progress towards this goal, they will be just as much out of business as teachers who cannot change their teaching methods, or universities that fail to change their learning environments. That is the way it is, it must be admitted that very few library managers, very few teachers and very few universities have realized this so far!

In short, the DTV management are aiming to implement several changes simultaneously:

1 Developing a one-stop shop – i.e. integrating as many relevant databases, table-of-contents services and electronic full-text journals as possible – primarily, but not solely, for the benefit of researchers. This is being done by min-

imizing the library 'paperwork' – i.e. if there is an electronic version of a journal, the library will no longer order the print edition.

2   Weeding out and displacing parts of the print collection to make room for:
    - the Learning Resource Centre, which provides support for multimedia
      education and presentations, integrating IT in educational processes, and
      distance education
    - the university's Centre of Didactic Methods, providing support for new
      teaching and learning methods
    - an IT-based learning and study environment with a number of worksta-
      tions, group-discussion and project-work rooms, a café etc.

The reason I have described this plan so extensively is that for obvious reasons it
has had great impact on the development of the JULIA project.

Furthermore, the initial implementation of the plan was accompanied by
changes in the organization of the library. It is clear, for example, that a staff
reduction of approximately 15% must inevitably lead to rearrangements in the
division of labour between departments and a reallocation of work responsibilities for the staff. The key features of this organizational change are a flattening of
the organization, with further delegation of responsibility and decision-making
to staff.

Just to complete the picture, a new nationwide salary system was launched
and the present director went on leave on 1 October 1997.

Project activities

The re-engineering plan and the other changes caused a lot of unrest during the
period from September 1997 until April 1998 when all 13 redundant staff had left
the library (although the majority had left earlier, thanks to the efforts made by
the replacement agency involved).

It was of course very difficult for the staff to become involved in the forward-
oriented measures of the project when faced with the insecurity triggered by the
re-engineering plan, and at least until the end of October, when the names of the
13 redundant staff members were released, most project activities outside the project group were brought to a standstill.

However, the project group continued its activities, the most important of
which was to gather information on current work processes in the 'paper-based'
library and the qualifications involved, as well as outlining the work processes in
the electronic library and the qualifications required. On the basis of these tasks,
the project group drew up a large number of topics for in-house training. One of
the problems encountered was that it was rather difficult to find external sources
for educational activities, work processes and qualifications related to the elec-

tronic library. Fortunately the DTV has had lengthy experience of offering courses in IT, Internet, WWW design etc., so in-house teaching resources were brought in to design and run the in-house training activities.

From November 1997 to date, a large number of courses have been held, most of which have consisted of short two-hour sessions. A number of them were repeated and tailored to the needs of different categories of staff.

Examples of courses are:

- network knowledge and general hardware knowledge
- PC and peripheral equipment – 'first aid' in case of technical problems
- 'use your browser' – browser functions, wallpaper, bookmarks, save to disk etc.
- the WWW OPAC for educated non-library staff
- Internet Pointer Guide: the DTV 'edition' of the Edinburgh Engineering Virtual Library – an Internet resource guide
- search engines
- in-house and external e-conferences – how to use them
- the DTV's Electronic Reference Guide
- electronic resources: databases and full-text resources (examples), contents and how to use them:
  - Cambridge Scientific Abstracts
  - EBSCO Academic Search
  - EI Village/Compendex
  - Standards.

Another major feature of the project was the WWW environment for information on the project, course and training offers, exchange of ideas and initiatives. A homepage was established on the DTV intranet with links to interesting projects – eLib and D-lib, for instance. All project group minutes, newsletters etc. are displayed. Initiatives for new courses, projects etc. are communicated and so on.

The homepage, with its electronic conferences, has in the course of the project developed into a central site for the exchange and testing of ideas, and thus has contributed to the overall training of the staff in handling electronic communication facilities.

Establishing facilities for continuous education, training and communication

One of the minor features of the project was to experiment with distance work and distance education. The project funding included a minor contribution (£3000) to support the purchase and installation of PCs in the homes of eight staff members. However, as a consequence of the re-engineering plan, it was decided to lease 70 PCs and install them in the homes of every single staff member during February 1998. The PCs are networked to the library and all telecommunication expenses are paid for by the library.

This action has proved to be very clever. It has boosted the activities of the staff, keeping them updated with developments on the net, has enabled participation in net-based distance learning, and has made individual staff members significantly more optimistic with regard to their future in the organization.

At present, 45 of the 70 staff members are engaged in obtaining an approved PC-user certification by means of distance learning: most of these 45 are the educated non-library staff.

Deployment of the PCs has also encouraged the staff to make use of the different electronic conferences installed by the library, such as for asking colleagues for advice or for exchanging and testing new ideas.

Indeed, a whole new attitude has developed towards the responsibility of keeping qualifications up-to-date. Earlier, staff were frequently of the opinion that the responsibility for their qualifications lay solely with the management. Now the majority of the staff say that now they have been given the facilities for continuous education, the responsibility is at least a shared one.

Job design in the hybrid library

Another of the major objectives for the JULIA project was to design the jobs in the 'electronic' library. The basic assumption was that the work processes in the traditional 'paper-based' library were well known and well described, and that it would be a difficult task to describe the work processes in the electronic library. The development of the project has proved that this was not the case.

What has been learned here is that the transition towards the hybrid library does not take place in a vacuum: the transition cannot be seen as an experiment in a laboratory, where all environmental conditions can be controlled. On the contrary, there is every chance that external forces will lead to modifications in the plans and prospects of the project, as indeed they did. The transition takes place in a very turbulent environment.

Furthermore, there seems to be very little help available on how to design more comprehensive jobs in an electronic library. As part of the project, the JULIA project group undertook a study tour of Tilburg, the University of Westminster, and Thames Valley University – to visit sites where the transition was already in progress towards the digital library, the Learning Resource Centre and related developments. They wanted especially to study changes in the division of labour between different categories of staff. Although the tour gave valuable insights into some aspects of the construction of the modern library and information services – for instance, in the physical integration of paper-based and electronic services, and 'new' teaching and learning support services – it became apparent that these sites still maintained a rather sharp division of labour between the different categories of staff, and especially between subject specialists, generalists (librarians) and clerical staff.

Increasingly over the years, the DTV has pursued a policy of creating overlaps between different categories of staff, in order to reduce the expense of higher-paid staff and create more comprehensive and challenging jobs for the less formally educated.

The fact that very few libraries to date have taken more radical steps towards the electronic library, plus the fact that the available technologies develop at a rapid pace, has made it rather clear that the 'new' library world will do best by saying farewell to the well-defined, very specific and therefore static job descriptions, and instead providing each staff member with the necessary means of continuously creating/updating their own jobs.

This can be done by implementing a combination of different 'tools', the most important of which are:

- inducing a certain level of pressure or competition with regard to the need to be up-to-date, inquisitive and self-reliant, in order to be valuable for the organization
- organizing the institution in such a way that the individual staff member has the competence to make decisions and take individual and group initiatives without having to pass several levels of management, thereby allowing staff to make mistakes and learn
- facilitating self-organized or group-organized education, or the development of competence on demand – i.e. at very short notice – by, for instance, establishing the technological conditions for distance learning and communication.

In short, instead of creating a set job description, the important thing is to provide the framework for the individual staff member to create and change the job on a continuous basis.

External evaluation

The evaluation of the project was handled by an external consultant company by means of a focus-group meeting. This meeting and discussion took place in April 1998, and the participants were 18 staff members, representing all categories of staff and all departments: all were 'customers' of the project – i.e. none were from the core project group.

The participants were asked to answer a number of written questions anonymously, and then to participate in a three-hour discussion with the consultant.

The main outcome of this evaluation can be summarized as follows:

1 All categories of staff reported that their present jobs resulted from the fact that the DTV was in a state of transition from a paper-based to a hybrid library: their current jobs consisted of 'old' and 'new' tasks.

2 They considered the DTV a good place to work in, with varied and challenging tasks that allowed them to use more of their own capabilities in their job.

3 It was a common viewpoint that the recent changes had led to a greater delegation of responsibilities and that they had more opportunity to make decisions by themselves, that problems with more than one solution arose more frequently, and that they experienced more involvement in the development of library services and in the use of IT to support this development.

It had been expected that the re-engineering plan, the staff reductions etc. would create defensive attitudes towards the changes and the implementation of new technologies in library services. The evaluation report suggested that the staff did not feel defensive, but that on the contrary they felt inspired to be in the forefront, exploring the opportunities which IT development offers, and they recognized that part of the responsibility lay with them as individuals.

The outcome: the lessons learned

Given the concurrent developments and changes during the course of the project period, it is very difficult to isolate very scientifically the specific outcomes of the JULIA project.

However, the most important lesson, in a project which has human resources as its main focus, is that it is possible to handle dramatic changes in an organization without encountering resistance from the staff, provided the management is committed to investment in, and provision of, an appropriate environment for personal growth that is responsive to bottom-up initiatives and ideas. This will make it possible for each individual to envisage an attractive future based on his or her own active contribution to this future.

From the managers' point of view it has been rather satisfactory, especially under the specific conditions which this project has faced, to discover that investments in people pay off.

We should of course be aware that the outcome of the external evaluation – no matter how anonymous (and it really was) – has to be considered very carefully and not over-interpreted. Nevertheless, one major outcome of the whole process of the JULIA project and the concurrent developments – and a very promising one for the many future problems to be encountered – is that the majority of the staff have become fellow-players in the process.

The future of the project

From the evaluation and many other comments received, there is a general consensus that the project should be continued. The JULIA project, both the project group and its activities, has certainly become a high spot within the organization.

No doubt the activities will go on, and the spirit of the project will continue to grow, in the future activities and undertakings that will be needed in the development of a hybrid library.

14

Maps, compasses and information skills

LOCATING A FUTURE PLACE FOR KNOWLEDGE AND INFORMATION

Biddy Fisher

Introduction

This paper sets out to explore some existing practice in the development of information management skills – existing practice which represents the future for those who are yet to take advantage of the information landscape which we already inhabit. It takes as its focus people – specifically those for whom the phrase 'lifelong learning' is a reality waiting to happen. In his guest address, Prof. Bob Fryer[1] set out a demanding agenda for us in terms of accommodating all of those who need to learn, not just those who successfully navigate entry requirements into higher or further education. His is a challenge which is already being met in his own area of Barnsley, and it is the initiatives which meet this agenda (illustrated below) which give a true way in for the future.

If you were feeling somewhat daunted by the size and nature of what needs to be done to achieve lifelong learning, remember that the best way to eat elephants is in small pieces. In the area of lifelong learning, it is important to do what can be achieved and plan for improvement, and not to be daunted by the scale of all that needs doing.

The impact of information on society

It is salutary to consider this impact in relation to major catastrophes – situations where individuals must rely on accuracy and factual detail in order to plan and live their lives to their best ability. Consider the need for information in significant events such as:

- the creation of a democratic system in South Africa
- the impact on society of HIV and AIDS, and the need for information to alleviate fear and to take evasive action

- the devastating effect which El Niño has had in areas of the world in 1998, and how information can assist people to plan for disaster
- on a local scale, how Yorkshire Water used information to highlight the need for conservation of water stocks and for some appreciation of the value of this essential commodity.

We will all have our own thoughts on how information plays a major role in maintaining society, and, as information professionals, how we can safeguard the access and availability of facts which assist planning.

To be truly usable, information must have some authority: people need to have access to undeniable facts. It is usually easier for people to obtain information which has been processed or synthesized in some way, like that which we receive from newspapers or from television reporting. These are secondary sources which choose a particular expression of fact or emphasis. We create our own information by our experience, and if we are involved in situations we offer that experience as truth, even though we are subjective in our assessment of any situation to the extent that we are either central or peripheral. We also receive information from those like ourselves who have some involvement with issues; this includes rumour and gossip, which may or may not be authenticated by comparison with factual sources. The Internet, or web, is an example of how sources of information can be compared against each other for 'truth' or reality, but how often do we restrict our sources to those which have been evaluated by sound methodologies? And if we are unable to do so, how much more difficult will it be for those without our professional training?

While we can make judgments about the authority of any source of information, it is as well to remind ourselves how easy or difficult it is for people to access the sources we consider to be authoritative. Compare the ease of the following:

- reading and understanding a government publication, a newspaper or television production
- speaking to other people (and judging whether or not they are 'informed')
- or searching the Internet.

In our working lives, accessing the Internet is commonplace, but it should be remembered that for many lifelong learners it is about as accessible as a first-class rail fare for a direct trip from London to Barnsley: that level of service is not available, there is no direct train service between those two places, and the financial resources for travel are limited.

Maps: access to information in libraries and on the Internet

In order to find information, people visit public libraries. In Sheffield this is a proven fact, illustrated by a recent study of attitudes to our public library system undertaken by Bob Usherwood at Sheffield University. The research was an affirmation of what everyone had hoped – that people need and use their libraries. The following comparison, shown in Table 14.1, between a real-time visit to a library and Internet access to obtain information serves to illustrate the different context of information searching in terms of the prerequisites for each type of search. There are common features, such as time, and search skills. But two quite different sets of search skills are involved – principally those of rigorous definition for Internet searching, and coping with classification schemes and the organization of knowledge for visits to libraries. Time factors are more directly comparable. What is notable is the different outlay that is required to find information, which is especially relevant given that neither of these sources guarantees access to the right information.

Table 14.1 *Comparison between obtaining information from a real-time library visit and Internet access*

Library visit	versus	Internet visit
Bus-fare	versus	Modem
Map	versus	Web searcher
Time to search	versus	Time to search
Photocopier	versus	Adobe Acrobat
Search skills	versus	Search skills
		PC/keyboard/disks etc.

Once information has been located, it still has to be assessed for its value and relevance to the question in hand. Judgment has to be applied before the information can be used. Pointers need to be in place before people can rely on the information they have found.

Library visits were far more commonplace in 1975, when people needing information were likely to see them as the authoritative place to go. The resources were, however, limited, and most people would use existing skills to attempt to find things. This led to people being more inclined to see library sources as the only ones they needed to use. The availability of information in electronic format, and the availability of Internet searching, has made the possible sources of information to search almost inexhaustible; the authority can be dubious; the skills required are new and not easily obtained; nor is the equipment required commonplace. Access to information is therefore constrained and made more difficult by technology. Yet our Prime Minister has stated that 'Technology has revolutionised the way we work and is now set to transform education.'[2]

Thus, our next question must be why are we about to embark on the extension of education by using technology? We are only able to do this with investment, collaboration and increasing understanding, and it is necessary to look at what the UK is doing to spread 'learning' to those who are currently excluded from it. The statistics for who is learning, shown in Table 14.2, are taken from the consultation paper on lifelong learning *The learning age*, published by the Department for Education and Employment in 1998. This, like many government reports, is available in hard copy as well as through the web.[3] The table shows the number of people that were in education last year.

Table 14.2 *Student numbers (all figures are for 1996/97, the latest complete statistical summary)*

Higher education	2.8 million students
Further education	3.8 million students
Adult education	1.2 million enrolments in November 1996
Workplace training	305,960 modern apprenticeships and youth training 'starts'

Of those students in higher education:

- 60% are mature
- 33% have alternatives to 'A' Levels
- 33% study part time
- there are equal numbers of men and women.

Amongst adult and vocational learners:

- 50% are under 40
- 90% are professional.

The nature of people in education is particularly important when it comes to providing appropriate skills development for information work. There is a wide variance in the IT and information handling expertise between school leavers and, for example, nurses undertaking degree-level courses who have had a gap since their last educational experience. This needs to be considered in the design and delivery of skills sessions, and that requires priority within the overall course content. We need time and opportunity to provide students with a learning experience in information use. The time when they are out of the lecture and seminar programme may have to be divided between the learning centre and time at work, earning the money needed for maintenance or for fees. Thus it is essential and important that information skills are integrated into the curriculum and given the priority to ensure that students acquire appropriate levels to support the academic content of their courses.

Bob Fryer found little reason to congratulate the UK with regard to the numbers involved in education in the late 1990s. The figures do prove that the more a person is exposed to learning, the higher the likelihood that he or she will want to carry on learning. This is supported by many initiatives that TECs support, particularly ELD initiatives, which get people hooked on learning something that they are really interested in to begin a process of lifelong involvement with learning.

Social inclusion for education

It would appear from the evidence in *The learning age*[3] that the major influences on those in any form of education (further, adult, higher or workplace) are:

- the social background they are from
- whether or not their parents received any further education
- which social group they come from.

There are particular issues for those from minority groups, those with disabilities and those from particular ethnic backgrounds. This is the challenge for lifelong learning: to reverse the effect of social exclusion and give individuals the opportunity and motivation to learn.

If we are to improve the numbers included in the education/learning cycle, we must tackle the excluded groups. Targeting education is one way; providing wider access points is another. We must accept that people are more inclined to learn if they have a social context for continuing learning. If parents and peers go on to further or higher education, it is seen to be more 'normal' than if you are the only one in your group. Social class and financial support for learning are important factors when it comes to maintaining learning – it is no longer free, and time and personal commitment are usually required to complete a course.

Government policy

At a national level we can examine the Government's response to the need for more learning. There have been a number of reports, of which three important ones are:

- the Kennedy Report[4] for widening (not increasing in volume, but directly targeting additional social groups) access to further education
- the University for Industry[5] with its plan to bring opportunities for educational activities to the attention of a larger number of people
- the Dearing Report on higher education.[6]

The Dearing Report may be seen by some to have been dropped from the priority list, but it contains some of the objective thinking and feasible ideas which found favour with many in higher education during its production and publication.

Compasses: how to find a learning opportunity in your community

People have to find their way to and around existing schemes. The range, level and nature of all available education opportunity is bewildering and confusing to those who are unfamiliar. Therefore they need some compasses to navigate the map of education successfully. The most common criterion to be met by any educational provision is that of access: education should be easy to locate, so is likely to be local in nature. What people want varies, but many are motivated by the qualifications at the end of a course rather than just the content. Understanding people's intentions for undertaking courses is as important as offering the right range of courses. Linked with this is the motivating factor for anyone taking on the commitment of a course of study. Many other factors will be taken into account, but one thing is certain: they will need the information skills to ensure that they make full use of the opportunity and make the most of their entry into education.

Case studies

What are the initiatives which are providing learning opportunities to people in local communities? The illustrations chosen represent a small proportion of the national enterprise, but all are local to Sheffield and are among those which are influencing people's attitudes to learning and to continuing the process into a lifelong habit. Most of these are described in web pages for the lead partner, but all are schemes for which collaboration is both desirable and necessary for success.

Barnsley's Education Information Network

The Education Information Network (EIN) was developed in Barnsley during 1997 as a response to the Single Regeneration Budget (SRB) strategy. Its aim was to enhance access to education through innovative approaches, and it was designed to improve the poor take-up of post-school education within the Barnsley area. Barnsley, in South Yorkshire, has one of the lowest participation rates in the country, and is a post-industrial town with a high level of unemployment and a low level of average earnings.

The EIN brought together libraries with the local Barnsley College to provide an infrastructure of support to those wishing to take advantage of open learning. Central to the initiative was the provision of materials, some print-based and others in hard copy, and there were plans to establish a distance learner support network with generic tutorial support for learners. Access points were established in ten library sites, three outreach facilities and one mobile workstation. Other links to the EIN included access to advice on education and training, management training opportunities for voluntary groups, neighbourhood development projects and 'Total Learning Communities', all of which were funded through the SRB route.

The main purpose was to improve access to education and information about education and training, thus increasing the numbers of people in post-16 education. However, a general enhancement to IT skills, and the improvement of education, cultural and leisure activities, were also provided for: Barnsley already had an IT strategy and it was important to complement that provision. The satellite village of Grimethorpe is best known for its brass band, but in this context it was to be the site for an electronic village hall. Other projects under design were a network for small and medium-size enterprises (SMEs) and City Challenge access points.

The project was awarded £450,000. It provided collaboration between Barnsley College, Barnsley Libraries Services and voluntary groups, with the lead being taken by the College. The Internet network and the development of the distance learning support were important strands to the initiative. There was a requirement for a fast and efficient communication system linking access points in town and the community. Materials needed development and distribution, and perhaps most important to the users was the provision of on-site tutorial support to assist those returning to studies or unfamiliar with study skills.

Sheffield's CITINET

In the city of Sheffield a new network has been developed. A smaller and more local 'University for Industry', CITINET was designed in direct response to the green paper, *The learning age.*[3] Some £300,000 has been directed towards the initiative from the Government's Skills Challenge fund, and the project has involved collaboration between employers and education providers in the widest sense. Again it is a further education college which has taken the lead.

CITINET exists to extend access to learning for all Sheffield's citizens. By engaging as many organizations as possible in the delivery of its aims, the founding partners have been assured of ownership and commitment from the start. The web page (<URL: http://www.citinet.org.uk/>) has a number of supporting statements from all types of organization and individuals who believe that this coordination is necessary to ensure that firms and individuals benefit from the large number of training and educational opportunities which exist within the Sheffield area. The joint effort put into this venture is likely to enhance the interest in, and take-up of, training as well as concentrating funding in the region.

Those familiar with the film *The full monty* may remember the backdrop for the scenes where the main characters first met up. They were getting to grips with new technology to complete application forms and CVs in what could have been a working men's club or local school. This is exactly the sort of venue that CITINET is intended to reach – a place to which people already go, as opposed to places that are unfamiliar.

Sheffield Libraries' Open for Learning

On a different scale, but nonetheless important to particular communities, is the Open for Learning initiative set up by Sheffield Libraries in 1994. National and local funding supported the project, and in 1998 over £22,000 was spent on materials and equipment. Like the other projects described, this one relies on the involvement of local employers as well as the individuals who participate as learners. There are other important initiatives which will complement the development of Open for Learning: the local CITINET (see above), the local government network, and national proposals stemming from the National Grid for Learning. It is important that the Sheffield Libraries were successful in their bid to run the Open for Learning initiative – the department has overcome some significant hurdles and decreased funding in recent years, and it is heartening to describe a project of this nature, starting in the Libraries Department, which affects people's futures in the information age.

The project aimed to provide open access to learning material which had a vocational bias, and to provide tutorial support for individuals working towards qualifications through study. The project used locally available sites (usually libraries) for the deposit of specialist materials, and in 1998 developed new homework centres to add to the number of sites where this service is available. As with the other projects described, encouraging the return to learning was an important objective for Open for Learning.

Sheffield Hallam University's Learning Centre

Against the backdrop of local initiatives is the creation of a department at Sheffield Hallam University known as the Learning Centre. Within this department a new building, designed to house a number of complementary teaching and learning units, was opened in October 1996. The Adsetts Centre has attracted considerable interest nationally and internationally, and in considering the landscape of information skills of the future, the Adsetts Centre exists as a model of modern practice for higher education. Its financing was derived from the fund established to upgrade library services following the Follett review of academic libraries carried out in 1994. Additional investment from the University ensured that the Centre embodied the University's aim to embrace new teaching and learning methodologies, using information technology to the students' advantage.

At the heart of the building is a library, but the department is much more than a collection of books. The information services include network and standalone electronic sources. Web information is collated and signposted following professional evaluation. The staff work at information desks to support users, not only in their search for, and use of, information but also by trouble-shooting software problems and offering advice on the best use of packages. The facilitation of computer-based learning (CBL) materials is the next challenge. The Learning and Teaching Institute works with academic colleagues to ensure good practice in the integration of CBL materials into course curricula and the subsequent assessment of students' work within the packages.

One of the important outcomes for any of the courses offered at Sheffield Hallam is competence in the use of IT and information. This work is part of the academic provision, and the course content is complemented by experience in the Learning Centre. Students gain information literacy – a skill that is important for graduates, as it is a vital element in their applications for jobs, for most of which IT experience is now a prerequisite. The economy needs graduates who are able to make an impact by using modern techniques and available technology. The information which can be accessed is vast, and companies need graduates who have had to evaluate and judge the usefulness of Internet sites. The availability of the University's web page on the Internet gives access to the Learning Centre's web page, and thus points to other sites already evaluated by information professionals who manage the Sheffield Hallam Learning Centre site. The Centre is providing the basics of knowledge management, and this is what will contribute to a company's success.

Information skills: successful navigation

The barriers to knowledge management or IT competency are a lack of skills coupled with an environment which does not provide the motivation or opportunity to learn. The Department of Academic Services Development at Sheffield Hallam University has recently completed a research investigation which measures a student's understanding of IT against his or her lecturer's understanding. The aim of this was to see if there was any correlation between the two, and the investigation included two or three case studies of schools where lecturers had good or less-good IT skills. The results were not conclusive, partly because the students who had access to IT and learning and who used it successfully relied on help and advice from peers and colleagues, including the Learning Centre and computing staff.

In the initiatives described above, one significant barrier is the availability of IT kit to provide an environment where the Internet can be accessed. PCs and software have to be constantly renewed. Virus checkers and maintenance software alone can be both time-consuming to install and monitor without major changes to Windows NT or Desktop 2000. Installing IT and Internet connections is not a once-and-for-all job.

A start, once made, has to be continued, and changes to the IT environment have to be faced. There has to be the conviction to continue, and the benefits to all need to be reviewed frequently. Once started the process of IT integration into our lives should be maintained. For us the process of continuing our professional development will attend to our work-based requirements. We have reviewed the way in which we establish priorities for staff development, and a recurrent need is for IT updating. We have developed much in-house expertise: just as we used to have subject specialists, we now have software specialists, with experts in e-mail, Word or PowerPoint. This is possible through investment in people as well as equipment. The forthcoming JISC funding for the people side of IT development is most welcome to those who appreciate the technology only inasmuch as it lends itself to application, and not for its own sake.

Challenges for librarians

As we speak, librarians are being presented with a huge challenge, which Grace Kempster outlines so eloquently (see Paper 15). The elements of this challenge are described below, but first we must start with a vision, for without any idea of what we are aiming for, we are indeed travelling on an uncharted map for which our compasses are redundant. There is risk attached, and to embark on this vision of the future requires us to forgo caution and proceed without always knowing the exact outcome. There needs to be some element of sustainability, and this will come from the involvement of librarians. The long-term storage of information in all its formats is of concern to libraries. Our skills must be practical and yet creative – there is nothing more soporific than words on a screen, which is why the multimedia productions in the Learning Centre are produced by artists using technology and not by computer experts attempting to design. Most of all, we need to draw on partnerships and collaborate with various experts to create the best possible learning environment for all those who need it.

Challenges for teaching staff

The issues for teaching staff and learners are much the same. The skills need is common to all: new materials have to be designed and integrated, and technology needs to be understood. The issues of independent learning, and the change from the lecture and seminar methods, have to be accepted, and time and opportunity for the much needed development has to be negotiated.

Challenges for learners

Learners have to understand that learning is not about listening to someone else who is an expert: there is much more personal responsibility; much more is expected of a learner; and there is a set of skills which has to be obtained before the new process can be fully exploited. Independent working has a higher profile than before, and group working is an accepted part of any learning process. The way in which people work is mimicked in education: we work collectively, drawing on the strengths of those who are the best and making up for shortcomings together. The practical skills of using IT and the intellect are complemented by the interpersonal skills, as in work, now in study.

Challenges for learning organizations

For any learning organization the challenges are:

- to develop programmes of study which meet new and existing needs (we must offer something to create a liking for learning)
- to meet the expectation of employers, who require people who know their way around IT and information
- to provide a mix of experience (it is no longer enough to rely on the lecturer as expert; people need the opportunity to test their own hypotheses and understand how to judge situations and knowledge)
- to exploit what is available, in terms of information and technology as well as information technology.

The challenge to society is lifelong learning

In the above illustrations of what is currently happening in Sheffield and its region to those in education and outside it, you will have seen a glimpse of the future. At the heart of all this is a belief that it is by education that we will achieve an information landscape peopled with those equipped for a learning society. In the preface to *Learning works*,[7] Helena Kennedy QC wrote:

> Education strengthens the ties which bind people, takes the fear out of difference and encourages tolerance. It helps people to see what makes the world tick, and the ways in which they, individually and together, can make a difference. It is the likeliest means of creating a modern, well-skilled workforce, reducing levels of crime and creating participating citizens.

This should be the aim for all of us – playing our part in an educational system that sets out to make us a society.

References

1   A special guest presentation given by Prof. R. H. Fryer (formerly Principle of the Northern College, now Director of New College and Assistant Vice-Chancellor for Lifelong Learning at the University of Southampton) entitled *Creating the learning age: challenges and opportunities* (the paper has not been included in this publication).

2   *Connecting the learning society: the National Grid for Learning*, London, HMSO, 1997.

3   *The learning age: a renaissance for a new Britain*, London, Department for Education and Employment, Cm 3790 HMSO, 1998. Available at <URL: http://www.lifelonglearning.co.uk.greenpaper/index.htm>.

4   Kennedy, H., *Learning works: main report of the Widening Participation Committee*, Coventry, The Further Education Funding Council, 1997.

5   University for Industry (UfI). Available at <URL: http://www.lifelonglearning.co.uk/ufi/index.htm>.

6   Dearing, R., *Higher education in the learning society: report of the National Committee of Inquiry into Higher Education*, London, HMSO, 1997. Available at <URL: http://www.leeds.ac.uk/niche/index.html>.

7   Kennedy, H. *op cit.*, Introduction.

Further reading

Higher education for the 21st century: the Government's response to the Dearing Report, London, HMSO, 1998. Available at
<URL: http://www.lifelonglearning.co.uk/dearing/index.htm>.

Fryer, R. H., *Learning for the twenty first century: first report of the Advisory Committee on Continuing Education and Lifelong Learning*, London, Department for Education and Employment, 1997.

Further education for the new millennium: the Government's response to 'Learning Works', London, HMSO, 1998. Available at
<URL: http://www.lifelonglearnng.co.uk/kennedy/index.htm>.

Brophy, P., Craven, J. and Fisher, S., *The development of UK academic library services in the context of lifelong learning*, Manchester Centre for Research in Library and Information Management (CERLIM), Manchester Metropolitan University, 1998.

The Net result: INSINC Report, National working party on social inclusion in the Information Society, 1997.

Morrison, M. *et al.*, *The role of libraries in a learning society*, London, The Library and Information Commission, 1998. Available at
<URL: http://www.lic.gov.uk/publications/learningsoc/index.html>.

University for Industry (UfI). Available at
<URL: http://www.lifelonglearning.co.uk/ufi/index.htm>.

Pathfinder prospectus for UfI. Available at
<URL: http://www.open.gov.uk/dfee/ufi/index.htm>.

Sheffield CITINET. Available at
<URL: http://www.citinet.org.uk/>.

Barnsley College Education Information Network. Available at
<URL: http://barnsley.ac.uk>
(e-mail a.best@barnsley.ac.uk).

15

Dawning of the age
THE HORIZON FOR POWERFUL PEOPLE-CENTRED LIBRARIES

Grace Kempster

Introduction

The purpose of this paper is to examine the future and share some thoughts on the issues that will be with affect libraries in the early years of the third millennium. It is a truism that ages are only named after they have happened and that only with hindsight can key decision nodes be identified such as the Renaissance or the Industrial Revolution. We would appear to be living at just such a nexus, the repercussions of which will be felt long into the future, as libraries transform themselves into virtual and actual information and knowledge exchange zones.

Although the changes ahead are technology-led, there can surely be no doubt that they will pioneer a transformation of both people and organizations. In this paper, I use an illustration of a possible future to consider the non-technological aspects of the impending changes and from these draw some further conclusions.

The political environment

Nearing the end of the first term of the current government, one can envisage a context of transformed local governance within a context of fused national governance across Europe – a new empire of regions still seeking to retain and champion cultural differences and preserve local identity and memory, against the tide of bland globalism.

In Australia this was expressed rather well:[1]

> As a society we have choices to make. If we ignore the opportunities of the information society we run the risk of being left behind as other countries introduce new services and make themselves more competitive: we will become consumers of other countries' content and technologies rather than our own.

There is a move towards a culture swamped by the global society – as Ted

Hughes says, 'to melt the folk into one puddle'.[2]

This Government will have achieved its resolve to create a National Education Service following on from the National Curriculum, the National Literacy Strategy and that rather quaint National Year of Reading back in the late 1990s. Private-sector influence will be widespread, while schooling will start earlier, go on for longer and be continuous throughout the year.

Lifelong learning had a slow start, but it is beginning to be unfashionable not to attend a people's university – there is always one nearby (it used to be a public library) – a college of further education or a university.

The battle goes on to merge the funding for publicly funded libraries (public and academic), even though they have been acting seamlessly for years, to the extent of including the interchange of staff. Learning choreographers are much in demand for individual navigation, rather like personal trainers back in the 90s. They come largely from arts and marketing backgrounds, but also include ex-teachers: ever since the playing field was levelled with upskilling for all library staff, the technological skills are a given (everyone has them), and it is the people skills that count. These learning choreographers sell their skills privately, and it is an attractive, high-profile line of work.

Public libraries have become trusts, and while all deliver the same core services through the people's network, they have developed differently across the country:

1   Some are really an 'arm's-length' democratic machine: a citizen shop, a local town hall where people vote, video-conference with their MEP and complete tax returns.
2   Others have extended their early development as homework centres, and now look more like schools and colleges combined, with many ages learning together.
3   Some have maintained through charging their pleasure/leisure role, and complement (and work closely with) the bookselling and publishing indus-tries, and act as culture houses.

At regional level, there is control of all libraries in a zone, and new librarians must know about rights negotiations and intellectual property management, as well as standards for ongoing skills enhancement, if they want to retain their permit to practise. Insurance is high since the first case was lost – someone did die of igno-rance.

Local government as we knew it is unrecognizable: direct-issues voting and referenda are the norm, and the elected mayors with a paid board maintain their power base through short-term, people-popular policies. It is a good thing that public libraries got out when they did and became regionally accountable. It also means that those which are now citizen shops are able to negotiate good and profitable deals on delivering electronic governance at arm's length from the Government.

The Government's mantra of opportunity for the many and not just for the few has credibility in one sense, but not in another. When public libraries were networked, they sold themselves short and allowed charging for electronic media. It is still free to go into what used to be a public library – and you can use the self-service facility for books – but the important electronic sources are only available for a fee. The staff there will help if they have time, but they are often too busy profiling multimedia learning packs for fee-paying customers on an individual basis.

This bitter-sweet pastiche of the future evokes a number of key issues for us now. Although the technological global glass web is the catalyst, few must doubt that enormous organizational change will follow.

People

New librarians will come from other backgrounds, and the emphasis will be on leadership, connectivity, innovation and creativity – making new and powerful connections increasingly on an individual basis between people and their knowledge needs. In 1995, Julie Sabaratnam foresaw the paradigm shift for librarians (see Table 15.1).[3]

Table 15.1 *Paradigm shift in libraries*

From		To
Custodians of books	→	Service-oriented information provider
One medium	→	Multiple media
Own collection	→	Library without walls
In good time	→	Just in time
In-sourcing	→	Out-sourcing
Local reach	→	Global reach
We go to the library	→	The library comes to us

Public libraries possess both a strength and a weakness in relation to this transformation: on the one hand, they are dealing daily with the greatest variety of humanity and need for knowledge – a powerful matrix that offers an enquire-within-upon-anything service and strength in diversity. The weakness is perhaps that some staff are closer to the custody of the product than to the service: unless they transform themselves into adaptive, outgoing, entrepreneurial people-focused workers, they will simply lose out. Many frontline staff are closer to the needs of users, and therefore able to suggest imaginative and new ways of service and product delivery.

New librarians will emerge both from the ranks of the current non-professionals and from a range of other professions.

Services

That old cataloguing adage 'the more you collocate, the more you scatter' rings true. For some global knowledge will be brought and woven together, while others will be left further and further behind, thus creating a potentially damaging and destructive underclass of non-learners, who threaten everyone by upsetting the apple-cart of economic prosperity.

Organization

This Government wishes to see through radical change and prizes above all innovation and 'third ways' of thinking. It would appear that trusts offer just that third way for public libraries, where their catholic learning role will engulf that of academic libraries; salaries can be commensurate with new skills; and hybrid alliances with the private sector can be managed more easily without the slow-to-change encumbrance of the local-authority bureaucratic machine.

Whether the power base for this new organization will be at regional or national level is not yet clear – perhaps it will be both. National accountability and common content will increase so that, at least potentially, 'Knowledge and learning for all without exception' becomes our mantra.

User power

It is salutary to recall that *New library: the people's network*[4] was and is championed by a non-librarian, Matthew Evans: his drive and energy stems from his standpoint as a user and a discovery of the sleeping giant that is the public library service. It seems to offer more potential for direct accountability – to users. The question is really this: will it be to the powerful few or the disenfranchised many? We are living in a new social climate where social inclusion does matter even to the people already included.

Choices today

The immediate danger is that public libraries will value themselves short in the imminent negotiations for bandwidth and universality, and that library leaders will lack the passion, impatience and perseverance to seize the future and defend the indefinable that makes public libraries such popular places. Geese and golden eggs come to mind.

The introduction to *New library: the people's network* conveys much of the argument:

> The library is an enormously powerful agent for change: accountable to and trusted by people and integral to education, industry, government and the community.[5]

We must not lose that trustworthiness of being on the side of all knowledge-seekers; we must use the technologies to assuage the disabilities of distance, and understand the psychology of choice and actual use.

If we make the right choices now, we can be the answer to social inclusion, the answer to the learning and knowledge society in creation, the answer to a future of bright independent thinkers and economic prosperity.

Libraries are about information and imagination: we must remain true to the underlying reasons for our existence. I once called us 'powerhouses of revolution and independent thought'[6] and I still believe that we are actually about freedom and finding out – places of choice, and people learning because they want to. If we don't exist, be in no doubt that others will leap in with a profit-centred rather than a learner-centred agenda, and those that have the wherewithal to find their way around the agenda-laden maze of learning will succeed, while others will not and will be left behind in an under-culture which threatens to implode.

The agenda of social inclusion matters – without it, we are all affected. As Bill Lucas of the Campaign for Learning has put it, 'It is those who do not have the capacity to learn who will be the new disadvantaged of the 21st century.'

Hannah Pollard (aged 12) expresses so well the 'libraryness' that can exist virtually as well as actually. We need to have the courage to fight for her vision, and to voice the meanings and values of the New Library, providing connected and very real opportunities for life:

My library's like a lighthouse
It illuminates my mind
With sunshine trips to far off lands
Enlightening journeys of every kind
Going to my library
I've travelled in space and time
In sounds and pictures, words and music
Prose and sometimes rhyme
When all is dark and black as night
My library shines its welcome light
A beacon on the dullest day
Taking me places far away.[7]

The future

The golden handcuffs of accountability may threaten the innate trustworthiness of the librarian, but the solution lies in the question. As we get ever closer to the personal librarian model of delivery, we can thrive on being uniquely on the side of the user.

We can manage robust and strong new alliances, leading to impact and life enhancement, new horizons, for the adult of tomorrow.

We have everything to gain by being accountable directly to our users. From this perspective will emerge radical approaches to the ways we structure and people our services. We urge Government to join up its thinking on lifelong learning and on the information society, but we need to plan for joined-up library and information services that actively lead people on to new services and new and changing expectations.

Conclusion

Librarians and information scientists will shortly be the most important profession in the country – think for a moment about what that means for you and your service, and for how you view yourselves – as the mainspring of national identity, as generals of memories bigger than armies.

At the close of that grand film *Gone with the wind*, Vivien Leigh stands at the hilltop, scans the horizon and says enigmatically 'Tomorrow is another day.' Tomorrow is our day – let's make it so.

References

1   Broadband Services Expert Group, *Networking Australia's future: final report of the Broadband Services Expert Group*, 1994. Available at <URL: http://www.dca.gov.au/pubs/network/toc.htm>.

2   Hughes, E., 'Hear it again', a poem written for the *New library: the people's network* report.

3   Sabaratnam, J. S., 'Transforming libraries to support change and growth' in Dempsey, L., Law, D. and Mowat, I., *Networking and the future of libraries 2: managing the intellectual record*, London, Library Association Publishing, 1995, 62–75.

4   Library and Information Commission, *New library: the people's network*, London, Library and Information Commission, 1997. Also available at <URL: http://www.ukoln.ac.uk/services/lic/newlibrary/>.

5   *Ibid.*, Introduction.

6   Kempster, G., 1996 National Libraries Week, Comment, Channel 4, broadcast November 1998.

7   [Unpublished poem written for library-run competition].

The future: widening the horizon

16

Unifying our cultural memory
COULD ELECTRONIC ENVIRONMENTS BRIDGE THE HISTORICAL ACCIDENTS
THAT FRAGMENT CULTURAL COLLECTIONS?

David Bearman and Jennifer Trant

Introduction

Networked access to cultural information resources

Despite promises that connectivity will result in universal accessibility of
resources for the public, students and scholars at all levels, the reality of networked access to cultural resources is, and will remain for quite some time, a
political aspiration. The barriers to universal accessibility of networked resources
are many. The ones which interest us in this paper are not those of social policy
– the vast effort and cost of converting our cultural heritage into digital form and
the provision of affordable access to users worldwide – but rather barriers intrinsic to the idea of access to resources under distributed control. Specifically, we will
focus here on the consequences of centuries of collecting and cataloguing the
documented history of the human race, of constructing reference resources about
people, places and things, and building an economic system to support commercial publishing. Ironically, many of these barriers to access have been created by
the very efforts to enable it.

This seems perverse when first encountered, but once considered it becomes
not only perfectly reasonable but obvious. By classifying a frying pan as a cook-
ing utensil, we don't consider it as a copper tool, or a potential murder weapon,
or a ladle, as certainly as by describing it in English we preclude access to it in
French. By describing a collection of many pots as the household belongings of
Benjamin Franklin, we call attention to only one aspect of their potential significance, while obscuring the fact that they include a pot for rendering tallow, which
could be of significance to someone researching commerce in candles.
Biographical dictionary entries will necessarily be too brief to tell us about a cook
in Benjamin Franklin's household. The economics of publishing on paper ensure
that more complete entries can never be financed; the mechanics of printing and

the cost of first-copy production ensure that new, tangential information cannot be contributed by a reader and made available to others.

In this paper we will explore some fairly regular distortions of this kind, which are related to the approaches society has taken to managing cultural heritage and to publishing. We will examine some possible strategies for bridging the barriers to access that have been created by specific traditions of custody and documentation. Our exploration of these issues will cross from theory into the arena of technology and practice and back again several times, because the methods which the community of humanities researchers has employed are intertwined with existing technologies and economic constructs.

Intellectual barriers

Actors in the discovery and retrieval process

In December 1994, at a seminar at the Getty Art History Information Program (subsequently renamed the Getty Information Institute) involving staff, consultants and members of the CIMI project, a structural model of the research process was developed (and articulated by Bearman) which represents the universe of information discovery, retrieval and use as consisting of three agents (see Figure 16.1):[1]

- users
- repositories
- reference resources.

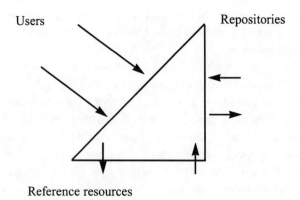

Fig. 16.1 *The universe of information discovery, retrieval and use*

The information discovery and retrieval process is a dialogue between these actors. *Users* formulate queries in their own terms, at their own level of granularity and with the preconceptions, capabilities and limitations of their own uses in mind. They put their queries to *repositories* – aggregators of material which have assembled collections of varying degrees of thematic or intellectual coherence, and where holdings are catalogued in a manner that best supports the mission and administrative requirements of each institution. Often repositories operate with a different frame of reference that does not conform in terminology, granularity or functionality to the requirements of the user.

Reference resources, including secondary and tertiary literature, provide one way to bridge the different historical and administrative perspectives of holding institutions. If the end-user receives a less-than-adequate response from the repository and is serious enough to continue researching, he or she is likely to turn to the secondary and tertiary literature in order to find other facts, concepts or terms, possibly at different levels of granularity, that might better match the cataloguing practices of the repositories. Thesauri, indexes, citations and bibliographic tools, biographies, gazetteers and other contextualizing resources, contain additional terminology and references that can be employed in a follow-up query.

Armed with the most complete set of relevant terminology and context, the user may still find query results less than satisfactory. Often the correspondences between (on the one hand) the user's mental model of the structures of the data and (on the other hand) the data structures implemented in each repository are imperfect. Ideally, repositories could map their view of the world to a common data model, through which the user's query would be translated to the repository and the response translated to the user. However, models may not map well: specific information available from the sources may not be known to the user. And those aspects of the sought-for evidence which are relevant to the user may not have been described in the repository as a consequence of its cataloguing practices. Each may be impeded by different missing data.

The purposes of the actors and their consequences

A model of the system of cultural documentation that takes into account the approaches to finding that documentation which can be taken by a user can be represented within this triangle.

The user seeks to satisfy a purpose

The first face of the triangle shown in Figure 16.1 represents the users and their questions.

In the simplest model of user interaction with the system, the user asks a question which he or she believes will yield an answer suited to the purpose. This question is directed to staff in a repository, who interpret the question and answer to the extent that they can with their documentation. Repository staff may refer to reference resources to try to understand the question better. If dissatisfied with the answer, the user may also look in reference resources to find additional terms, related concepts and other clues to an improved formulation of the query. But in the most direct use of an information resource, the query/response dialogue is unmediated.

Typically, user profiles (in an anonymized form) and users' queries are collected for analysis. We are interested in:

- who uses systems
- what classes they might belong to
- what resources they are reviewing
- what searches they make.

Sometimes repositories are also interested in whether or not these searches are successful. Too often these two tangible aspects of the user are all that is represented to a system.

However, between the user and the query is the user's *purpose*. This purpose reflects the actual problem that led to the question reflected in the query, *and* it is what must be satisfied if the interaction between the user and the system is to be perceived as successful. The user's purpose dictates what information content and form will satisfy the user, but it does not express itself directly.

Different repositories: documentation purposes and disciplinary schemas

One of the major reasons why this simple model often fails to produce a result that satisfies the user is a mismatch between the documentation and control methods employed by the repositories and the user's sense of the questions. Documentation and control methods are the strategies for organizing knowledge employed by the publishers of the reference resources and the staffs of the repositories. These methods are optimized to serve the kinds of users each resource anticipates and the management requirements of the materials which the methods document. Not surprisingly, these methods work less well for users with points of view and purposes for inquiry other than those traditionally served by the repository or reference resource, or considered in the design of an information management system.[2]

The second face of the triangle model represents the many types of repositories which collect various genres of cultural documentation (see Figure 16.2). Genre is the critical aspect of this documentation; while each repository may also collect many different media, we emphasize their intellectual characteristics rather than their physical ones, because these are what lead to most of the barriers to providing access. The physical media may create conservation difficulties, require special care in copying or delivery, or require users to acquire special systems to use them, but each of these problems can be overcome (possibly though increased investment). Genres – which can be defined as information packages distinctive because of the manner in which their content is presented – include poetry, prose, song, paintings, motion pictures, numeric data etc. More detailed prose genres distinguish, for example, between scientific articles, diaries, laboratory or field notes, and correspondence. Genres of motion pictures include, among others, feature films, documentaries, newsreels, cartoons, previews and nature films. Visual works may be paintings, sculptures, installations or drawings, and drawings themselves may be architectural, preliminary studies or cartoons.

Each genre has characteristics which are crucial to a correct 'reading' of its content. These characteristics can be described, and may be the subject of inquiry, but typically users are expected by repositories to understand the nature and limitations of the genres they use and to interpret their information content with a sophisticated understanding of these constraints.[3] In addition, for many valid intellectual and historical reasons, different types of cultural repositories have developed distinctive documentary practices, even though they may hold the same genres. Rationales for diverging practices include different requirements for

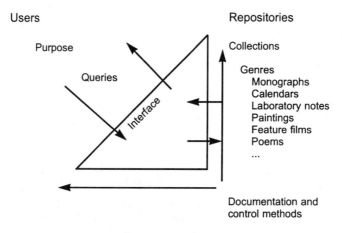

Fig. 16.2 *The many types of repositories*

control, preservation and access, and the expectations of their primary user group, which may have a distinct disciplinary background, and therefore a particular tradition of using particular kinds of documentation.

Consider, for example, the treatment of a large body of diverse materials from a single estate. The business and personal records of the donor would be housed in the archives. Archives traditionally accession large collections of paper, which have been organized by their original owner to reflect the way in which the owner conducted business and his or her life. These might be described using the ISAD(G).[4] Archivists do not reorganize these collections internally, nor do they index the items within them, because their coherence is provided by the life and/or processes that they supported. The same individual's books would be given to a library, which will treat each volume individually, making decisions about which, if any, are duplicates, and which unique copies require special care. Each work will be described separately, indexed by author, title and subject, and most likely catalogued using AACR2 in the MARC format (see **Select list of acronyms**). The volumes will be reorganized on the shelves with other volumes of similar subject matter. This reflects the perspective of library clients, who seek individual titles for the content they hold, not for the fact that they were part of an estate. Artefacts from this estate might be accessioned by a history museum and treated in two quite distinct ways: those artifacts collected purposefully 'as a collection' might be kept together, while those artefacts which the individual collected in the course of everyday life might be dispersed among their holdings. If the individual was extremely important historically, the items collected in everyday life might also be kept as a unit. In either case, they are likely to provide provenance as only one access point among many, and to catalogue the items themselves at least superficially. If the collection of our donor was one of art, an art museum would describe each work separately, providing a number of access points including artist, title, medium and donor. However, it is unlikely that any two museums would treat the same collection in exactly the same way.[5]

These major distinctions between archives, libraries, and cultural or art museums can be refined and extended to explain methods prevalent in slide collections, zoos, botanical gardens, local history societies and many other types of institution. In addition, we can overlay on these rough differences practices which relate directly to the specific types of clients served by the institution. Thus, Winterthur Museum, a historical museum with a clientele of connoisseurs and graduate students in decorative arts and museology, is notable for providing access to its collections according to the artisans who made the artefacts, the designers, the owners and many other methods of concern to students of high culture. Most local historical collections would be happy to provide approaches by decade, by social class and by types of objects.

Suffice it to say, at this point, that these purposes – that is, the specific purposes of the curators and clients – are combined with the mission of the repository itself in determining methods and granularity of control. These perspectives affect such basic functions as the conservation and preservation of works themselves. Many art museums can provide an account of all the storage and exhibition spaces in which a particular work has resided over a number of years, and the number of lumens to which it was exposed. A very exceptional rare book library may also be able to provide such data. Most libraries know how often a work was checked out, but they don't know how frequently it was consulted and (usually purposefully) do not collect information about who used it. Archives, on the other hand, can usually account for all uses, and users, of a particular record group for many years.

Recording documentation about things serves many purposes, and institutions that do not share purposes tend to accumulate different data. The attributes of things recorded in one institution differ significantly from the attributes of these same types of things collected by other institutions. In the end, none of these may be the salient aspects sought by the researcher.

Part of learning the methodology of research is developing a familiarity with different kinds of documentation and control methods.[6] Library user training in North America will teach you that library catalogues can be searched by author, title and subject term. Visiting an archivist and becoming oriented to a finding aid system will show that archival records can be searched by who owned them and sometimes by who received them, and how they are organized. But special needs in subject-specific institutions extend these generalities.[7] Film libraries can often be searched by names of actors as well as directors and producers, script-writers, cinematographers, etc. These differences in methods of documentation and control reflect the management requirements of the collecting organizations. But they may not support the needs of potential users for access to materials in these repositories.[8]

Organization of materials, physically and/or intellectually, is based on a schema or logical construct. The schema employed by repositories or reference resources of a particular type tend to be quite similar to each other – libraries like libraries, archives like archives, gazetteers like gazetteers etc. Users also have schemas – art historians may focus on the visual output of individuals, archaeologists are interested in the items collected at a particular site, material historians study artefacts in use in a particular time. Indeed, the same user will employ many different schemas depending on a particular purpose. And because users have been trained in research methods and want to get results, they also employ schemas that they believe are used in the systems they are trying to use. In this case, they become victims, both of the difficulty in translating between their own schema and that of the repository, and of any mistake they make in understanding the schema used by the repository.

Knowledge models and reference data resources

The third face of the triangle model represents the many reference resources that a person could consult in search of an answer to a question (see Figure 16.3). Reference resources could be used in place of, on the way to, or in addition to, primary materials in cultural repositories. Typically, these reference resources answer questions about people, places, events, things or ideas, and provide definitions, alternative terms, citations to other resources, and pointers to parallel, similar or related concepts.

Users, quite rightly, are often catholic about what kind of repository holds the information they need in their research. They are aware that the same kinds of sources, or different kinds of sources about the same theme, can be found in many kinds of repositories, even if they are unaware of the particular accidents of fate, politics and time that have influenced what a particular repository holds. But they have learned that they cannot be indifferent to the tradition by which the evidence they seek is being managed, or they will not find it. As any reference librarian knows, they have learned to approach each institution by asking questions that do not directly reflect what they hope to learn, but rather what they expect to find. They try to translate their own model of the problem into what they imagine will be the language and organizational schema of the collecting institution.

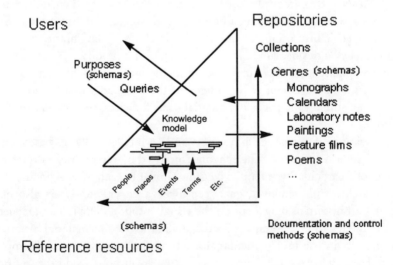

Fig. 16.3 *The knowledge model*

The mismatch between descriptive standards and user needs is sometimes acknowledged:

This focus on provenance, as a means of providing access to archival holdings, has produced archival descriptive tools that are largely creator and document oriented. As such, these descriptive reference tools frequently fail to adequately describe the content of material for researchers.[9]

Needless to say, this process is fraught with pitfalls, and continually amazes the reference staff, who often do not understand why this seemingly indirect strategy is regularly employed. But the reference librarian's complaint – 'Why don't they just ask for what they want?' – reveals an ignorance of the limitations imposed by the schemes that libraries employ to describe their holdings. Users are often right in realizing that if they asked for what they wanted, in their own terms, they would not receive an answer.

It is relatively easy to imagine a simpler strategy that would produce a more precise result. Users would translate their own models into a common form of expression and ask questions against a documentary model expressed in that same form. But are such translations possible?

Well, maybe. A more complex model of the relationship between users, reference resources and repositories is one in which the schemas of the documentation (both the genres and the methods of control) are explicitly declared to a *knowledge model* (see Figure 16.3). The user's query criteria could also be mapped to the knowledge model. The knowledge model thereby mediates between the points of view of the user and the resources. The cross-walks developed in the Dublin Core discussions are first-generation versions of such tables of equivalent concepts in different documentation systems.[10]

A shared knowledge model with common 'categories' in queries also makes it possible to position reference resources between the user and the information repository. Mapping to the model enables the user's query to be deconstructed by the system and put first, and automatically, to the reference resources. In this first stage of query processing, additional references, terminology and context can be included, to enable the query to succeed in repositories where, for example, more specialist terminology is used. The commonly modelled query can then be put to the repositories in terms of their known (declared) schemas. The result of this enhanced query can be expressed in terms of the user's schema, offering the user a much more complete and precise result, in a form that is easily understood.

Very simple examples of the use of model-mediated inquiry can be seen in user requests for primary documents about the author Mark Twain, or maps of the city of St Petersburg: Twain was, of course, a pseudonym for Samuel Clemens, and most documentation about the life of that individual will be found under his own name; St Petersburg is a place that has been known by many names throughout history. Looking up Mark Twain first in a biographical dictionary (or 'authority file' that collocated alternate names), and St Petersburg in a geographical thesaurus, historical atlas or gazetteer, would provide the alternative names that should be searched.

The goal of integrated access

There are several different kinds of problems encountered when attempting to translate between schemas. Examples are necessary to explore each of these points, since the principles here seem very abstract. The Getty/CIMI examination of users' questions is helpful:[11]

1 The simplest problem is that the value assigned to an attribute being sought is not in the vocabulary of the user. Karol Schmiegle recounted the following observations from the Winterthur Museum: 'We may record that the object is made of leaded glass, but the person seeing this material may wonder why, if the object is made out of lead it can be so transparent.'[12]

2 The attribute may be present in both the user's model and the documentation system, but no value has been assigned by the cataloguer. 'Do you have any film of the last V-1 to fall on London?' requires a knowledge of both the nature of a V-1 and a complex temporal inference.

3 The attributes being sought by the user, though present in the user's world view, may not be present in the world view of the repository. 'What images of women are there that are created by gay men?' implies a level of detail in both biographies of artists and image subject analysis that may not be documented.

4 The attribute may be present, but it may belong to a different entity. 'What items were found in the Sutton Hoo horde?' may require searching documentation of the excavation in order to find it by its vernacular name, and then finding objects that were excavated at a particular, scientifically identified site.

But many other questions required a knowledge far beyond that of one information resource:

1 'Do you have any miniatures depicting the "churning of the milky ocean"?' requires a detailed knowledge of Indian iconography to know where, in what object genres and which contexts this might be shown.

2 'When were fish knives first used?' requires us to determine the questioner's meaning of the word 'fish knife', and to understand the concept of 'first use' and the purpose of the questioner. It could be answered equally well by a Brueghel image of fishing that shows a knife, a Victorian fish service, or a fish slice (which is a serving tool).

3 'What is the essence of minimalist art?' may not be answerable, and certainly wasn't asked to generate a list of titles linked to examples of minimalist art. An article on the subject might be more appropriate.

4 Knowing the purpose of the user is essential to determining an appropriate answer. 'When was the Mona Lisa on exhibit at the National Gallery of Art?' takes on a new meaning when it is asked by the Andy Warhol Museum.

But often this survey revealed that real questions reflect assumptions and misconceptions, and that providing an appropriate response often involves a number of stages of refinement and disambiguation. A favourite question from a teacher, 'Do you have any pictures of interiors designed by Mr Rococo, suitable for framing?' revealed just how bundled concepts are in some users' minds. Once the confusion of 'Mr Rococo' had been dealt with, the attributes of what is really being sought here are very complex. Queries about the availability of a reproduction, genre of art, implied subject matter, audience interest level would return little from traditional collections documentation systems.

It is easy to dismiss 'Mr Rococo' but we can't ignore other more accurate queries for 'paintings by modern French artists suitable for copying for my tenth grade world history class study of inter-war France'. These create equally complex problems. The copyright status of the works of modern European painters is highly unlikely to be recorded anywhere, because it is known as a consequence of the general provisions of copyright laws. Subject matter is seldom recorded in art museums, and here the user is seeking a subject with an implied relevance to history beyond being art. Genre terms such as 'painting' are correctly applied only to the painting itself, so a photograph or poster of the work (which is in fact what the user is seeking) would, in art repositories, be described as a photograph and not as a painting. Finally, the nationality of the artist is an attribute of the artist and not of the painting, and is, in addition, not as straightforward as generally imagined, since the nationality of an artist at the time of painting a particular picture may not be that which is generally recorded in biographical databases (the nationality at time of either birth or death). Information recorded as an attribute of the painting which looks like the nationality of the painter may relate to the place the work was painted.

With correct knowledge of the values being sought by the user in a normalized model of the domain, the system can begin to seek resources that might satisfy the inquiry. Note, however, in our example that the operative term is what the teacher wants to do with the result. It could have been a publisher seeking an illustration or a dealer seeking to buy the work of art itself – the limitations of a successful inquiry are that it must yield a result suited for the stated purpose of use. Models must recognize that the goal of the query may not be an object or artefact, but a process or procedure that will guide a future action, or provide context for a past one. McCorry and Morrison report that 'Information relating to procedures – activities involved in the acquisition or management of the object ... represented 13.3% of those queries sampled that fell into their broad category of "information about the objects" '.[13] The verbs are as important as the nouns.

If we again imagine our schoolteacher looking for 'modern French paintings', the system could reasonably assist this user at the discovery phase of research by correctly modelling the query itself. Is the user really interested in an artist whose nationality is French, regardless of location during the inter-war years? Or is he or she more interested in art created in France, regardless of the nationality of the artist, or perhaps (and this is most likely, given the target audience and pedagogic purpose) in artists whose subject matter was France? By explicitly displaying the mapping that the system presumed, and perhaps prompting to show (from previous discourse frames recorded in a query database) that other possible models exist, the system could disambiguate the initial query, and help the user to refine the question into one that could produce the desired result.[14]

Mechanisms: metadata declarations, common models and shared vocabularies

Bridging the intellectual perspectives of users and documentalists will require explicit declaration by the creators of documentation of the schemas (formal rules and data models) which they are employing, and methods to assess the attributes of each user's requirements. These schemes operate at the levels of data structure (what attributes are described) and data values (what terms are used). The data structure reflects the sum of all elements deemed relevant to discourse in a domain – in this case the domain of the management of this documentation rather than the domain of the disciplines whose research questions the documentation is intended to support.

On the surface, the declaration of such schemes by content creators is fairly simple.[15] Each repository will need to define its methods (or at least its methods with respect to any given type of data source). Information resources, in the same genres, documented by the repository will have the same attributes. The cataloguing and documentation standards we now implement provide the key building blocks in this part of the solution. Tools such as the 'Categories for the description of works of art'[16] and the CIDOC Data Model (in both relational and object-oriented form)[17] provide prototypes for the more generalized expression of information content.

However, the problem of identifying the perspectives of the user is more complex. Schemes reflecting user needs including the user's language, age/interest, purpose and knowledge as reflected in those terms are essential to understanding a query. Determining language is quite easy, though bridging it as a barrier to access could require a significant long-term investment in the translation of access. Establishing the age level and interest of a user is only possible with repeated interactions, so the system must build such knowledge over the course of the 'reference interview'. Correctly defining the user's purpose, on which much of the success of the research strategy depends, requires the explicit recognition of objectives as a separate component of the query formulation. Plotting terms posed by a user on the knowledge landscape that the user wishes to traverse, and providing the appropriate map, requires that the system be aware of templates for a wide range of known discourse structures and that the user be involved implicitly or explicitly in the selection of structures appropriate to the search.[18]

Users employ terms in their queries which identify attributes of the resources they seek that distinguish those resources from the general universe, but these attributes are most likely not the ones that are actually of interest to the user (since they are going to be common to all the resources which the user wishes to examine). In searching, the system must not only find resources, however documented, which are most likely to have the attributes identified; it must report them by displaying terms actually used in their documentation and additional attributes usually present in the discourse frame of the user. If the user provides enough terms as part of the query, it is possible that a sufficient breadth of attributes will be selected to define this discourse frame, but users have learned that search systems are unlikely to return results if given too many of terms, so sophisticated searchers do not provide language that defines their domain. Instead, only a few attributes will be specified in a query.[19]

Other terms could be proposed to a user based on a partial match with one or more discourse profiles. What would need to happen in this scenario is that discourse frames defined and stored in the system will be mapped against queries. If the user is employing (mentally) a discourse frame that has previously been registered with the system, then the system can automatically fill in the 'slots' (attributes) of that frame not specified by the user's query but implied by the form of the question. In effect, the system means proposing a number of schemas to the user so that the user can select that which fits closest to his or her needs.

Alternatively, a more experienced or sophisticated user could explicitly declare the schema in which the user is working. This declaration would likewise define relevant discourse frames and enable the system to seek to identify attributes missing in the user query. Network architectures, and software applications, to support this kind of functionality are in the early stages of discussion as part of the implementation of the Resource Description Framework (RDF) in XML. Front-ends would be required to negotiate user schemas in an intelligent way.

Key here is the abstract declaration of a series of schemas that characterizes the points of view of users and the documentation practices of repositories. These would need to be expressed in a formal language, and mapped between disciplines. A means of establishing consensus between those holding this viewpoint would need to be established to ensure that it correctly reflected their assumptions. In developing and articulating schemas, the abstract model must be pushed far enough so that its concrete implications for all the stakeholders are clear. Task groups of representative professionals from appropriate institutions with the correct leadership could achieve framework schemas in a year or two. Such groups would be defining the abstract types of user discourse frames, identifying repository documentary practices, and determining the relevant genres of primary, secondary and tertiary documentation structures.

But such conceptual models will only define a possible path; implementation requires that the institutions and individuals in the system perceive advantages, indeed sufficient economic advantages, in implementing the system. In practical terms, this means they must either be pushed by the costs imposed on users by inefficient searches in distributed environments (this has been the impetus for the Dublin Core activity) or pulled by the competitive advantage of offering a better searching functionality. The potential exists for a fully integrated information space, within which scholarly humanistic research could be enabled. The triangle model provides a framework for parsing the problems we must overcome, and where we need to go to find the answers. But it doesn't suggest how to provide a solution that will fit into the social process of the user's research.

Social barriers: the humanities research process

Integrating access to, and use of, diverse primary, secondary and tertiary documentation in the humanities requires an understanding of the research process; different functional and documentation requirements apply to different phases of the research process. To design systems that address the intellectual distance between the potential user, the documentation needed, and the methods of control employed by publishers and repositories, requires us to imagine, and implement, a system that translates between knowledge models. However, without a better understanding of what kinds of knowledge are germane to what kinds of inquiries, and the way in which that information is ultimately processed, the task of developing a sort of universal 'knowledge translator' becomes completely unmanageable. Limiting the scope of the task, by dividing it into phases and then understanding the specific requirements of each phase, may make it more manageable.[20]

We begin at a disadvantage in understanding humanities research processes. The humanities have not generated the same kind of self-conscious research programme that we find in courses in the history, philosophy and social study of science or medicine. We cannot readily point to a literature that describes for us 'how humanists work' in the way that Woolgar and Latour[21] describe how scientists work in their seminal book *Laboratory life*. We have some multidisciplinary surveys of changing research methods, such as the Research Libraries Group studies of the early 1990s[22] and a few penetrating and interesting anecdotal reports, such as the Brown University studies on which *Object, image, inquiry*[23] was based, but nowhere, to our knowledge, is there a detailed, self-conscious, scholarly report on how humanists 'do it'.[24]

Stages in the research process

Research is a multi-stage iterative process involving a series of tasks. These typically take place in sequence but may occur out of order. We think of research as taking place in two realms: that of the information provider (where the researcher is *getting* information), and that of the user (where the researcher is *using* information). Getting information can be divided into two phases: discovery and retrieval. Using information can be subdivided into collation, analysis and re-presentation. In each stage, metadata about an information resource provides critical support for the research process (see Figure 16.4).[25]

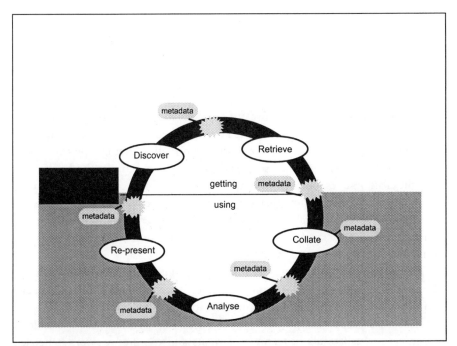

Fig. 16.4 *The research process*

Finding information

Discovery

Information discovery is the identification and location of relevant resources. An initial query, formulated in the user's space as a 'research question', is put to a provider's information. Embedded in the query are the user's schemas and the user's purpose in asking the question. These interact with the description of information resources provided by repositories. As pointed out earlier, correspondences between these two schemas, and their exact interrelationships, will often be difficult to identify or extricate.[26]

Except in the case of *browsing*, information discovery is entirely dependent upon metadata, whether that provided by the resource creator, the repository, a subject gateway or a subsequent documenting agent. As with the traditional library card catalogue, a repository's holdings are communicated to the researcher by means of the metadata provided about them. The answer to a metadata-based discovery query should enable the user to take the next step, and decide whether to obtain some or all of the cited resources.

If the query produces a result which the user cannot interpret, or from which the user cannot decide whether to retrieve the cited objects, then another discovery query will follow until the user gives up. If, however, one of the metadata sets returned by a discovery query cites information objects that appear to be promising for the user's purposes, the user will follow it with a retrieval request.

Retrieval

A retrieval request reflects the conscious choice to move a copy or subset of a digital source into a user-defined space. Like checking a book out of the library, the retrieval process provides the research with information that can be used (read, played, sorted, integrated, analysed, refuted and so on). Unlike the book, however, the electronic resource need not be 'checked out' in its entirety, may be reformatted in the process of downloading, or may be selectively retrieved from and directly imported into local resource management systems at any level of granularity. Metadata plays a critical role in a retrieval decision and ensuring that the resultant request produces a satisfactory result.

Through metadata, a particular resource is identified for retrieval – possibly through unique identifiers, or through a URL. But sometimes more metadata is required prior to actual retrieval, in order to identify a resource with a particular 'fitness for purpose'. That purpose may be rendering user hardware available, in which case metadata about technical formats and required viewers is needed. Indeed, the dialogue may need to discover not only the present technical characteristics but the functionality present at the source system that could enable the resource to be reformatted or an entirely new resource to be generated in response to the user's request prior to retrieval. The researcher may wish to assess whether a statistical data set has the coverage required to support his or her research; a more accurate description may be needed. An art historian may wish to view a work of art from a particular vantage point; descriptive information about an image view would be required. Terms and conditions metadata, including costs and restrictions, may come into play. In all these instances, detailed metadata called about specific works prior to their retrieval allows the researcher to identify if a discovered resource is appropriate for use, and if it can be retrieved and used successfully in the researcher's workspace.

Using information

Collation

Collation organizes information from various sources into a uniform conceptual order or schema maintained by the researcher. It requires knowledge of the structures of retrieved information resources in order to integrate them with the researcher's prior knowledge base. At its simplest, this involves mapping data content structures (fields in the retrieved resource) to those in the research database – integrating a citation into a bibliography. More often, for research within a single discipline, this involves additional sorting of search results according to the values in a particular field – for example, ordering botanical illustrations according to their genus and species. For less structured data such as text files, it may require mapping of genre-typed headings or SGML DTDs. In an interdisciplinary environment, collation frequently requires the establishment of conceptual equivalencies between and among differing knowledge representation structures, such as is required to reassemble data about cultural objects from early 19th century France, from sources which associate them with the 'Napoleonic era' or the 'neoclassical style'. For any of these tasks, metadata becomes important which documents the structure and syntax of the resource and its schemas in considerably greater detail than is required for discovery. Participants at the 1998 Museums and the Web Conference were invited to populate a virtual model of Berlin in various time periods with representations of objects from their museum collections appropriate to the time and place. Needless to say, significant structural metadata and interoperability are required to make this possible, especially in a distributed environment.

Since the information resources being provided in our model are digital data, the retrieval process needs to have returned interoperable files and definitive metadata, or the user will not be able to exploit the retrieved resources. In some cases, collation may necessitate file format conversion, character set mapping, code translation or term explosion. Only if the retrieved files are accompanied by metadata declarations will they carry with them information the user needs to use them. Without knowledge of the schemes employed in the intellectual construction of the retrieved resources and the data structures used to represent their content, the researcher will be unable to correlate them with other data to evaluate their information content.

These metadata make it possible for the user to bring the new resource into the context of resources already available in the user space, and 'organized', indexed or understood with respect to local schemas. Such collation, which can involve various degrees of integration, is at least minimally necessary if the user is to be able to correlate the new information with existing knowledge in a usable way.

Analysis

Once coherent research knowledge bases are constructed through the collation of disparate resources, discipline-specific methodologies are employed in the extraction of the meaning inherent in the content of resources. The methods by which the underlying data have been gathered, prepared and previously analysed become critical issues in determining the validity of subsequent analytical methods, and metadata documenting these processes will be required if analysis is not to introduce artefacts. For example, the gamma of the capture of a colour image is critical to its interpretation or comparison with other images. The methods of interpolation of census data are crucial to their combination with other data sets in a statistical test.[27]

The knowledge representation processes that were applied by the creators or custodians of the information resource are crucial to the subsequent use of that resource in another context. If these metadata were not delivered at the time of the initial retrieval, the user will need to go back to the provider to obtain additional meta-information. Just as the analysis process is iterative, the user may need to return to the provider many times to obtain different or more detailed metadata to support subsequent analysis and assessment. Having access to detailed documentation about the manner in which a source was represented may be critical to assessing its authenticity or its utility as evidence in a particular argument. As we are at a stage where capture and representation of analogue objects in digital form is far from standardized, we can assume there will often need to be significant dialogue between the source system and the user's system about the data capture, knowledge representation and documentation methods. We can expect there to be disconnects between the perspectives of a resource's creator and the disciplinary schema of a subsequent user. Bridging these will require an explicit declaration of the nature of the source, and a self-awareness on the part of the researcher of his or her own process or methods.

Re-presentation

The goal of the research process is to create new information – to provide an answer to the research question. Of course, in the process of analysis the user hopes to add new knowledge, establish a personal synthesis, or create a revised schema that will bring new meaning to the previously collated information. If the researcher is successful, a new information resource will be created. The researcher will want to communicate this new idea, re-use the information obtained from the provider, and cite or quote or adapt some or all of the acquired resources. Additional metadata may be required, particularly metadata about rights and permissions and documentation of the analysis methods employed.

The subsequent re-presentation of the information will be a new information package, and as such the user will need to create new metadata for it as well. If the communication involves publication of the new ideas, the published resource will, eventually, become part of the universe of information resources provided by others and subject to the same cycle of discovery, retrieval, collation and re-use by other users.

Some genres of scholarly communication are discipline-specific. Others are specific to the type of research process being reported, and all involve formalisms in the representation of knowledge. Much of the metadata sought by future researchers in the discovery process will be created at the re-presentation, or in the formal publication of results. While scholarly traditions have long demanded that some 'metadata' be reported in footnotes – e.g. stanzas or line breaks, the edition used in word-frequency or textual analysis, the length of the light waves in medical diagnostic procedures such as MRI (Magnetic Resonance Imaging) or the density of laser beams – future researchers will need guidelines and methods for reporting this information in ways can be systematically used by others. The significance of this becomes particularly obvious when we consider types of distributed publication in which the new knowledge is in fact only the imposition of a new method, as defined by its metadata, on an existing information resource or data set. Such 'publications' are being created today in electronic 'collaboratories' and remote medical consultation.

Scholarship is a communal process of discussion and debate, involving links between resources and the addition of value by one work to those which preceded it. The linking mechanisms, such as citation, acknowledgement and quotation, use metadata and author-stated relationships at the level of the information resource itself. Its additive mechanism, such as annotation, criticism, summarization or indexing, often refers to specific content or structures within the individual information resource. These will become important in information discovery. Consider the simple example of a resource used in a particular context, such as a photograph that appeared on the front page of the *New York Times* on a particular day. Post-hoc metadata packets, created by others but linked to the photograph, reflect subsequent re-use and provide further knowledge essential to an appreciation of its social significance.

Metadata declarations and dialogue

An example of metadata in a process

Consider the example of a professor working on the creation of a multimedia study-guide to be used in his course on Egyptian history and culture.[28] He queries a database of Dublin Core records, hoping to find works with an appropriate temporal and spatial coverage. He discovers a number of representations of art and artefacts in museums around the world. Because his students' technical environment is limited, he uses format metadata to limit his retrieval request to only those works that are depicted by images that his classroom lab computers can display.

His retrieval request returns a catalogue record and an image file depicting the relevant works of art, as well as an image metadata file. With the aid of an explicitly declared descriptive schema, he is able to integrate the catalogue record from each museum into his own working database, by mapping their fields to the ones he uses. He finds the metadata for images particularly useful in distinguishing the versions he acquires for his students from his own, higher-resolution study images.

Following the integration of the new works, he begins his analysis. Sorting and grouping functions enable new comparisons. Struck by several points about the nature of the hieroglyphics on a number of works, he queries again to find out if the differences he is seeing are a result of transliteration methods, or if indeed he has discovered a new formal variation. Unfortunately, the class is tomorrow, and this insight will have to be explored later. (See Figure 16.5.)

Now ready to write his next study unit, the professor queries for the terms and conditions of use for the representations of several comparable sarcophagi. Each will prove his point equally well, and he hopes that one will be within his budget. He easily discovers that several are part of licensed resources delivered on his campus (which he can use freely in his own teaching and research) and that one has no restrictions on educational use. Citing the required credit line, he incorporates several images into his study unit, glad that his authoring tool extracts their metadata and automatically builds him a table of contents that lists all of the

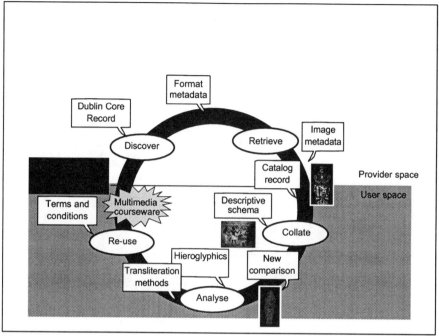

Fig. 16.5 *Examples of metadata*

components of his course. He has already had a query from an educator at a museum about his research: she had found one of 'their works' in a previous course pack and had e-mailed to discuss ideas for explaining Egyptian iconography.

Towards models and methods

This discussion of the process shows that metadata have a pivotal role to play that extends far beyond that of 'simple resource discovery' as identified by the Dublin Core. Table 16.1, while by no means exhaustive, begins to position various 'packages' of metadata at particular stages in the process.

The challenge, in constructing methods that will support the process, is to provide each user with the metadata that he or she needs at the time needed. The kind of detailed analysis of the research process which is required – in various disciplines, with users of differing levels of expertise, and in both formal educational settings and informal lifelong learning settings – has not been undertaken. Thus we are still guessing when we design information discovery and retrieval systems, or propose frameworks for metadata delivery.

Table 16.1 *Metadata packets in five stages of research by layers in the reference model for business-acceptable communications* [29]

	Discovery	Retrieval	Collation	Analysis	Re-Presentation
Handle	Publisher or distributor	Identification number			
Terms and conditions	Access, use, rights statements	Access terms, fee structures, use restrictions	Acknowledge-ments	Anonym-ization requirements	Terms and conditions, fees
Structure	File type, size, format	Resolution, compression method, arrangement, hardware or software dependencies	Data structure and representation methods	Data capture and manipulation methods	
Context					
Creation	Functional provenance, creator name, date	Links, functional dependencies		Value tables and organizational schemes	
Relations	Collection/site/item/association	Toolsets and analytical methods	Disciplinary schemas		Credits/citations
Content					
Classification	Object type, class		Disciplinary schemas		Conventions of representation
Subject	Subjects, coverage, topics or themes		Disciplinary methods	Methods, data values	
Use history	Publication or citation history	Captions and citation details			Citations

To elucidate requirements, we must systematically ask the following questions:

1 What metadata are required at each stage in the process?
2 When is knowledge of the presence of data necessary to make a decision about whether to proceed to the next step in the process?
3 If orthogonal packages can be defined so as to be present where and when they are needed in the process, what are the most efficient methods for delivering metadata from multiple sources to where they may be required?

4 When can extensibility be achieved through reference to disciplinary extensions (conceptual schemas) that support the processes of collation, analysis
   and representation, and how is the metadata management process to obtain
   these schema and employ them in support of research?
5 Where and how will these genres of information structuring and communication be defined?
6 If there are shared processes and concepts across disciplines that require
   generic tools and may provide conceptual bridges, what metadata would best
   support them?

What we do know is that different users require different metadata, and that during the life of an information resource people and organizations playing quite
different roles will create metadata that may be germane to future users.
Designing distributed mechanisms that can support on-going metadata creation
and responsive metadata delivery will continue to be a challenge, especially to the
cultural heritage community, where the variety of users and uses is so much
greater than in more narrowly targeted research domains such as medicine or
aeronautic engineering.

Conclusions

There are many impediments to implementing such an integrated system, not
the least of which is cost. It is no surprise that the costs of scholarship are high or
that scholars are unable to pay the full cost. Society has, through various means,
subsidized knowledge creation and use, and networked use will require continued subsidy. New models are required, however, to provide access to digital culture.[30] Means can be invented to share the costs of sophisticated access between
parties desiring to receive such services. The Art Museum Image Consortium
(AMICO) represents such a new model of cost sharing between users and creators of scholarly resources. In this model, AMICO member institutions, which
hold primary materials of interest to scholars, bear the full cost of creating digital
representations that have the properties which users desire. A variety of content
distributors, already providing services to the appropriate educational user community, bear the costs of developing applications that will satisfy user needs.
Users pay the costs of compiling information provided by individual repositories
into value-added product and of delivering that to their chosen distributor, as well
as the costs which the distributor needs to recover for having developed delivery
services. In the end, subscribing institutions pay only a fraction of the full cost,
much of which has been borne by the AMICO museums and the distributors.[31]
    Systems that enable a dialogue between information providers and users are
the best way to build our knowledge of research processes, and to ensure that the

requirements of those processes are considered in the creation and distribution of digital documents. A call for this collaboration ran through the *Research agenda for networked cultural heritage*,[32] and has resurfaced in discussions sponsored by the American Council of Learned Societies.[33] We hope that the technical dialogue about metadata delivery, the social investigation of changing communication patterns and needs, and the economic innovations required to support scholarship, can be advanced by the models presented here, and that further research will lead us along these paths to truly integrated cultural heritage resources over the Internet.

Notes and references

1   Bearman, D., 'CIMI entertains new framework', *Archives and museum informatics*, **9** (1), 1995, 120–3. (A preliminary version of the 'triangle' is reproduced on p. 121.)
    For another version of this diagram see Sledge, J., 'Points of view: multimedia computing and museums' in Bearman, D. (ed.), *Selected papers from the Third International Conference on Hypermedia and Interactivity in Museums (ICHIM 95/MCN 95)*, Pittsburgh, PA, *Archives and museum informatics*, 1995, 335–46.

2   This has been made painfully apparent to museums, which have found great difficulty in making databases that were constructed primarily for collections management into resources that can provide pubic access to their collections. The Catechism Project, at the National Museums of Scotland, surveyed questions asked of museums, and found that almost one-third of these could not be answered by a museum database. See McCorry, H. and Morrison, I., *Report on the Catechism Project*, National Museums of Scotland, 1995. This issue was also investigated by the Consortium for the Computer Interchange of Museum Information. See particularly the section 'Formulating typical questions' in Janney, K. and Sledge, J., *A user model for CII Z39.50 application profile*, September 1995. Available at
    <URL: http://www.cimi.org/documents/Z3950_app_profile.0995.html>.

3   See, for example, Bearman, D. and Sigmond, P., 'Explorations of form of material authority files by Dutch archivists', *American archivist*, **50**, 1987, 249–53.

4   The International Standard Archival Description (General) is maintained by UNESCO. See <URL: http://www.unesco.org/webworld/ramp/ramp_isa.htm>.

5   While there are many reference sources and standards for the documentation of museum collections (such as *SPECTRUM: The UK Museum Documentation Standard*, Museum Documentation Association, 1994, available at
    <URL: http://www.open.gov.uk/mdocassn/spectrum.htm>).
    local collection documentation systems structure records in distinct ways.

6   See, for example, the chapters 'From questions to sources' and 'Using sources' in

Booth, W. C., Colomb, G. C. and Williams, J. M., *The craft of research*, Chicago and London, The University of Chicago Press, 1995, 64–84.

7   One scholar conceived an international guide that she thought would be of great use to both new and experienced researchers. ' I . . . imaging . . . some sort of publication . . . Let's say you pick[ed] ten major libraries in Europe, and you just said how they worked, how they were set up . . . you would probably be several weeks ahead of yourself.' From Bakewell, E., Beeman, W. O., Reese, C. M. and Schmitt, M. (eds.), *Object, image, inquiry: the art historian at work* (report on a collaborative study by the Getty Art History Information Program (AHIP) and the Institute for Research in Information and Scholarship (IRIS)), Brown University, Santa Monica, CA, Getty Art History Information Program, 1988.

8   This problem has been acknowledged at Harvard University. See the Visual Information Access Project, particularly the report of the Task Group, May 1997. Available at
      <URL: http://www.peabody.harvard.edu/VRTG/report.html>.

9   Beattie, D., 'Retrieving the irretrievable; providing access to 'hidden groups' in archives' in Cohen, L. B. (ed.), *Reference services for archives and manuscripts*, New York and London, Haworth Press, 1997, 85.

10   See, for example, <URL: http://www.loc.gov/marc/dccross.html>.

11   Sledge, J. and Case, M., 'Looking for Mr Rococo: Getty Art History Information Program Point of View Workshop', *Archives and museum informatics*, 9 (1), 1995, 124–9.

12   Sledge, J. *op cit.*, 342.

13   McCorry, H. and Morrison, I.O., *Catechism: study of museum enquiries*, National Museums of Scotland, 1995, 7.

14   Such dialogues are essential to assure the accurate choice of homonyms (e.g. glass as a material versus Glass as a name), and to refine common English language uses (e.g. drawings by Italian architects executed in the 18th century).

15   In practice, scholarly knowledge representations have made very complex choices, which can be quite hard to represent in formal declarations. See Prescott, A., 'Constructing electronic Beowulf' in The British Library, *Towards the digital Library*, London, British Library, 1998, 30–49.

16   College Art Association and Getty Art History Information Program, 'Categories for the description of works of art', *Visual resources*, 11, 1996, 241–429. Also articles on aspects of its development and application, edited by Baca, M. and Harpring, P. Also available at
      <URL: http//www.gii.getty.edu/cdwa>.

17   International Council of Museums, International Committee on Documentation, *CIDOC Relational Data Model*, 1997. Available at
      <URL: http://www.cidoc.icom.org/model/relational.model/>.
      CIDOC Documentation Standards Working Group, *CIDOC Conceptual*

Reference Model, 1998. Available at
<URL: http://www.ville-ge.ch/musinfo/cidoc/oomodel/>.

18   The concept of frames, and of the discourse of disciplines building from common frames, grows out of the seminal writings of Marvin Minsky, which influenced 20 years of AI research. See Minsky, M., 'A framework for representing
knowledge', *MIT-AI Laboratory Memo,* **306,** June 1974. See also Minsky, M.,
Society of mind, New York, Simon and Schuster, c.1986.

19   See, for example, the preliminary results obtained by Andrew Gordon of
Northwestern University, in the definition of what he calls 'expectation packages'
within the *Library of Congress Thesaurus of Graphic Materials,* for building links in
descriptive metadata and aiding retrieval in his 'Deja-vu' Thesaurus Browsing
System. Andrew Gordon, 'Accessing image collections by browsing through standard thesauri', a paper presented in the session 'Theory and practice in the organization of image and other visuo-spatial data for retrieval: from indexing to
metadata', American Society for Information Science, 25–6 October 1998,
Pittsburgh, PA.

20   Elsewhere we have found this helpful in understanding the issues of 'authenticity' in digital documents. See Bearman, D. and Trant, J., 'Authenticity of digital
resources: towards a statement of requirements in the research process', *D-Lib
magazine,* June 1998. Available at
<URL: http://www.dlib.org/dlib/june98/06bearman.html>.
(The definitions of the phases in the research process that follow are based on
those in this article.)

21   Latour, B. and Woolgar, S., *Laboratory life: the social construction of scientific
facts,* London, Sage Publications, 1979.

22   Gould, C., *Information needs in the humanities: an assessment,* Mountain View,
CA, Research Libraries Group, 1988.
Gould, C. and Handler, M., *Research needs in the social sciences: an assessment,*
Mountain View, CA,: Research Libraries Group, 1989;
Gould, C. and Pearce, K., *Research needs in the sciences: an assessment,* Mountain
View, CA, Research Libraries Group, 1991.

23   Bakewell, E., Beeman, W. O., Reese, C. M. and Schmitt, M. (eds.), *Object, image,
inquiry: the art historian at work* (report on a collaborative study by the Getty Art
History Information Program (AHIP) and the Institute for Research in
Information and Scholarship (IRIS)), Brown University, Santa Monica, CA,
Getty Art History Information Program, 1988.

24   A useful text which explores these issues within the domain of art historical
research is 'Linking art objects and art information', a special issue of *Library
trends,* **37** (2), 1988 (see especially articles by Markey, K., Bearman, D. and
Giral, A.).

25   Our analysis assumes the existence of orthogonal packages of metadata, as

described in the Warwick Framework. See Lagoze, C., 'The Warwick Framework: a container architecture for diverse sets of metadata', *D-Lib magazine*, July/August 1996. Available at <URL: http://www.dlib.org/dlib/july96/lagoze/07lagoze.html>. See also Lagoze, C., Lynch, C. and Daniel, R., *The Warwick Framework: a container architecture for aggregating sets of metadata*, Cornell Computer Science Technical Report TR96-1593, 1996. Available at <URL: http://cs-tr.cs.cornell.edu:80/Dienst/UI/2.0/Describe/ncstrl.cornell %2fTR96-1593>.

26   Bates, M., 'Indexing and access for digital libraries and the Internet: human, database and domain factors', *JASIS*, **49**, 1998, 1185–205.

27   Gurbaxani, V. and Mendelson, H., 'The use of secondary analysis in MIS research' in Kraemer, K. (ed.), *Harvard Business School research colloquium on information systems research challenge: survey research methods*, **3**, 1991, 71–106.

28   The images in this example are drawn from the online Thumbnail catalogue of the Art Museum Image Consortium. Available at <URL: http:// www.amico.net>. They are: *Mummy Case of Paankhenamun*, Third Intermediate Period, Dynasty 22, c. 945–71, No. 1910.238, Art Institute of Chicago, Willner, W. M. Fund, Copyright Art Institute of Chicago, 1998. *Wall Fragment from the Tomb of Amenemhet and His Wife Hemet*, Middle Kingdom, Dynasty 12, c.1991–1784 BC, No. 1920.262, Art Institute of Chicago, Museum Purchase Fund, Copyright Art Institute of Chicago, 1998. Egypt, Akhmim (?). *Mummy Case*. 30 BC-AD 395, No. 1914.715, Cleveland Museum of Art, Gift of the John Huntington Art and Polytechnic Trust, Copyright Cleveland Museum of Art.

29   For further context of this table as it relates to the reference model for business-acceptable communications, developed for electronic archives, and the requirements of Dublin Core image data, see Bearman, D., 'Possible contributions of the reference model of metadata required for evidence to a reference model of metadata required for image description', *Archives and museum informatics*, **10**, 1996, 295–302; See also Bearman, D., 'Item level control and electronic record-keeping', *Archives and museum informatics*, **10**, 1996, 195–245. Also available at <URL: http://www.lis.pitt.edu/~nhprc/item-lvl.html>.

30   Kahin, B., 'Institutional and policy issues in the development of the digital library' in Kenna, S. and Ross, S. (eds.), *Networking in the humanities*, London, Bowker-Saur, 1995, 127–40.

31   See the Art Museum Image Consortium web pages at <URL: http://www.amioc.net> for full background on their programme. See also Bearman, D. and Trant, J.,

'Economic, social and technical models for digital libraries of primary resources', *New review of information networking*, 1998 (forthcoming).

32   *Research agenda for networked cultural heritage*, Santa Monica, CA, the J. Paul Getty Trust, 1996.

33   *Computing and the humanities: summary of a roundtable meeting*, Computer Science and Telecommunications Board, National Research Council, in collaboration with Coalition for Networked Information, National Initiative for Networked Cultural Heritage, Two Ravens Institute (American Council of Learned Societies, Occasional Paper No. 41), 1998.

17

Democracy and information in a network society

Frank Webster

There is a pervasive political demise infecting Western democracies. Voter turnout is at an all-time low, and parties struggle even to get enough candidates to contest available seats, while many intellectuals seem to prefer to talk more about 'EastEnders' and Armani fashions than the machinations of New Labour. Opinion surveys regularly rank politicians only marginally above journalists when it comes to occupational prestige, yet the latter are amongst the least-respected of all professionals. There is widespread contempt and even disdain for political representatives – a commonly expressed attitude that 'they're only in it for themselves'. To the likes of Francis Fukuyama this is a consequence of people having it all: no longer having to struggle for regular elections and the secret ballot, people have lost the will to fight and prefer to wallow in their consumer products.[1] Others might think that it is a disillusion stemming from the recognition of corruption, sleaze, careerism and the impotence of political action in face of the triumph of global capitalism.

Whatever the most persuasive explanation, the problems of apathy and disengagement from the democratic process are widely recognized, and various remedies are proposed. For example, every so often, right-thinking advisers recommend the insertion of classes on civics into the school curriculum (Bernard Crick, the eminent political thinker, has been advocating this on and off for several years now); again, pop singers and celebrities occasionally appear on television and in the press urging their admirers to use their votes; another proposal, recently influential in Britain, involves devolution from Westminster to the regions in order to promote the relevance of politics to the public. I would not want to disparage such endeavours: they seem to me well-meant, virtuous and potentially helpful. Yet the panacea most frequently offered, and which I plan to deal with in this paper, is the much spoken-about democratizing potential of new technologies. Information and communications technologies (ICTs), and the information revolution more generally, are presented, nowadays quite routinely, as a privileged means to revitalize and rescue politics from the present morass. In the network society, runs a common refrain, electronic democracy will stimulate participation, empower the citizenry, and shake up complacent politicians. For example, American Vice-President Al Gore states that the global information infrastructure will in fact promote the functioning of democracy by greatly enhancing the participation of citizens in decision-making.[2]

This technical fix solution (for it is no other) has a long history, and one which ought to put us on our guard against today's techno-boosters. It is salutary to recall, for instance, the early educational promise of radio and television in the USA during the opening decades of the 20th century. It was then commonplace to enthuse about the educational potential of radio – something widely regarded as a means whereby knowledge could readily be taken to the most dispersed of places and, moreover, a technology with the capability of delivering 'lifelong learning' [sic] to the American people.[3] We know now that the sponsor quickly took over the reins of American broadcasting, turned it into the world's most sophisticated entertainment vehicle, and emptied it of any credible educational content. That reminds us – if we should need reminding – that technology on its own is never sufficient to improve things when it comes to informational matters.

In what follows I will examine recent expressions of the claim that technology may encourage democratization with a questioning – perhaps even a jaundiced – eye. I will consider in particular two key areas in which ICTs, it is claimed, are set to play a crucial role in boosting democracy:

- the claim that ICTs will lead to greater **knowledgeability** amongst the public
- the suggestion that improvements in **communications** will transform democracy for the better.

Knowledgeability

To claim that more knowledge is of itself a good thing has the sound of revealed truth. This is an assertion which is frequently bolstered with the much quoted epigram of Francis Bacon: 'Knowledge itself is power'. In a healthy democracy, so runs a popular argument, if citizens are to play a full part in the political process, then they must have the knowledge made available to them that allows for effective engagement. It is self-evident that one cannot participate meaningfully in debate, say, about law and order without reliable information about delinquency patterns, assaults and arrest rates. It follows logically that appropriate information is a mainstay of the democratic process. Commentators frequently evoke here the dictum of the fourth United States President, James Madison, that ignorance threatens democracy, since the uneducated and uninformed, because they are incapable of exercising positive influence over the polity, are easily disempowered.[4] For much the same reason information has been called a fourth right of citizenship (after food, shelter and work) since it is the prerequisite of understanding and involvement in public affairs.[5]

It seems almost perverse to dissent from this principle. Without knowledge as to the character of one's society, or of the elements underpinning a particular policy, then it is impossible to exercise much meaningful influence. A deliberative democracy – one in which people are able to exercise their civic rights and responsibilities both thoughtfully and effectively – requires that the citizenry be equipped with the means of deliberation. This surely is a major reason why, in even a rudimentary democracy, government agencies are charged with responsibility to gather information about society and, in turn, to make this available to the wider public. The information that is generated in government censuses and surveys – on wage rates, patterns of inequality, employment trends, distribution of consumer goods, family composition, criminal activity, divorce, educational attainment, skill levels, industrial structures and so forth – is absolutely essential to the democratic process. Incidentally, this is also information which is capable of aggregation to provide national trends and comparisons through time and space, but it is also applicable to local situations so that people may know about, say, housing conditions, health patterns or the age distribution of inhabitants, in order to arrive at considered and robust decisions about the provision of services such as schools, hospitals and welfare organizations in their own areas.

The major way in which a society knows about itself is through these information-gathering activities of state agencies. Of course, other organizations contribute to this process – newspapers, international agencies, charities, even university research projects – but all are bit players (and are frequently parasitical) when compared to government information agencies which have developed ethics of 'public service' and impartiality to support this important task.[6] There are plenty of other information-gathering agencies – credit verification companies, direct mail companies, retailers, credit-card handlers, banks and insurance corporations – which amass enormous amounts of information about the population. They do not, however, make (or even think of making) any of this information available, even in anonymized forms, either to the general public or to its representatives, having quite different interests and agendas to pursue compared to those of state organizations.

While I would not dissent from the view that what might be called 'social information' is a prerequisite of democracy, I am reluctant to endorse the argument that more knowledge, per se, is a positive development. In the late 20th century, the key issue is not the fact of more information being available, but rather questions about its quality. This is, of course, to make an elitist critique of our 'information society' insofar as I am insisting on the need to discriminate between types and orders of information. Moreover, as will become clear, I consider that today's 'information society' is one in which an enormous amount of the information available is deeply *uninformative* – 'junk information' analogous to the junk food that is plentiful but not nutritious.[7] Some no doubt will respond to this with the accusation that I am old-fashioned, dull and grey – contemptuous of the thrill of 'popular culture'. To this I can only plead guilty, at least if this means insisting that the character of democracy is a sober and serious matter that is ill-served by those who celebrate the trivial, ephemeral and escapist. Democracy requires of citizens thought, commitment and effort – civic responsibilities if you will – if it is to work effectively.[8]

If I am unwilling to agree that more information, per se, is valuable, this does not mean that I subscribe to the converse, that ignorance is bliss. Rather it means that we may usefully be reminded of ancestors who, struggling to extend democracy in difficult circumstances, often did so with precious few information resources beyond elementary schooling, a few books and the odd pamphlet. When techno-boosters insist that in future ICTs will ensure that we will enjoy an information abundance which in and of itself will mark progress, it is as well to be reminded of those splendid trades unionists, Chartists, Primitive Methodists, reformers and autodidacts in the past who made much of so little. They had little beyond the Bible, perhaps Shakespeare and some Dickens, plus a few free-thinking tracts.

Thinking of them will also remind us of what they struggled for. Not least they worked for the establishment of an information infrastructure – though of course they would not have used such a term – that would be a foundation of democracy. Two key elements of this were *access* and *provision* of knowledge. These remain axial to a healthy democracy. Access to knowledge has long involved the primacy of making education available for all, but it also extends to agitation for the creation of public libraries and museums, and later on to ensure that radio and television were available to all at minimal individual cost. Provision involved ensuring that information and knowledge was reliable, was as free as possible from censorship, and as comprehensive as was humanly feasible.

There are those today who see in ICTs the means by which we might massively increase the information infrastructure of contemporary democracies. Visionaries of an 'electronic democracy' see in the 'information superhighway' the potential even for reversing the current 'disillusion' which has 'generated an atmosphere of cynicism and alienation' from politics.[9] This quotation comes from a report, *New library: the people's network*, prepared by the Library and Information Commission and published in April 1997. The report expresses the familiar hopes and aspirations of techno-enthusiasts. The predominant theme is that libraries need urgently to become electronically connected, the 'networked public library' becoming 'an entry point to the information superhighway'.[10] This 'digital library network' ensures ready access to knowledge for everyone, wherever they may be located. Digitalization of British libraries – imagine 5000 of them hooked together, their treasures accessible with a few strokes on the keyboard to anyone and everyone – will mean that 'even the most remote rural library will offer access to the same facilities as a large urban library, providing a means to draw in those people who, through geography, are furthest removed from the opportunities offered by the Information Age.'[11] Thus the 'library *without walls*' means that everyone has access to all knowledge on an equal basis, wherever they might happen to be – 'an opening to the networked society which will promote a healthy democracy'.[12] The vision is of Parliamentary proceedings, Government reports, Select Committee minutes, Blue Books, departmental guides, all flowing electronically to wheresoever they are required.

Ultimately it means far more even than this. With still more technological innovation the digital library network will 'reconstitute the visual into the virtual and deliver it from its custodial home to the widest community in local libraries.'[13] Here we have the 'death of the book' superseded by the birth of the 'virtual library': the conversion of texts into bits means that any manuscript may be easily moved anywhere without itself being physically transported.[14] How splendid, how easy, how readily this technology improves the knowledgeability of every man and woman.

These proposals have been connected with New Labour's much-publicized plans for a National Grid for Learning, which aims, in conjunction with British Telecom, to network schools, colleges, universities and libraries, with the primary goal of promoting 'lifetime learning'. Chris Smith, the Minister responsible for much of this, argues that 'public libraries will be a crucial part of the National Grid since they are 'colleges for ordinary people'. So the 'library network' will simultaneously enhance educational opportunities and improve the democratic process. So long as the local library is connected to the net, then no one need be excluded from the 'knowledge society'. Networking the 'library service means access for all, not just the few. It's the best possible way to avoid creating a society of information haves and have-nots.'[15]

Ready access to information, wherever one may be and however little money one might have, is certainly an enticing prospect. But will it revitalize the democratic process? I have my doubts, and these centre on two large questions:

1 How can we have faith in the capacity of new technologies to bring about a much-improved information service when the **established information systems** have demonstrably failed to fulfil their potential?

2 On what grounds can we have confidence that the arrival of a 'network society' will provide a high-quality information domain when we examine major characteristics – and palpable flaws – of today's **information environment**?

Established information systems

Public libraries are popular and much used. Well in excess of half the British population are members of their local public library, one-third of them regularly borrow from it, taking away nine books per year, and together they made almost 400 million visits to libraries in 1995/6 (more than ten times the total attendances at professional football games). Founded in the mid-19th century, they have spread throughout the land, and have been required by government to provide an information service which is free to users and comprehensive in its service (should what a user requires not be in the local library, then the interlibrary loan service would supply it without cost). Ordinary citizens, from children to pensioners, could visit their library confident in receiving a public service, whether they were seeking reference material on a school project, advice on planning applications, or simply a novel to read. Truly, the public library service was the jewel in the crown of the United Kingdom's information infrastructure for the overwhelming majority of ordinary citizens.

There have, of course, long been tensions within the library service about, notably, what and what not to provide. While the national stock might have been comprehensive, at the branch level the librarians had finite budgets which had to be spent with care. Inevitably, then, the librarians were gatekeepers, and just as inevitably there were arguments about what should be let through and what debarred. Agatha Christie perhaps, but not Jeffrey Archer? Charles Dickens certainly, but perhaps not Stephen King? More Roald Dahl than Enid Blyton? These questions of judgement, decisions about quality, range of local stock, and perceived requirements of users, are difficult and often fraught, and this necessarily so. They cause argument, dissent and debate on library committees, but cannot be side-stepped since they are a proper concern of any acquisitions policy. So long as libraries were structured as a public good, funded from taxation with a mandate to supply a full and free information service, then it was right and proper that a library's purchasing policy was set by criteria that ranged far beyond those of a market-oriented information business (which would, in principle at least, supply anything that was saleable at a profit, and nothing that was not). The criteria would vary somewhat according to local circumstances (as well as in relation to regional and even national stocks), the dispositions of the librarians, committee members and school curricula, and perhaps even the recommendations of especially respected users – but what cannot be doubted is that they were much more generous than those operating in the commercial realm. Not surprisingly, the commercial subscription libraries run by the likes of Boots, W. H. Smith and Mudies, providing a much narrower range of information, and that at a direct (if quite small) fee, went out of business since users favoured the public library service.

However, while public libraries have remained well used and popular, over the past 20 years they have had to face attacks which make disputes about acquisitions appear petty. What can only be regarded as an assault on their raison d'être has been mounted from three main quarters:

1 There has been the matter of sustained reductions in funds from the public purse, resulting in fewer book purchases, fewer available staff, fewer current periodicals (and frequently no daily newspapers), declining opening hours in many places, as well as more dowdy and unkempt surroundings.[16] A corollary has been a shift towards commercialization of services – chiefly at the margins, since librarians' professional ethics and government legislation inhibits the process – as an attempt to recoup diminished resources.[17] Thus orders for specified books, interlibrary loans, and some reference services now command a fee, while the fines system for overdue books is increasingly calibrated as a mechanism for generating funds rather than to encourage prompt return of materials. Not surprisingly, between 1986 and 1996 there has been a 20% decline in book lending from libraries.[18]

2 There has been an attack from the political right (armed with a general enthusiasm for 'the market' in all things) that regards public librarians as being unaccountable to anyone other than themselves – something which lets them foist their values on library users (since they determine what stock to purchase), and, moreover, allows them to allocate most of the library budget to their own salaries. In addition, the Adam Smith Institute[19] believes that nowadays people are well able to satisfy their information needs by paying for them, as witness the 'paperback revolution' that has brought cheap books to everyone, and the boom in video rental chains which customers seem happy to use. Yearning for a return to subscription-based services, and admiring the success of the Blockbuster video company, the ideology of 'the market' – increasingly articulated as the voice of the 'real world' as well as representative of popular choice and responsiveness to ordinary people[20] – cast a dark cloud over the library system during the 1980s as it bowed under heavy and hostile cuts.

3 Currently, and loudest of all, comes the accusation that public librarians have failed to move with the times, and are outdated custodians fixated on books rather than on the modern forms of electronic information delivery. This is a critique which comes readily from post-Thatcherite sources – from groups whose emphasis may be more on the cultural inadequacies of the old-fashioned, inflexible and fuddy-duddy library system than on economic stringencies and market opportunities. The complaint here is motivated by a conviction that new technology-based information, multimedia delivery, and above all the Internet, are the only future for public libraries, and that adjust-

ment to these bounties requires, before anything else, a change in mind-set – of outlook, expectations and organizing principles – from those working in the library service.[21] The message here is that libraries must invest in ICTs, brighten up the paintwork, install PCs, relegate old and tatty literature, and sideline the old guard. The 'Miss Smiths' with their hair in tight buns, dressed in grey cardigans and sensible shoes, and with undue reverence for books and 'library silence', have for far too long acted as custodians of the library. They must go and the library 'modernize'.[22]

This tone permeates *New library: the people's network*.[9]
Consider Sheila Pantry's view:[22]

> The problem is the continuing universal image of the information worker *The Librarian*. It does hinder the acceptance of the information service as core to the organisation because other professions do not accept the information worker on the same level. So we must develop a modern image, which includes professional skills coupled with business acumen.

This enthusiasm for new means of information delivery strikes me as nothing short of astonishing. This is in part because it egregiously ignores the recent history of attacks on the library system and its servants (for good measure, it adds its own), but it is chiefly because, enthused by ICTs' facility of information handling, it fails to consider key questions such as *what information* is to be delivered, of *what quality*, for *what purposes* and on *what terms?* Each of these questions, when seriously addressed, must raise doubts about any technological salvation of libraries. Ambitions to put half a dozen computer terminals in each library will not rescue or even resuscitate an information service currently straining to provide basic book and reference materials. Moreover, what the Internet offers, and on what terms information is made available, must be carefully scrutinized *before* libraries irrevocably commit themselves. The information it offers is not in and of itself valuable – it may be worthless or even noxious. For instance, it is well known that unscrupulous groups, sinister political schismatics and pornographers – as well as myriad cranks and self-publicists – have websites, just as it is common knowledge that the most valuable current sites have been constructed by public institutions such as universities, which aim to make freely available information from their library catalogues, researchers and teachers. These latter share with public libraries an ethos of disseminating information on the basis of user need, as against ability to pay, and this is manifested in the high quality of information they make available with no economic commitments required of the user. Contrast this with the countless commercial websites that, when offered free, are cluttered with advertisements and created for no other reason than to celebrate the sponsor and/or cajole the user into making a purchase. Pioneered earlier, but now converging on the information superhighway, online information services are being developed, primarily, as a commercial service, and thus many of them are either charged at premium rates and/or placed there for the purposes of business propaganda. It may sound wonderful that one can access *The New York Times* or *California Today* electronically, but they cannot be read for free online, and costs for most public libraries are prohibitive.

To be sure, at present connect charges on the Internet are low and a good deal of information there is freely available, but the likelihood is that commercialization will advance with great rapidity as private interests combine with strapped public institutions to make a 'business of information'. Already annual connect charges to each library or school – and this at special cheap rates – range between £600 and £800, and these, run by the likes of British Telecom and private cable contractors (with Microsoft waiting in the wings), are likely to rise rapidly once institutions are tied in to a given technical system.

A related matter concerns official statistics. On the surface ICTs seem to be a marvellous opportunity to increase public knowledgeability because they enable immediate access to mountains of the statistical information by which we know ourselves as a society. Such virtuoso technological possibilities lead futurists like Don Tapscott to announce the immanence of 'real-time, participative democracy' since the 'new technology holds the promise of open government.'[23] Moreover, word search facilities enormously ease the citizen's capacity to find what he or she is after, since a few letters sift and sort all relevant information. Thus, without leaving the computer terminal, the user is taken through the repositories of all available statistical holdings, and they are neatly presented on screen.

This is rather appealing, but such a positive scenario has to be set against the recent history of official statistics – a history which demonstrates an accelerated tendency (following a review of the field by Sir Derek Rayner,[24] a manager from retailers Marks and Spencer) towards:

- charging, at well above rates of inflation, for what is being offered (whether in electronic or hard form)
- a distrust in the veracity of the information available following political interference to restrict and reshape unpleasant data (for example, those on unemployment, poverty, and wealth distribution)[25]
- reductions in the frequency with which some important statistical data will even be gathered[26] (for instance, in 1997 the General Household Survey, an annual review of a sample of 10,000 households which provided information on a range of matters, from contraceptive use and telephone availability to home ownership, was 'suspended').

What I am raising here are questions concerned with the quality of statistical information, of the principles that underpin its dissemination, of how frequently and how accurately it is collected and made available. Of course, new technological means could, potentially, improve public access, but accounts which focus on technology and technology's promise to the exclusion of other matters are surely inadmissible. They substitute crucial issues of informational quality, access and availability with superficial matters of techniques of storage and delivery.[27]

The information environment

There is a great deal more information available nowadays – of this there can be no doubt. From this fact stem a good many assertions that we must, in consequence, be a more knowledgable people than our predecessors. To be sure, much depends here on one's point of comparison in the historical frame. We are certainly better informed today than our early 19th century forebears, who suffered from widespread illiteracy, little or no formal education, arduous and time-consuming labour, as well as a dearth of available information. But if the timescale were to be 30 years – and thus prior to the spread of ICTs and the information explosion it heralded – then the question of our superiority is much more debatable. I have already expressed some doubts about this – doubts which resurface when we begin to reflect on the contemporary information environment.

People have many ways of gathering knowledge: from their own experiences, from their family and friends, from work relations, from advertising hoardings, from letters, from reading newspapers and books, and from listening to the radio. These involve extremely complex forms of knowledge distribution and acquisition, and I would not want to oversimplify matters. However, what is surely indisputable is that television is a primary element of just about everyone's information environment in Britain today. All available figures are telling: saturation of television ownership (many homes have two or more sets), each set on for several hours of every day, provision of round-the-clock programming. Given the enormous amount of information currently distributed on the five terrestrial stations alone, to which must be added the thriving video hire and sales business as well as the rapidly expanding cable and satellite services, along with the multitude of video games which play through the TV monitor, then it might seem impossible to make any statement which might be accepted as generally true about this television phenomenon. It is not. The general picture is clear, and it looks like this.

Since the early 1980s we have witnessed a shift away from public service television, with its commitment to 'inform, educate and entertain', towards television organized as a business whose prime aim is, accordingly, to provide information which turns a profit. Ineluctably, then, we are moving away from a television service which provided material to what was largely an imagined audience, which was offered programmes judged to be most appropriate by the television makers themselves, who were, in crucial respects, independent of their viewers (who were obliged, through legislation, to pay for their television through the license fee). In place of this, we are moving towards a television system reliant on subscription charges from viewers, sponsorship support and advertising (or a combination of these three). These commercial services must offer either programming which has mass appeal (and thus has an audience size that appeals to advertisers) or, less frequently, which is targeted to groups which have specific characteristics that make them willing and able to pay a premium rate for what they watch (for example, a world title boxing fight) and/or especially attractive to a sponsor (for example, the rather well-heeled audiences for the Ryder Cup).

There are complicated reasons why all this should be happening, and on the ground things are still more involved, what with the continued (if increasingly entrepreneurial) survival of the BBC,[28] the particular public service features of Channel 4, and commercial television's distinct statutes.[29] Any full explanation would need to take into account the decline of national sovereignty in broadcasting and beyond, an enthusiasm for marketization, new technologies, some disillusion with public service broadcasting, as well as the emergence of competitors such as News International and MTV. However, what cannot be gainsaid is that 'the 1980s were the Passchendaele of public broadcasters'[30] – and not just in the United Kingdom – and the results of this slaughter are readily seen. Television programming is now dominated more than ever by soaps, action adventure, drama documentary, magazine news and quiz shows, all of which is accompanied by a squeeze on news and current affairs (which itself leans heavily towards 'sound-bite news' and sensationalized coverage of events as it responds to the competition for audiences),[31] and by burgeoning cable television services offering a stolid diet of 'infotainment', movies and, above all, sport (at a price at least 300% above that of public broadcasting's license fee).

At least three consequences of all this are evident:

1 Despite the increased output and availability of television, the information provided represents not an improvement, but rather a decline, in informational quality, at the least in terms of knowledge about the key issues of social, economic, political and cultural life. Only if one considers that lengthy TV coverage of snooker, ice hockey and, especially, premier league football provides insight into important elements of our conditions of existence, can one argue that citizens' knowledgability has been extended.[32] To some, of course, the very coverage by television of long-neglected sports is indicative of 'democratization'. In this sense hour upon hour of televised darts, doubtless watched by several million people, represents the democratic recognition of

popular pursuits long neglected by the elitist television producers who once filled the BBC. I find such reasoning – at root the same line of argument which sees in *Brookside* and *Neighbours* an engagement with life's everyday issues, and thereby part of a 'democratic conversation' – perverse. One may argue along such grounds only by emptying the concept democracy of any notion of seriousness and responsibility – by ultimately treating with contempt both the citizens of society today as well as their antecedents who struggled for the extension of democracy.

2 One becomes aware that, in spite of all the technological improvements in television programming and delivery that there have been in recent years, sophisticated technique cannot substitute for high-quality content (though low-quality technique may limit the efficacy of high-quality content). For instance, when one looks across the Atlantic to the USA – which is the direction of all television systems – one cannot but be struck by the low quality of content coexisting with the highest-quality technique. Years ago, American television was depicted by one of its own critics as a 'cultural wasteland', and still it remains so, amongst its finest achievements in the 1990s being a hospital soap opera (*ER*) and an updated cops-and-robbers show (*NYPD Blue*). Breathlessly paced, expensively written and innovatively filmed, their substance contributes little if anything to public knowledgability. Such are the most-lauded products of the world centre of television.

3 We may also see a trend towards the increased fragmentation of television audiences – a move towards the 'targeting' of programmes to specified consumer niches (though simultaneously creating a uniform category of audiences as 'consumers' who pay for the information they receive) – which means that the nation cannot be engaged as a collectivity except in the most unusual of circumstances. There is a suspicion today of this notion, and an associated denial of the possibility that a nation might come together in a democratic dialogue through television. Television broadcasting to the nation as a whole, on matters of common concern,[33] smacks nowadays of sinister propaganda and control[34] – the antithesis of audience 'choice'. Thus the inexorable spread of more programming, and a more differentiated audience, is encouraged, and with it goes the possibility of 'talking to ourselves' about important issues of the day.

I do not yearn nostalgically for a return to public service broadcasting's golden age (which never existed and can never be reinstated anyway). With Michael Tracey, I feel rather that 'a certain hopelessness sets in as the triumph of the banal and the morally and creatively impoverished appears complete.'[35] I do, though, treat with contempt those who persist in arguing that new technologies will radically improve public knowledge while television continues on its dismal path.

Communications

A close correlate of increased knowledgeability is the emphasis placed on the improved communications which ICTs portend. With this goes the assertion that better communications will lead to better democracy, since, goes the reasoning, what else could there be if Members of Parliament are readily accessible by e-mail, if pressure groups are able to organize through their web pages, if each and every one of us has the opportunity to engage, courtesy of the new interactive technologies? American Vice-President Al Gore summed up these hopes in his idealization of the 'information superhighway': 'Our goal is a kind of global conversation in which everyone who wants can have his or her say.'[36]

The logic underpinning this faith is one spelled out by British Telecom in recent advertisements: 'It's good to talk.' From this self-evident starting point, new information and communications technologies take on an enormous significance: talking is good because talking is the way to resolve conflicts and to include the excluded by engaging them in conversation; ICTs make communications easier than ever, hence it follows that all problems of discord and division are more readily overcome than before because communications are so much better now. In this way, the democratic process may be revitalized because people:

- can 'reach out and touch' others like (and unlike) themselves
- they can make their representatives more accountable by tracing them electronically and getting them to respond to their queries
- can reach politicians directly without going through intermediaries[37] (and we all know that 'talking straight to the person' is the best way to sort out difficulties)
- can feel a genuine sense of participation in the political process (they may even recreate the Jeffersonian ideal of direct democracy in a 'Virtual Town Meeting)
- can arrive at resolutions to problems because that, after all, is what discussion is all about.

Let me concede immediately that communication is a prerequisite of democratic decision making. Moreover, one may also agree that new technologies have, in some cases, enhanced communication processes, and thereby enriched democracy. For instance, the spread of local radio might well be thought to have opened up public spaces for discussion about issues of consequence in many people's lives.[38] Nevertheless, I remain deeply sceptical of the faith invested in ICTs' capacity to transform democracy in any profound sense.[39]

First of all, one must wonder what is so much superior about e-mail than, say, letters or the telephone (or even attendance at constituency surgeries) in communicating with one's political representatives. E-mail will, of course, reach the MP a few hours before the postal delivery (should he/she choose to read it immediately), but the electronic communication is just as likely (or unlikely) to evoke a response as is a letter. Bluntly, why should we invest hope in ICTs to galvanize democracy when existing communication systems, with similar functions, are in place, yet are presently not sustaining high levels of democratic conversation?

This takes us to a second objection – to the technical fix attitude so much in evidence here. Communication has long been presented as the means by which disorder will be replaced by equilibrium, and each new technology of communication is considered by someone or other to be the privileged means of rescuing order from disequilibrium.[40] Well, no one can be opposed to communication, but what grounds have we for believing that this can resolve perhaps irreconcilable differences of ideology or of interest? Rich and poor may converse until the cows come home, but I doubt that it will lead to a mutually agreed redistribution of resources. Furthermore, communication as salvation ignores the forces which have led to social divisions in the first place – forces such as the investment patterns that demand geographical dispersal, lifestyles which express the fragmented people that we have become, ways of work that exacerbate social isolation for many people today. These phenomena are so deep-rooted and profound that improvements in communication cannot hope to resolve the problems that emanate from them, and it is wishful thinking to suggest otherwise.[41] It may even be that communications technologies encourage these divisive trends – for example, by encouraging Internet users to stay at home, content to make only 'virtual' contact with others, though this only insofar as communication is with the 'parts' of strangers with whom the user has a personal interest. It is significant here that Robert Putnam's influential diagnosis of a fall in 'social capital' identifies computerized entertainment as one of the causes of the decline in neighbourliness, communal involvement, active citizenship and civic concern.[42]

Whatever the weight of these objections, Manuel Castells is surely correct to note that ICTs have contributed towards politics being conducted differently nowadays from in the past. He refers to 'informational politics' as those which are pursued, necessarily, through electronic networks, and especially through television. In Castells' view, ICTs are the 'privileged space of politics', so much so that 'outside the media sphere there is only political marginality'.[43]

This observation alerts us to a further difficulty for those enraptured by the possibilities of 'communication': just who are the major communicators in the era of informational politics, and what and why are they communicating? Here attention turns necessarily to organized politicians and their parties, and to the media industries themselves. And what one encounters from the politicians is public relations, spin-doctoring, image-projection, sound-bite argument, negative campaigning, media massage and manipulation, and dissimulation of information whenever there is advantage to be gained from it[44] – and from the media one encounters an obsessive concern for trivia, scandal and sleaze.[45]

The interrelationship between professional politicians and contemporary media, conflict-ridden and adversarial though it frequently is (though there is collusion too), hardly contributes to the democratic process by enhancing communication between citizens and their representatives. Indeed, for a long time in the USA, but also in Britain in recent years, we have had from politicians a strangely apolitical form of politics (arguments revolve around the ability to contemporary capitalism rather than around alternative political philosophies), with a focus on 'managed' communication eager to make no gaffes, and strategies aimed at destroying the credibility of opponents rather than presenting a distinct political programme of one's own. A similar absence of political debate is evident in the media themselves. This reflects, of course, the comfortable 'post-ideological' politics of the contemporary world, where no one appears capable of challenging, or even willing to try to contest, market presumptions, private property and global capitalism.

But this does leave the media in something of a fix, since they must retain their audiences' interest, and their own credibility as investigative and energetic information agencies. The consequence is that much of their efforts go into gathering and disseminating information about personalities and the personal frailties of all and any celebrity, politicians included. The upshot is that, in 1998, we learned much more about the wart on President Clinton's penis than about his State of the Union address, and more about Robin Cook's marital distress than about his role as Foreign Secretary, while in 1997 we learned much about President Clinton's sexual behaviour, Neil (and Christine) Hamilton's venality and Jonathan Aitken's duplicity, but little about their voting behaviour and political actions.

To review these constituents of 'communication' in modern-day politics is to be reminded of a concern expressed by both Walter Lippmann and Harold Lasswell in the inter-war years – the concern that democracy provokes the 'management' of public opinion by those expert in such matters. Lasswell[46] especially felt that mass media were a prime resource for 'opinion management', for what Edward Bernays, a devotee and key architect of 'public relations', called the 'engineering of consent'[47] and what Walter Lippmann[48] referred to as the 'manufacture of consent'.[49] To be sure, 'opinion management' is often far from successful, and it is often stymied by media exposure of some personal peccadillo or other amongst politicians and their associates, but the ambition to effect it drives an enormous amount of politics today, and it is a reality against which all futurist talk of better 'communication' enriching democracy must be compared.

Conclusion

It is right and proper that concern should be expressed about the widespread cynicism towards, and lack of involvement with politics in the advanced democratic societies. It is depressing, dispiriting and even potentially dangerous that so few citizens appear to be interested in, still less engaged with, public issues and affairs that only one in three turned out to vote in the UK local elections of May 1998. Nonetheless, I cannot share the view that this might be transformed by the judicious application of ICTs and the abundance of information this network society promises to make available and transmit. The technical fix solution is widely suspect, and this rightly so. Yet it will keep reappearing with attendant hype and fervour. I have endeavoured in this paper to restate some of the objections to techno-enthusiasm in this regard. By way of conclusion, all one may say is, bluntly, that an information explosion, and no end of super information and communications technologies, do not make for an informed public.

However, let me make clear that I do not wish to argue either that technology has no role to play in reinvigorating politics or that there is no serious problem of political disaffection nowadays. What I do wish to suggest, though, is that technology has no special claim to resolve the crisis of democracy in which we find ourselves as we reach the end of the millennium. On the contrary, while democracy will be conducted in an advanced technological society – as it is today, so will it continue – I would insist that the resolution of dissatisfaction with politics lies in reform of politics itself rather than in an infusion of technologies into political affairs.

References and notes

1   Fukuyama, F., *The end of history and the last man*, London, Hamish Hamilton, 1992.

2   Gore, A., 'Forging a new Athenian age of democracy', *Intermedia*, 22 (2), 1994, 4–6. See also Ward, D., *Rewiring democracy: the role of public information in Europe's information society*, MacLennan Ward Research, 1995.

3   Barnouw, E., *The sponsor: notes on a modern potentate*, New York, Oxford University Press, 1978. 12. For a more detailed treatment, see Barnouw, E., *A tower in Babel: a history of broadcasting in the United States*, New York, Oxford University Press, 1966. See also Barnouw, E., *The golden web: a history of broadcasting in the United States, Volume 2: 1933 to 1953*. New York, Oxford University Press, 1968.

4   'Popular government without popular information . . . is but a prologue to a farce or tragedy, or perhaps both. Knowledge will forever govern ignorance, and a people who mean to be their own governors must arm themselves with the power which knowledge gives'. James Madison to W. T. Barry, 4 August, 1822. Compare

Lupia, A. and McCubbins, M. D., *The democratic dilemma: can citizens learn what they need to know?*, Cambridge University Press, 1998.

5   Haywood, T., *The withering of public access*, London, The Library Association, 1989.

6   Webster, F., *Theories of the information society*, London, Routledge, 1995, 120–4.
    Bulmer, M., 'Why don't sociologists make more use of official statistics?', *Sociology*, **14** (4), 1980, 505–23.

7   Hoggart, R.. *The way we live now*, London, Chatto and Windus, 1996.

8   Barber, B., *Jihad versus McWorld: how globalism and tribalism are reshaping the world*, New York, Ballantine, 1995.

9   Library and Information Commission, *New library: the people's network*, London, Library and Information Commission, 1997, para. 1.22. Also available at <URL: http://www.ukoln.ac.uk/services/lic/newlibrary/full.html>.

10   *Ibid.*, para. 1.1

11   *Ibid.*, Introduction.

12   *Ibid.*, para. 1.21.

13   *Ibid.*, para. 1.41.

14   In April 1998, £60 million was committed to this project from Lottery funds (*Guardian*, 17 April, 1998).

15   Smith. C. (1997), 'New technology will enhance library services', 15 October 1997. Available at
     <URL: http://www.ukoln.ac.uk/services/lic/new library/dcms-15oct97.html>.

16   West, W. J., *The strange rise of semi-literate England: the dissolution of the libraries*, London, Duckworth, 1992.

17   Usherwood, B., *The public library as public knowledge*, London, The Library Association, 1989.

18   *Due for renewal: a report for the library service*, London, Audit Commission for Local Authorities in England and Wales, 1997.

19   Adam Smith Institute, *Ex libris*, Adam Smith Institute, 1986.

20   Harris, R., 'Some issues in political economy' in Gerard, D. (ed.), *Libraries in society*, London, Bingley, 1978, 49–57.

21   Greenhalgh, L. and Worpole, K. with Landry, C., *Libraries in a world of cultural change*, London, UCL Press, 1995.

22   Pantry, S., 'Whither the information profession? challenges and opportunities: the cultivation of information professionals for the new millennium', *Aslib proceedings*, **49** (6), 1997, 170–2.

23   Tapscott, D., *The digital economy: promise and peril in the age of networked intelligence*, New York, McGraw-Hill, 1996, 170.

24   Rayner, D., *Report to the Prime Minister*, Central Statistical Office, 1981.

25   Columnist Melanie Phillips, the most assiduous critic of interference in official statistics, recently observed that 'Every policy area is now stained by sleights of hand

from the statistical box of tricks . . . [I]n official statistics, [the market] has brought a vandalism of public knowledge and the iron grip of central government which has corrupted that knowledge to its own ends', *Observer*, 23 March 1997.

26   Much detail is provided in Levitas, R. and Guy, W. (eds.), *Interpreting official statistics*, London, Routledge, 1996.

27   Schreibman, V., 'The politics of cyberspace', *Journal of government information*, 21 (3), 1994, 249–80.

28   See Barnett, S. and Curry, A., *The battle for the BBC: a British broadcasting conspiracy?*, London, Aurum Press, 1994.

29   See, for example, Seymour-Ure, C., *The British press and broadcasting since 1945*, Oxford, Blackwell, 1996, Ch. 4.

30   Tracey, M., *The decline and fall of public service broadcasting*, New York, Oxford University Press, 1998, 199.

31   Postman, N., *Amusing ourselves to death*, London, Methuen, 1985.

32   A tee-shirt, popular in Europe, carries the message 'Football is Life, the Rest is Mere Detail'. It is intended as an ironic joke.

33   For discussion of how this developed in Britain, see Scannell, P. and Cardiff, D., *A social history of British broadcasting, volume 1: 1922–1939*, Oxford, Blackwell, 1991.

34   On the rare occasions that it now occurs – for example, on the funeral of Diana, Princess of Wales, in September 1997 – there is wonder at the degree of reverence and sentimentality of the television coverage.

35   Tracey, M. *op cit.*, 261.

36   Gore, A. *op cit.*, 6.

37   Enthusiast for electronic democracy Don Tapscott refers to this as 'disintermediation': see Tapscott, D., *The digital economy: promise and peril in the age of networked intelligence*, New York, McGraw-Hill, 1996.

38   Keane, J., *The media and democracy*, Cambridge, Polity, 1994.

39   In what follows I ignore the idea of the 'electronic ballot box' when it is used to suggest a move towards plebiscitary or 'direct democracy', chiefly on grounds that 'representative democracy' is generally accepted as the most desirable and acceptable.

40   See Alan Ryan's insightful discussion of John Dewey's optimism about the potential of mass media to increase democracy during the 1920s. Ryan, A., 'Exaggerated hopes and baseless fears', *Social research*, 64 (3), 1997, 1167–90.

41   Gray, J., *Endgames: questions in late modern political thought*, Cambridge, Polity, 1997, 136–40.

42   Putnam, R. D., 'The strange disappearance of civic America', *The American prospect*, 24, 34–46. See also Putnam, R. D., *Making democracy work*, New Haven, Princeton University Press, 1993.

43   Castells, M., 'Informational politics and the crisis of democracy' in *The power of identity*, Oxford, Blackwell, 1997, 310–2.

44 Franklin, B., *Packaging politics: political communications in Britain's media democracy*, London, Edward Arnold, 1994.

Cockerell, M., *Live from number 10: the inside story of prime ministers and television*, London, Faber and Faber, 1989.

Jamieson, K. H., *Packaging the presidency: a history and criticism of presidential campaign advertising*, New York, Oxford University Press, 1984.

45 Fallows, J., *Breaking the news*, New York, Pantheon, 1996.

46 Lasswell, H. D., *Democracy through public opinion*, Wisconsin, George Banta Publishing Company, 1941.

47 Bernays, E. I., *The engineering of consent*, Norman, University of Oklahoma Press, 1955.

48 Lippmann, W., *Public opinion*, Allen and Unwin, 1922.

49 See also Robins, K., Webster, F. and Pickering, M., 'Propaganda, information and social control' in Hawthorn, J. (ed.), *Propaganda, persuasion and polemic*, London, Arnold, 1987, 1–17.

Closing keynote address

Civilizing the information ecology
VIEWS OF INFORMATION LANDSCAPES FOR A LEARNING SOCIETY

Clifford Lynch

Introduction

This paper is an extensively revised version of the presentation that was originally intended, both building on and reacting to ideas offered by colleagues at the conference.

Two major themes – both highlighted in the conference title – have emerged repeatedly through the conference. The first theme was the idea of an *information landscape* and its role as a potential organizing metaphor for information collections and systems of information creation, management and delivery.

The second theme of the conference was that of a *learning society*, and the part that libraries and networked information might play in facilitating such a society. Some cautions are in order here, which were highlighted by colleagues. The term 'learning society', much like the older and less circumscribing term 'information society,' is in fact an ill-defined and politically charged code word for a whole range of sometimes conflicting values, visions and principles. Most people, particularly policy makers and politicians, agree that an information society is a good thing and a noble goal, and perhaps even a matter of survival in an increasingly competitive and globalized economic environment. Those who question this may find themselves characterized as Luddites or worse. It's hard for anyone to disagree that a learning society is a good and probably even necessary *goal*, particularly if kept to the level of slogan and not defined in detail. The idea – or perhaps ideal – of a learning society was offered as a source of goals and needs around which we might shape our developing information landscapes.

I will use metaphors for information collections and delivery systems as a point of departure, both to highlight and to put into context a number of current issues that will determine our ability to meet the needs of all readers, creators and citizens in the emerging networked information age. I will also explore some of the specific requirements that might be attributed to a learning society, and how they interact with broader information needs; and I will comment on the ability of current networked information technologies to respond to those needs. As a conclusion to this paper, I will talk about the role of libraries as potential mediators in the new world of electronic information.

Metaphors for information

Landscapes – perhaps bringing to mind the work of the great landscape painters of the 19th century – are a powerful metaphor for a world of information and information delivery systems. We can think about landscapes as intrinsic or consensual representations of an information world (perhaps echoing the notion of visual and immersive cyberspace as consensual hallucination portrayed by authors such as William Gibson). Or we can think of them as personalized perspectives, views, or representational and organizational tools that individuals might use to manage, visualize, navigate and perhaps even manipulate information. We can imagine different kinds of landscapes that externalize our feelings about information and the character of information collections – the wilderness that Peter Lyman described (see **Chapter 5**), perhaps merely grand and scenic, or perhaps turned hostile, with nature 'red in tooth and claw' (one cannot help but recall the preservation community's characterization of the life of digital information as 'nasty, brutish and short'); Arcadian and bucolic images; domesticated landscapes; cityscapes; and surreal and fantastic worlds.

These are powerful images and metaphors, but I find them largely unhelpful. Even though they are so visual, we have been largely unsuccessful in developing a useful visualization of large-scale spaces of information *resources*. Certainly, aided by computer graphics, visualization technology and supercomputing, we have made vast progress in the visual presentation and understanding of many kinds of simulations and numeric or observational databases or data sets. Recently, there have been interesting research projects in visualizing specific collections of textual data (for example, the work of Schatz[1] and his colleagues at the University of Illinois at Champaign-Urbana, or the work of Card[2] *et al.* at Xerox Palo Alto Research). But these are research prototypes, and are mainly concerned with the visual portrayal of snapshots of constrained, bounded information collections. They fail to capture much of the dynamic, interdependent evolution and commerce of information creation, management and use, and in particular the roles of autonomous parties within an information life cycle – elements that are essentially part of a landscape of information resources.

The metaphor of ecologies is more helpful because it suggests these characteristics. One can then think of a landscape (for the visual sense) as a captured snapshot of the state of the ecology. One occasionally hears the neologism 'infosphere' used in somewhat the same as the ecology of information, its creation and management, and its use; 'infosphere' parallels more common ideas such as atmosphere, biosphere or ecosphere.

It is possible to push these metaphors too hard and to examine them too closely. We understand so little of the intrinsic nature of information and documents. (Consider, for example, the work of Michael Buckland,[3] who has built on the tradition of the great pre-World War II documentalists such as Otlet, in trying to clarify these foundational issues.) Our taxonomies of information flow and utilization are so tentative and unsystematic that very close scrutiny will, probably, cause any analogy to disintegrate. At the same time, a lack of critical examination of our metaphors may mean that we are talking past each other. It's not clear to me that there is consensus about what the objects are within an information landscape, or the species and interactions within an information ecology: are they artefacts, services, institutions, flows, phenomena, or transactions and commerce? There are also fascinating questions of scope. In the old physical world of information artefacts and geographically bound communication and human interaction, it was reasonable to think about localized information landscapes or ecologies. Today, in a world of global communications networks and global media, the older local landscapes and ecologies seem almost like specialized case studies; ecologists and evolutionary biologists studied physically isolated island ecologies because they were helpful in providing insights and validating theories, even though they were not directly relevant to real-world systems. As we examine information creation, management and use in primitive societies, are we looking at the intellectual analogue of the Galapagos Islands for evolutionary biology? If we want to continue to use these metaphors, we need to refine and focus them, even while remembering that they are only metaphors.

It is worth noting that ecologies and landscapes in the physical world have been civilized by humanity over time. Landscapes have been shaped, altered and conserved. Ecological systems have been occasionally managed and often unpredictably disrupted by the introduction of new species, the elimination of old species, or the change in the balance and interaction among species. All of these processes are characteristic of what is happening today in the world of information and information use.

We also have notions, not just of *natural* ecologies, but of social systems and systems of commerce as ecologies. In some sense, each of these ecologies can be overlaid on the others, just as physical and political geography are significant overlays superimposed on landscapes and, increasingly, on information space. Each layer contributes to our understanding of the whole. All of these forms of ecologies are significant as we try to understand the evolution of the information landscapes.

Civilizing information landscapes and ecologies

Over the last few thousand years, we have developed societies that have brought civilization, management and stewardship to landscapes and ecologies, and we have wrecked quite a few of them in the process. We have seen the development of agriculture, and the domestication of animals and crops. More recently we have seen a series of legal developments to structure the landscape according to the needs and expectations of societies: cadastral maps that establish property boundaries and ownership; concepts of easements and rights of way and even condemnation of property to the public use, and of 'open skies' for satellite surveillance in international relations. We have developed a theory of public spaces and of commons; we have established the public good of parks and monuments. We have structured the ecology of commerce and social activities through law and regulation, custom and politics.

We, as a society – indeed, as a diversity of societies worldwide – are struggling to create the same sort of structuring of the information ecology, or to extend our current structures there, in order to bring it into greater conformity with the expectations and needs of the public and the society. We are attempting to accomplish this much more quickly than the slow evolution that characterized the domestication and civilization of landscapes, commerce and earlier societies. And there are many powerful vested interests trying to shape the process, as assets and controls that existed in the physical world are transmigrated into the electronic world.

Consider just a few of the key policy debates that are currently underway. Their resolution will fundamentally shape the information ecology, and will have broad-reaching implications for authors, readers, citizens and the society at large. They are establishing the cadastrals, easements and national parks of the landscapes – the species and predator–prey relationships of the information ecology. It's important to recognize that, while the immediate forum for many of these issues is legal or legislative, they are really wide-reaching issues of cultural and social norms, behaviours and expectations. The resolution of these issues will determine whether we will have access to a cornucopia of inexpensive, readily accessible information products that can be shared fairly casually, or whether information will be scarce, costly and constrained in its use. It will determine whether the digital culture will include a very rich and public historical record, or if that historical record will be fragmented, redacted and rearranged easily, and only referenced and accessible in very constrained ways. The resolution of these issues will ultimately help define what sort of civilization we will have in a digital world.

There are a series of profound debates growing about the construction, meaning, and assignment of authorship and ownership, in the digital culture and in the new genres it supports. We still cling to a definition of authorship that is granted by the exercise of what are essentially reproduction technologies – literal photography, videotaping and sound recording (consider C-SPAN in the USA), and now in the digitization of physical artefacts such as manuscripts and photographs. Yet we also struggle with a second layer of rights that are held by the targets of this reproduction technology: the people filmed, photographed or recorded; or the rights pertaining to the material being digitized. We are now beginning the digitization of our out-of-copyright cultural heritage from the 19th century and earlier; will the process of digitization return these materials to copyright in the networked environment under the newly-lengthened terms of copyright protection? We are on the threshold of an era of routine, ubiquitous capture of events such as lectures and public meetings through digital video; will the speakers and participants, or the camera operators, become the toll collectors for wide distribution of these materials? Further, digital genres expand to encompass 'captured' collaboration and interaction in the form of meetings and scientific activities that can subsequently be replayed, annotated and reused; authorship again becomes a complex and unclear issue.

In the USA, it appears that architectural designs are now protected, and that one cannot safely take pictures of certain buildings and republish them. There are debates about the patenting of life forms and genomic information on the one hand, and of business processes or software structures on the other. Indeed, in a multimedia environment we may see authors constrained, not just by copyright in reusing the work of others, but also by patents. There is also an emerging set of rights of publicity in the USA, designed to protect public figures (for example, ensuring that the estate of Elvis Presley can gain license revenue from commercial Elvis impersonators). Finally, there is discussion within the EU and the USA, among other nations, of a new set of rights for compilations of information – databases – which may reach well beyond traditional copyright approaches. All of these developments threaten to lock up more information more tightly than the historical norm, to constrain use and discourage reuse. And because so many of the proposed legal regimes and interpetations are novel, they give rise as well to uncertainty about what is permissible; in a world of risk-adverse, litigation-shy institutions, this may chill innovation and the exploitation of the rich digital information ecology.

A second series of questions concerns the social, cultural and intellectual records and the public domain, including the right of creators to reuse freely material created by others, and the right of the society as a whole to preserve and ensure access to these records. The questions here include:

- the duration of ownership rights in copyright (and also rights of publicity)

- national deposit mechanisms, and the ability of libraries to take measures to preserve materials
- the ability to make reference to 'public' materials.

Part of the difficulty is that we seem to have abandoned the notion of publication (that is, making public) of information as a relatively irrevocable act. At least in the USA, there appears to have been a social (though perhaps not legal) understanding that there is a public domain, which everyone is free to use fully, and a much larger and more recent 'published' or 'public' sphere, containing works which are still protected under copyright but which can be consulted, referenced and built upon in real but limited ways.

Another series of questions revolves around rights to reuse, to build upon existing works in a rich collective whole with other authors and creators – 'fair use' in the USA – and the broader social practices of quotation and reference to works. These issues are poorly understood for non-textual materials – what does it mean, for example, to 'quote' a passage from an image? And they are poorly understood in a digital environment, where references (links) are actionable rather than passive citations, and where access to information can be mediated by protective software that attempts to prevent certain uses of the information it protects.

Questions are emerging about the rights and expectations of readers (for example, whether readers should have the right, ability or opportunity to read anonymously, and if not, what constraints should exist on the use of records of their reading behaviour). In the print world, people can browse and read (or listen, or view) anonymously at two levels. Through libraries and stores, readers can access materials without the publisher knowing who they are. Readers can browse in library and bookstore; they can purchase a work with cash in a transaction that does not involve the rightsholder. Once they have obtained access to the materials (that is, have taken the work off the shelf in a library, or taken it home from a bookstore), no details on the specifics of their use is collected; there is a sphere of privacy, of personal use. In the digital environment, we have the potential to deploy systems for protecting and managing commerce in intellectual property which are stunningly invasive, tracking who obtains access and the details of their access: how many times an individual summons a specific passage to the screen, or plays a specific song. And not only can these new systems track, but they can constrain and block practices that, historically, have been within the personal sphere: copying a track from an audio CD to a cassette to play in one's car; loaning a book to a colleague; or taking a videotape to a friend's home for viewing. Any or all of these practices may be impossible, prohibited by software and hardware protective mechanisms, under some of the content protection schemes currently being developed.

Decisions about these fundamental issues will shape the commercial and social ecologies of information creation, access, distribution and management in the digital culture. Among other things, these decisions will determine the extent to which libraries can continue to play a meaningful role in the access and management of electronic information. They will also help shape the value and distribution chains, and the forms of intermediation (for selection, rating, resale, tracking, personalization and brokerage), that will form these chains.

Readers, citizens, and the nurturing of a learning society

I have to confess that I have no clear vision of what constitutes a learning society. There is no question in my mind that we need to build a society where individuals are able and empowered to learn, in the broadest sense of finding information or developing skills. This is an issue about self-determination and independence based on information literacy and, increasingly, an information technology literacy. Access to information and training and teaching – if not always free, then at least affordable, and if not all information and learning materials, at least a very substantial set of offerings – must be ensured. But it's also important to be realistic and understand that most learning and information seeking will be directed rather open-ended scholarly inquiry. Most of the proponents of the 'learning society' are not advocating a broad-based public policy to develop a society of learning-obsessed dilettantes who spend their time learning dead languages, obscure historical information and abstruse mathematical theories because it's fun. They are concerned with the ability of the populace to access information and to learn in order to solve problems at personal, business and even perhaps public policy levels, and in order to compete more effectively in the marketplace.

There are some fundamental questions here about whether and how to create communities of learners. People often learn better when they collaborate with other people who are also trying to learn about the same subject at roughly the same level of knowledge, perhaps with a teacher or guide. At the same time, a community based on learning a specific set of skills is rather transient, and it is not obvious that it is useful for this community to interact directly with researchers and teachers in a field, except in very structured and controlled ways. Here is a concrete example. A lot of people every year need to learn basic algebra and calculus, and sometimes working in groups to solve problems is an effective way to help master these skills. Most of these people are not interested in pursuing mathematics beyond the acquisition of the skills they need. While it's clear that setting up physical or electronic 'classes' of such people is useful, at least for some learning styles, it isn't clear whether it's either helpful or productive to connect this community of learners to the on-going discussions of the mathematics research community. It's easy to get carried away with the rhetoric of learning communities, and to confuse what's appropriate for advanced students, predominantly in higher education, with the broader questions of how to make effective use of network-based collaboration and community-building opportunities to support learning across a broad spectrum of needs.

Michael Schrage,[4] who has spent many years studying collaborative processes, makes an important point that while we know how to *deliver* information electronically to large communities, and we know how to use information technology to create discussion and collaboration among small communities, **we don't know how to scale this up**. Very large-scale collaboration, or dialogue involving tens of thousands of people works no better when mediated by information technology than it does in the physical world. Networked information technologies can create 'virtual' classes that achieve critical mass by drawing from a region, a nation or even the entire world rather than a geographically constrained area, permitting groups of learners to come together to study very specialized subjects in a way that has not been feasible historically. But for more commonplace subjects, we still want reasonably small learning communities, be they traditional classes or network-based learners. Information technology enables us to increase vastly the number of learning opportunities and to make them relatively independent of participant location. It will allow groups of learners to learn more effectively through collaboration, but it will not totally restructure how we teach commonly needed subjects, at least given the current state of the art.

Mastery of skills is only a small part of a learning society information programme, however. A much larger part deals with problem-solving (often through collaboration), or very focused location of facts, opinions and other information. I'll make only two comments here.

My first point is that very few of the information resources that are available today are oriented towards *answering questions* in a balanced, authoritative way. This is a difficult problem, and one that the designers of information systems have largely avoided in favour of the much easier one of identifying literature that pertains to a question. It is much easier to identify a mass of information and leave it to the reader to synthesize and evaluate, than to have the information resource directly provide the synthesis and evaluation. We are going to see a much greater demand from information seekers for answers, synthesis and evaluation, rather than simply literature bibliographies. This is problematic in many ways. The choices made in synthesis and evaluation are very powerful, and questions of authority and fairness are crucial. Libraries have historically been cautious about providing a patron with an answer, instead offering a wide range of evidence from which the patron can develop a conclusion. Yet information seekers are demanding answers and synthesis, and will happily purchase it commercially if libraries won't provide it.

My second comment is that collaboration among a diverse group of experts in various areas is a tremendously powerful way to solve problems. To facilitate these collaborations, however, it's necessary not only to develop information technology that makes it easy to conduct the collaboration across geographical boundaries, but to find ways to identify appropriate experts and provide them with some incentive to participate. I'm sure that many of us have received e-mail from someone we don't know asking a question that would take many hours to answer well, and where we know that much of the answer is available somewhere in the literature, and have simply deleted the e-mail. We don't have time to respond to an endless set of questions that do not assign any value to our time, efforts or attention. Solving this problem is a complex economic and social issue.

Finally, it is important not to let the vision of the learning society unduly dominate the design of information services and resources. There are many reasons why people use libraries today, and why they seek out and use electronic information resources. It's not just about learning new skills and solving problems. There's a substantial amount of research done for scholarship, intellectual curiosity and the sheer pleasure of knowing, rather than narrowly focused problem-solving. There's also a tremendous amount of information that is used primarily for entertainment in all media. The demarcation between learning and entertainment is always blurred. Understanding the history of our society and reading popular novels of two decades past or of the last century have elements of both scholarship and entertainment.

Moreover, a substantial amount of information use is for routine activities that hardly seem worthy of glorifying as the achievements of a learning society. Checking the daily weather report to decide whether to carry an umbrella does not reflect a major social shift to a learning society.

Of course, the boundaries between routine information use in daily life and the pervasive, creative use of information that is characteristic of a learning society or an information society are not well understood and are clearly continually shifting. It is frequently said that a good daily newspaper today contains more information than someone might have obtained in a decade two centuries ago; while I might question the specifics of this observation the continually growing infusion of information of various kinds into daily life is clear. I suspect that many individuals are routinely making somewhat more extensive use of health and personal finance information than they did a generation ago. The growth of access to information and of social explotiation of this access are desirable trends, and we need to ensure that they continue; but it's unclear when or how we should decide that an acceleration of these trends has brought us to the state of a learning society.

There is also an implication that the information resources that can support the activities of today's learning society are the most important and the most valuable, and should receive the majority of the funding for publicly available information resources. Presumably these are the information resources that improve economic competitiveness and personal, business, organizational and social problem-solving. While this may be a short-term political and pragmatic truth, the broader and longer-term activities of capturing and maintaining the scholarly and cultural record are of very great importance to both present and future generations. We must make the case that today's learning society should not cannibalize society's longer-term information resources in the name of economic competitiveness.

A coda: libraries as mediators in the information ecology

I have not spoken much about libraries and their role in the new networked information ecology. Their role is uncertain, and will be defined largely by the public policy decisions about authorship, personal use, the public domain and related issues that have been discussed earlier. It is also unclear how libraries will support the learning society. They could become key players in creating these learning communities, and in providing access to information resources that nurture them, and that also provide for the knowledge-seeking style of the solitary learner so out of fashion today. Or they could abdicate – by choice, or under the compulsion of wide-reaching legal and economic changes – these roles to educational institutions (in the case of academic libraries, to other organizational units within their host educational institutions).

Some of the issues are clearly economic. In a learning society, one might underwrite libraries as a public good, or one might assume that information and learning resources will be provided commercially, and then follow a public policy that subsidizes learners directly, rather than support libraries as providers of learning opportunities. In the latter case, libraries would compete in the marketplace to serve learners. There are many forces trying to move the vast majority of the transactions in information access to a more purely commercial basis in the electronic world. Libraries also have to make strategic choices: whether to continue to invest the vast majority of their resources into textually based content, or whether also to embrace, engage and invest heavily in the new digital genres that are emerging, such as video capture of lectures and other public events that may be key materials to a 21st century learning society and to future scholarship.

As we consider the broader issues, including the protection of the private use sphere and the vital societal mandate for the preservation of the cultural and scholarly record, it seems clear that libraries can play pivotal roles as mediators and trusted parties, as agents of society at large within the information ecology.

As computer communications networks increasingly factor out geography and its inconveniences as organizing principles in the information ecology, so libraries seem to be ideal institutions through which to formalize social and economic compromises about author and publisher rights, access and preservation. Rather than battling out these compromises in legislation and in the courts through case-law, there are real opportunities for all stakeholders to empower libraries to serve as trusted mediators for the collective long-term good.

At the same time, libraries will need to recognize that in the new networked information ecology, the public and commercial information landscapes overlap and interpenetrate in more complex and intimate ways. It is not unreasonable to envision a library that provides an information access system offering patrons the choice of borrowing or personally purchasing information, or of a commercial information provider that gives the customer the option of borrowing information from his or her local library as well as purchasing it. There are very large areas (in particular, the provision of information to drive the activities of a learning society) where libraries and the private sector can, and perhaps should, reasonably be viewed as sharing common goals and common cause. Recognizing these commonalties will, I believe, make it easier for libraries to establish their roles as mediators for public policy objectives. They should face little or no competition from the commercial sector in activities such as underwriting the expectation of readers to read anonymously when necessary (a vital activity, but perhaps not a common one) or the maintenance of the intellectual and cultural record for the very long term.

References

1   <URL: www.canis.uiuc.edu>
2   <URL: www.parc.xerox.com>
3   Buckland, M. K., *Information and information systems*, London, Greenwood, 1991.
4   Plenary Address given by Michael Schrage at the American Society for Information Science 1998 Mid-Year Meeting, 'Collaboration across boundaries: theories, strategies and technology', May 17–20 1998, Orlando, Florida, USA.

A select list of acronyms

AACR2	Anglo-American Cataloguing Rules, second edition
ACTS	Advanced Communications Technologies and Services
ADS	Archaeology Data Service
AHDS	Arts and Humanities Data Service
AMICO	Art Museum Image COnsortium
API	Applications Programming Interface
BIDS	Bath Information Data Service
BUFVC	British Universities Film and Video Council
CAIRNS	Co-operative Academic Information Retrieval Network for Scotland
CBL	Computer-based Learning
CCTA	Central Computer and Telecommunications Agency
CHIC	Cooperative Hierarchical Indexing Coordination
CHIO	Cultural Heritage Information Online (a CIMI project)
CIDOC	International Committee for DOCumentation
CIMI	Computer Interchange of Museum Information
CIT	Communications and Information Technology
CMC	Computer-Mediated Communication
COMPASS	Collections Multimedia Public Access System
CSCW	Computer-Supported Collaborative Work
CSV	Comma separated value
CWIS	Campus-Wide Information Service
DALI	Document And Library Integration
DCMS	Department for Culture, Media and Sport
DETR	Department of the Environment, Transport and the Regions
DfEE	Department for Education and Employment
DNER	Distributed National Electronic Resource
DTD	Document Type Definition
DTI	Department of Trade and Industry
DTU	Technical University of Denmark
DTV	Technical Knowledge Centre and Library of Denmark

EAD	Encoded Archival Description
EAFA	East Anglian Film Archive
EARL	Electronic Access to Resources in Libraries
EDDIS	Electronic Document Delivery: the Integrated Solution
EDI	Electronic Data Interchange
EDINA	Edinburgh Data and Information Access
EEVL	Edinburgh Engineering Virtual Library
EIN	Education Information Network
ELD	Employee-Led Development
ELEN	Extended Learning Environment Network
ELISE	Electronic Library Image Service for Europe
EUAN	European Archival Network
FIGIT	Follett Implementation Group for Information Technology
FOI	Freedom of Information
GAIA	Generic Architecture for Information Availability
GILS	Government Information Locator Service
GIS	Geographic Information Systems
HDS	History Data Service
HLF	Heritage Lottery Fund
HTML	HyperText Markup Language
HTTP	HyperText Transfer Protocol
ICT	Information and Communications Technology
IFLA	International Federation of Library Associations and Institutions
ILL	Interlibrary loan
IMS	Instructional Management System
IRC	Internet relay chat
ISAD(G)	International Standard Archival Description (General)
JANET	Joint Academic Network
JISC	Joint Information Systems Committee
LAN	Local Area Network
LASER	Library Access to Selected Electronic Resources
LASER	London And South East Region
LASH	Library Access Sunderland scHeme
LIDDAS	Local Interlending and Document Delivery Administration System
LTM	London Transport Museum
MAGUS	Museums And Galleries User System
MARC	MAchine Readable Cataloguing
MDA	Museum Documentation Association
MIA	MODELS Information Architecture

MIDAS	Manchester Information Datasets and Associated Services
MODELS	MOving to Distributed Environments for Library Services
MOO	MUD, Object Oriented
MUD	Multiple User Dimension/Dialogue
MUSIMS	MUSeum Information Management System
NCC	Norfolk County Council
NGfL	National Grid for Learning
NISS	National Information Services and Systems
NRO	Norfolk Record Office
OECD	Organisation for Economic Co-operation and Development
OPAC	Online Public Access Catalogue
OTA	Oxford Text Archive
PADS	Performing Arts Data Service
PDA	Personal Digital Assistant
POD	Place Of Deposit
PRIDE	People and Resource Identification for Distributed Environments
PRO	Public Record Office
RDF	Resource Description Framework
RLG	Research Libraries Group
ROADS	Resource Organization And Discovery in Subject-based services
SCAN	Scottish Archival Network
SCONUL	Standing Conference of National and University Libraries
SCRAN	Scottish Cultural Resources Access Network
SDI	Selective Dissemination of Information
SET	Secure Electronic Transactions
SGML	Standard Generalized Markup Language
SME	Small and Medium-size Enterprise
SOCITM	Society of IT Managers in Local Government
SQL	Structured Query Language
SRB	Single Regeneration Budget
STM	Science, Technology and Medicine
TAP	Total Access Project
TEC	Training and Enterprise Council
TEI	Text Encoding Initiative
TLTP	Teaching and Learning Technology Programme
UEA	University of East Anglia
UfI	University for Industry
UKNDAD	UK National Digital Archive of Datasets
V&A	Victoria and Albert Museum

VADS   Visual Arts Data Service
VTC   Virtual Teacher Centre
XML   eXtensible Markup Language
YHUA   Yorkshire and Humberside Universities Association

Index